Workbook

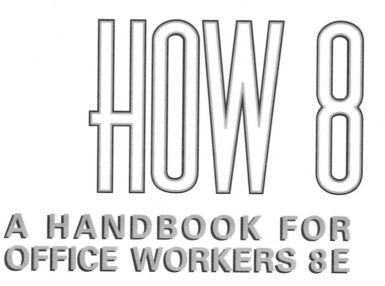

HOW 8

A HANDBOOK FOR OFFICE WORKERS 8E

James L. Clark
Professor, Business Department
Pasadena City College

Lyn R. Clark
Professor, Office Administration Department
Los Angeles Pierce College

SOUTH-WESTERN College Publishing

An International Thomson Publishing Company

Publishing Team Director: John Szilagyi
Developmental Editor: Susan Freeman Carson
Production Editor: Kelly Keeler
Manufacturing Coordinator: Sue Kirven
Marketing Manager: Steve Scoble

Copyright © 1998

by SOUTH-WESTERN COLLEGE PUBLISHING
Cincinnati, Ohio

All Rights Reserved

The text of this publication, or any part thereof, may be reproduced for use in classes for which *HOW 8: A Handbook for Office Workers,* by James and Lyn Clark, is the adopted textbook. It may not be reproduced in any manner whatsoever for any other purpose without prior written permission of the publisher.

   3 4 5 PN 0 9 8
Printed in the United States of America

ISBN: 0-538-87042-7

International Thomson Publishing
South-Western College Publishing is an ITP Company. The ITP trademark is used under license.

CONTENTS

PREFACE

The worksheets in this book, *Workbook for HOW 8,* have been developed to correlate specifically with the principles in *HOW 8: A Handbook for Office Workers,* Eighth Edition. Each section in this workbook corresponds with a specific chapter in *HOW 8.* In fact, the section references containing the information needed to complete each worksheet are shown in parentheses in the introductory heading.

Workbook for HOW 8 is divided into four parts, with some parts containing several sections. Instructions for completing the worksheets in each section precede the exercise materials. Answers or solutions to the initial learning activities are given in Part 4. Other keys and solutions are contained in the *Instructor's Manual and Key* for *HOW 8* (ISBN 0-538-87042-7). The worksheets are perforated so that they may be removed from the book and turned in to the instructor.

Students may use this workbook independently, or they may use it as an organized class activity. If the worksheets are to be completed independently, the students should first complete the Familiarization Exercise presented on pages 3 to 11. Then, they should use the information presented in *HOW 8* to complete the worksheets. Class sets for distribution of the key may be made from the camera-ready copy in the *Instructor's Manual and Key* for *HOW 8,* should the instructor wish to do so.

If *Workbook for HOW 8* is to be used as a regular classroom learning activity, the transparency masters contained in the instructor's manual may be used to present the major principles before the corresponding worksheets are completed.

Regardless of the instructional method employed, however, the practice materials contained in *Workbook for HOW 8* will reinforce the knowledge and skills needed to prepare business documents.

James and Lyn Clark
E-mail: ClarksHOW@aol.com
(818) 701-9770
(818) 772-8108 (Fax)

Part 1

Part 1

Familiarization Exercise for *HOW*

Instructions: Use *HOW 8* to locate the correct answers to the following items. Place the letter or letters corresponding to the correct answer in the answer column provided. Indicate in the second column the number of the section (or page number when no section number is given) where you found your answer. When you have completed this exercise, check your answers with those on page 311.

	Answer	*Section*

1. In using *HOW* to obtain solutions to any questions, which of the following places would you consult first?
   a. Index
   b. Solution Finder
   c. Back cover
   d. Table of Contents

2. If you are unable to locate needed information because you do not know the name of the chapter in which it might be contained, which section of *HOW* would you consult?
   a. Table of Contents
   b. Solution Finders
   c. Preface
   d. Index

3. The page-edge chapter divider tabs are used for
   a. Making *HOW* more attractive.
   b. Locating the Solution Finder for each chapter.
   c. Referring to the Table of Contents.
   d. Locating specific chapters from the Index.

4. Which of the following is the most efficient plan recommended by the authors to locate information in *HOW?*
   a. Consult Table of Contents, turn to page listing for chapter needed, and use Solution Finder to locate specific section that contains answer.
   b. Turn to back cover, locate chapter needed, use page-edge chapter divider tab to reach Solution Finder, and use Solution Finder to locate specific section that contains answer.
   c. Turn to Index, locate major heading in Index, locate topic under major heading, and use page-edge divider tab to locate chapter and specific section.

5. Which of the plans described in Question 4 should be used if the information cannot be located through the chapter titles?

6. If you wanted to know how to address a letter to the mayor of your city, which chapter would you consult?
   a. Capitalization
   b. Business Letters and Memorandums
   c. Address Format and Forms of Address
   d. Mail and Electronic Messaging

7. If you wished to know how to locate information on the Internet, which chapter would you consult to assist you?
   a. Information Sources
   b. Mail and Electronic Messaging
   c. Business Letters and Memorandums
   d. Address Format and Forms of Address
   _____ _____

8. If you wanted to obtain information on how to prepare an itinerary, which chapter of *HOW* should you consult?
   a. Employment Application Documents
   b. Business Letters and Memorandums
   c. Reports and Other Business Documents
   d. Mail and Electronic Messaging
   _____ _____

9. If you wished to know how to calculate a percentage of increase, which chapter of *HOW* would you consult?
   a. Number Formats and Applications
   b. Abbreviated Forms
   c. Spelling, Proofreading, and Editing
   d. Information Sources
   _____ _____

10. If you wanted to know whether the word in a letter was to be spelled *affect* or *effect,* which chapter of *HOW* would you consult?
    a. Grammar and Usage
    b. Business Letters and Memorandums
    c. Hyphenating and Dividing Words
    d. Words Often Confused and Misused
    _____ _____

11. Which one of the following sentences has the correct ending punctuation mark?
    a. Will you please send us your check by the end of the month?
    b. Will you please send us your check by the end of the month.
    _____ _____

12. Business organizations and divisions are usually divided into departments. How would you handle the capitalization of department names? Indicate which of the following sentences are correct. Select all correct answers.
    a. Our department of human resources hired three new accountants today.
    b. Our Division is planning to enlarge its facilities.
    c. We will forward the forms to the Research Department next week.
    d. When can we expect to receive the reports from the Accounting Department?
    _____ _____

13. Related numbers are handled similarly in the same format. According to *HOW,* which of the sentences below have been expressed correctly? Select all correct answers.
    a. Our 4 salespersons sold 32 houses this week.
    b. We will be able to fill your order for 26 chairs, 9 dining tables, and 4 sofas.
    c. Of the 12 entrees listed, only four were priced under $10.
    d. Last year our subscribers increased from 2 million to 2,800,000.
    _____ _____

14. Some compound numbers are always hyphenated; others are not. Locate the correct rule in *HOW*. Then indicate which of the following numbers are expressed correctly. Select all correct answers.
    a. twenty seven
    b. one hundred nineteen
    c. eighty-three
    d. two hundred fifty-seven
    e. one-hundred forty-three _____ _____

15. Pronouns are used in the subjective case under certain circumstances. Select all the correct circumstances from the ones described below.
    a. As the complement of a "being" verb
    b. Following a preposition
    c. As the subject of a sentence
    d. After *to be* when this infinitive does not have a subject
    e. As the subject of any infinitive other than *to be* _____ _____

16. In comparing adjectives, which of the following sentences are written correctly? Select all correct answers.
    a. John writes letters more better than I.
    b. This men's suit line is the most handsome one I have seen this season.
    c. Our reception area is more cheery since it has been redecorated.
    d. The hard disk on your computer is more nearly full than the one on mine. _____ _____

17. Which of the following geographical locations are expressed correctly? Select all correct answers.
    a. Our next flight to New York City will leave at 10:05 a.m.
    b. We took float trips down the Colorado and Snake rivers.
    c. Last year the State of Colorado initiated new election procedures.
    d. Most of our new business has come from the South. _____ _____

18. Select the correct format or formats for expressing the name of the following book. Select all correct answers.
    a. *HOW: A Handbook For Office Workers*
    b. HOW: A Handbook for Office Workers
    c. How: a Handbook for Office Workers
    d. <u>HOW: A Handbook for Office Workers</u>
    e. *HOW: A Handbook for Office Workers*
    f. HOW: A HANDBOOK FOR OFFICE WORKERS _____ _____

19. Which **one** of the following sentences shows a short direct quote punctuated correctly?
    a. "All overtime work has been canceled", said Mr. Stevens.
    b. "All overtime work has been canceled" said Mr. Stevens.
    c. "All overtime work has been canceled," said Mr. Stevens.
    d. "All overtime work has been canceled;" said Mr. Stevens. _____ _____

20. Which **one** of the following sentences shows a parenthetical
    expression punctuated correctly?
    a. You may wish in addition, to order from our new catalog.
    b. You may wish, in addition, to order from our new catalog.
    c. You may wish in addition to order from our new catalog.
    d. You may wish in addition; to order from our new catalog.

    _____ _____

21. If you were asked to address a letter to R. Lewis, how would
    you begin the salutation? According to *HOW*, which of the
    following salutations would be correct?
    a. Dear Mr. Lewis
    b. Dear R. Lewis
    c. Dear Mrs. Lewis
    d. Dear Ms. Lewis

    _____ _____

22. According to the rules for forming noun plurals, which of the
    following words are spelled correctly? Select all correct
    choices.
    a. attornies   d. monies
    b. notaries   e. companys
    c. valleys   f. secretarys

    _____ _____

23. Which of the following uses of *among* and *between* are
    correct? Select all correct choices.
    a. Please distribute these supplies among the two
       departments.
    b. This information should remain between the three of us.
    c. Place the lamp between the two tables.
    d. The invoice was found among the legal documents.

    _____ _____

24. Locate in *HOW* the correct two-letter postal abbreviation for
    the state of Massachusetts. Which **one** of the following
    answers is correct?
    a. MA
    b. MS
    c. MC
    d. MT

    _____ _____

25. There are specific rules regarding subject-verb agreement for
    sentences beginning with *There* and subjects indicating
    portions. Locate this section in *HOW*. From it determine which
    of the sentences are using the principles correctly. Select all
    correct choices.
    a. There is three people in the lobby waiting to see
       Dr. Lyons.
    b. About one half of the packages has been shipped.
    c. There is only one blank check left in the book.
    d. Some of the contracts were destroyed in the fire.

    _____ _____

26. Which of the following statements are true about E-mail messages? Select all correct answers.
    a. E-mail messages may be used to replace all business letters and memorandums as long as the recipient has an E-mail address.
    b. E-mail messages are secure and protected from network hackers as they make their way through the Internet.
    c. E-mail messages are sent through both intraorganizational networks and the Internet.
    d. Creating and sending E-mail messages through the Internet is more convenient and economical than using conventional mailing methods.

    _____   _____

27. Which one of the following dates is expressed correctly?
    a. Please send us your check by March 22nd.
    b. We must have your check by the 22 of March.
    c. The audit was conducted on March 22nd, 1998
    d. May we have your reply by March 22.

    _____   _____

28. In the modified block letter style, the date may be placed in all the positions listed below except one. Use *HOW* to determine which one of the positions listed below is incorrect.
    a. Aligned with the right margin
    b. Centered
    c. Begun at the center of the page
    d. Begun at the left margin

    _____   _____

29. Which of the following statements are true about dividing words at the end of a line? Select all correct choices.
    a. The last words appearing in two consecutive lines in the middle of a paragraph may not be divided.
    b. The last word of a paragraph may never be divided.
    c. The last word appearing on a page may never be divided.
    d. The last word in the first line of a paragraph may never be divided.

    _____   _____

30. Sometimes professional titles are capitalized; other times they are not. Which of the following sentences are written correctly? Select all correct choices.
    a. May I please have an appointment to see the President of your company?
    b. Please ask Professor Ripley to call me.
    c. Sally Abramowitz, the President of Allied Enterprises, attended the conference.
    d. Yes, we did receive a response from the vice president of the United States.

    _____   _____

31. Which of the following uses of *principal* and *principle* are correct? Select all correct choices.
    a. The principle of our school resigned yesterday.
    b. You must reinvest this principal within 90 days.
    c. Please take time to review these accounting principals.
    d. My principle concern is that we retain the same high quality in our products.

    _____   _____

32. Sometimes nouns appearing with numbers or letters are capitalized; other times they are not. Which of the following sentences are written correctly? Select all correct choices.
    a. Please return policy 381294 to us in the enclosed envelope.
    b. Ask Ms. Mann to delete line 5 from the first paragraph.
    c. Our committee plans to meet in Room 52 at 1:30 p.m.
    d. The graph was located on Page 4.

    _____ _____

33. Which one of the following dates is punctuated correctly?
    a. By August 15, we must complete our inventory.
    b. By August 15, 1999 we must complete our inventory.
    c. By Tuesday August 15, 1999, we must complete our inventory.
    d. By Tuesday, August 15, 1999, we must complete our inventory.

    _____ _____

34. Sometimes compound adjectives are hyphenated; other times they are not. From the information contained in *HOW,* indicate which sentences are correct. Select all correct choices.
    a. Your thoroughly-documented report has been read by the research staff.
    b. Because your records are up-to-date, we have been able to contact members who have not paid this year's annual dues.
    c. Use 4- by 6-inch cards for this invitation.
    d. Only three high-school students applied for the scholarship.

    _____ _____

35. Which of the following statements are true about the format of an attention line in a letter? Select all correct choices.
    a. The attention line may be typed after the salutation.
    b. The attention line may be included in the inside address.
    c. The attention line must always be underlined.
    d. The word *attention* may or may not be followed by a colon.

    _____ _____

36. In indexing names to be filed in alphabetical order, which of the following statements are true? Select all correct choices.
    a. Hyphenated last names are considered as separate filing units.
    b. Suffixes and titles are not used as filing units unless they are needed to distinguish between or among identical names.
    c. Two-word first names are considered as a single filing unit.
    d. Middle initials are not considered filing units.

    _____ _____

37. What are the dimensions of a No. 10 envelope?
    a. 6.5 inches x 3.63 inches
    b. 9.5 inches x 4.13 inches
    c. 7.5 inches x 3.88 inches
    d. 5.94 inches x 4.63 inches

    _____ _____

38. Which **one** of the following choices is an Internet address for the World Wide Web site of an educational institution?
    a. http://www.law.usc.edu
    b. http://cgi.amazing.com
    c. http://entisoft.earthlink.net
    d. http://www.usps.gov
    _____ _____

39. If you were to write the governor of your state, which form of address would you use for the salutation?
    a. Dear Mr. Harris:
    b. Dear Governor:
    c. Esteemed Honorable Sir:
    d. Dear Governor Harris:
    e. Dear Excellency:
    _____ _____

40. Which of the following statements are true about placing delivery notations in a business letter? Select all correct choices.
    a. Delivery notations always appear in all capital letters.
    b. Delivery notations may appear in a combination of uppercase and lowercase letters OR in all capital letters.
    c. Delivery notations may appear a double space below the date.
    d. Delivery notations may appear a double space above the inside address.
    e. Delivery notations may appear directly below the copy notation.
    _____ _____

41. Most verbs form their parts in a regular way (*ask, asked, asked*), but others do not follow the regular pattern. From the information contained in *HOW,* indicate which of the combinations given below are correct. Select all correct choices.
    a. go   went   gone
    b. catch   catched   catched
    c. pay   payed   payed
    d. do   done   done
    e. throw   threw   thrown
    _____ _____

42. Which of the following sentences are expressed correctly in their capitalization of academic subjects, courses, or degrees? Select all correct choices.
    a. Will you enroll in History 12 this semester?
    b. I plan to take a course in Mathematical Analysis.
    c. When will you earn your Associate in Arts degree?
    d. What grade did you earn in your conversational Spanish class?
    _____ _____

43. Second-page headings for business letters and memorandums include the following information:
    a. Complete address of addressee
    b. Page number only, centered
    c. Name of addressee, name of sender, page number
    d. Name of addressee, page number, date
    _____ _____

44. Which of the following amounts of money are expressed correctly? Select all correct choices.
    a. We received invoices for $101.87, $395.00, and $62.50 today.
    b. The postage for your two packages was 87 cents and $1.73.
    c. Has the retail price of your pens increased from 89 cents to 99 cents?
    d. The construction costs for this building were estimated to be $3,000,000.

    _____ _____

45. Which of the following statements are correct about using the dictionary to locate the proper spelling of words. Select all correct choices.
    a. When the dictionary offers two spellings for a word in the same entry, use the first spelling.
    b. When the dictionary shows a compound word spelled as one word and two words in different entries, use the spelling shown in the first entry.
    c. The spellings of irregular plural nouns appear in the dictionary directly after the root word in the entry.
    d. The spellings of all verb forms appear in the dictionary directly after the root word in the entry.

    _____ _____

46. Which of the following movie titles are expressed correctly? Select all correct choices.
    a. Next week "Father of the Bride" will be shown on television.
    b. Next week <u>Father of the Bride</u> will be shown on television.
    c. Next week FATHER OF THE BRIDE will be shown on television.
    d. Next week *Father of the Bride* will be shown on television.

    _____ _____

47. According to the general rules for expressing numbers, which of the following statements are true? Select all correct choices.
    a. Numbers *ten* and below are usually written in word form; numbers above *ten* are usually written in figure form.
    b. Approximations above *ten* are always written in figures.
    c. Numbers above *ten* may not be used to begin a sentence.
    d. Round numbers in the millions or billions are usually expressed in a combination of figures and words.

    _____ _____

48. Which **one** of the following compound sentences containing a transitional expression is punctuated correctly?
    a. All our salespersons are attending a sales meeting in Chicago, therefore, no one will be available to call on your company until next week.
    b. All our salespersons are attending a sales meeting in Chicago, therefore no one will be available to call on your company until next week.

    c. All our salespersons are attending a sales meeting in
       Chicago; therefore no one will be available to call on your
       company until next week.

    d. All our salespersons are attending a sales meeting in
       Chicago; therefore, no one will be available to call on
       your company until next week.   _____ _____

49. Which of the following statements are **not** true about forming
    possessives? Select all correct choices.
    a. Nouns not ending with a pronounced *s* form the possessive
       by adding *'s.*
    b. All nouns may show possession.
    c. When two or more persons own a single item, show
       possession only on the last person.
    d. Ownership on compound nouns is shown on the main
       word, e.g., *sister's-in-law.*   _____ _____

50. Which of the following uses of *lose* and *loose* are correct?
    Select all correct choices.
    a. Did you loose any money in the stock market this year?
    b. The springs on the garage door are loose.
    c. When did you lose your watch?
    d. This lose screw must be tightened.   _____ _____

Check your answers with those given on page 311.

Part 2

Section 1 Punctuation

The following materials contain 20 sets of exercises for each of the major uses of the comma, the semicolon, the colon, and the dash. These sets include *Practice Sentences,* a *Practice Paragraph,* and a *Reinforcement Letter.*

Each principle is labeled by name at the beginning of the exercise series. The section in *HOW* that explains the use of the principle is shown in parentheses.

For *Practice Sentences* use proofreaders' marks to insert punctuation marks where they are needed. (See Section 8-5 or inside back cover of *HOW* for proofreaders' marks.) Only the punctuation mark illustrating the principle under consideration is correct. After you have punctuated the sentences, check your answers on pages 313–320.

Practice Paragraphs use mainly the punctuation mark presented in the current section. Insert the necessary punctuation marks, and **label them using the abbreviations listed below.** Then check your answers on pages 313–320.

Punctuation Labels

Comma

Series	ser
Parenthetical	par
Direct Address	da
Appositive	app
Date	date
Address	add
Coordinating Conjunction	cc
Independent Adjective	ia
Introductory Clause	intro
Introductory Phrase	intro
Nonrestrictive	nr
Contrasting Expression	cont ex
Omitted Words	omit
Clarity	cl
Short Quotation	sq

Semicolon

No Conjunction	nc
Coordinating Conjunction	cc
Transitional Expression	trans
Series	ser
Enumeration	enum

Colon

Enumerated or Listed Items	list
Explanatory Sentence	exp

Dash

Summary Statement	summ
Appositive With Commas	app
Emphasis	emph

An illustration of an edited *Practice Paragraph* appears below:

We *par* of course *par* are concerned about the production problems Deco Designs has encountered during the past year. We cannot *par* however *par* allow its unpaid balance of $324 to continue much longer. You can perhaps understand the difficult position in which suppliers find themselves today. We *par* too *par* must meet our financial obligations. Therefore *par* we must turn over this account for collection unless we receive payment by May 1.

PUNCTUATION   15

Reinforcement Letters are cumulative; that is, once a punctuation principle has been covered in a previous exercise, it may appear in any of the following *Reinforcement Letters.* For the *Reinforcement Letters* use proofreaders' marks to insert any necessary punctuation marks. Label each mark with the reason for its use by selecting one of the abbreviations shown on page 15. Check your answers with your instructor. An example of an edited *Reinforcement Letter* follows:

Dear Ms. Davis:

We appreciate receiving your April 8 letter. Because we want you to be pleased with

your selection for many years to come, your china is available on an open-stock basis. If you
_{intro}

need to replace a broken piece, you may do so at any time. Also, you may purchase additional
_{intro}   _{par}

pieces at your convenience.

Enclosed is a brochure describing your china pattern. This brochure features the

available money-saving sets, and it also shows all pieces that may be purchased individually.
_{cc}

If you are interested in purchasing additional sets or individual pieces, use the enclosed order
_{intro}

form. You may include a check with your order, charge it on a bankcard, or have it sent c.o.d.
_{ser}   _{ser}

We hope this information has been helpful to you. However, if you have any other
_{par}

questions, please let us know.
_{intro}

Sincerely yours,

Comma Placement, Series (1-1)

Practice Sentences 1

1. The latest weather reports show rain sleet and ice in New York City.

2. The administrative assistant in our office uses a word processor prepares spreadsheets and answers numerous telephone inquiries.

3. This particular travel group is scheduled to tour Arizona Nevada Utah and Montana.

4. We changed all the locks barred the outside windows and installed a burglar alarm system last week.

5. Trees shrubs and ground cover are needed to complete this project.

6. Call Henry Smith offer him the job and ask him to begin work July 1.

7. Many doctors dentists and lawyers are among our clientele.

8. The contractor obtained a permit purchased the building materials and hired several additional workers to complete the job within the specified three-week period.

9. Proofread the report make three copies and mail the original to Ms. Williams.

10. Sheila was late because she stopped at the stationery store post office and grocery store before reporting to work.

Check your answers with those given on page 313 before completing the following exercise.

Practice Paragraph 1

We must correspond with Mr. Jones regarding our inventory sales and profit picture.

Ask him to let us know how our high inventory low sales volume and declining profits during

the last quarter will affect our status for the entire year. Write the letter sign it and mail it.

Check your answers with those given on page 313 before completing the following exercise.

Reinforcement Letter 1

To: John Cole

Our assistant collected the facts Mr. Phillips researched the case and Ms. Watson prepared the brief. This team of experts was instrumental in our receiving a favorable court decision. They are to be congratulated on their ability patience and success.

Please continue to rely on Mr. Day for collecting the information Mr. Phillips for conducting the research and Ms. Watson for preparing the briefs. We will be able to develop a steady group of business industrial and professional clients by using the special talents of these three people.

The answers to this exercise appear in the **Instructor's Manual and Key** *for* **HOW 8: A Handbook for Office Workers,** *Eighth Edition.*

Comma Placement, Parenthetical Expressions (1-2)

Practice Sentences 2

1. In fact Mr. Ryan has called our office several times.

2. We feel nevertheless that you should honor your original commitment.

3. The committee has rejected his proposal fortunately.

4. Yes we are planning to revise the previous edition.

5. Perhaps you would like to purchase this set of encyclopedias on a free 10-day trial basis.

6. The chapter was not in other words well presented and thoroughly documented.

7. Between you and me I would be surprised if Canton Industries bids on this project.

8. We are therefore closing your account until the overdue balance has been paid.

9. We will without a doubt have your order shipped to you in time for your fall sale.

10. You can indeed receive a full refund within 30 days if you are not fully satisfied with any of our products.

Check your answers with those given on page 313 before completing the following exercise.

Practice Paragraph 2

We as a rule do not employ inexperienced accountants. However Mr. Williams has so many excellent recommendations that we could not afford to turn down his application. Perhaps you will wish to meet him personally before assigning him to a supervisor. I can of course have him stop by your office tomorrow.

Check your answers with those given on page 313 before completing the following exercise.

Reinforcement Letter 2

To: David Post

Next month we will open new stores in Los Angeles San Francisco and Phoenix. Publicity releases consequently have already been sent to the major newspapers in these cities. In addition we will advertise a number of grand opening specials that should attract a large number of customers.

Plans for opening our new stores are contained in the attached report. You may however wish to contact the store managers for further information on their sales promotions present merchandise inventory and progress in hiring personnel. Such additional information will perhaps be of help to you in your new assignment.

Your assistance needless to say will be important in assessing marketing trends in Los Angeles San Francisco and Phoenix. May we rely on you then for information regarding consumer preferences buying habits and purchasing power? The results of your research will indeed assist the staff in ensuring the success of these three new stores.

*The answers to this exercise appear in the **Instructor's Manual and Key** for **HOW 8: A Handbook for Office Workers,** Eighth Edition.*

Comma Placement, Direct Address (1-3)

Practice Sentences 3

1. Brett please reword the final paragraph of this letter to refer to the enclosures.

2. You may continue class with the assigned lessons shown in your syllabus.

3. Your staff is certainly efficient Mrs. Davis.

4. We can ladies and gentlemen promise you increased dividends for the next fiscal period.

5. Have you Gary decided on the dates for your vacation this year?

6. Yes fellow citizens of Spokane Senator Winfield's voting record is open for public scrutiny.

7. We plan to ask Ms. Stevens to complete the billing for this month.

8. Only you can help us solve this problem Dr. Bush.

9. Will David Kloss be leaving for Michigan next week?

10. Only you friends and neighbors can prevent further crime increases in this city.

Check your answers with those given on page 313 before completing the following exercise.

Practice Paragraph 3

Would you Ms. White please review the financial report. I would appreciate your doing so too Ms. Smith. Gentlemen please check with both Ms. White and Ms. Smith for their advice before making any further financial commitments.

Check your answers with those given on page 314 before completing the following exercise.

Reinforcement Letter 3

Dear Mrs. Smith:

We welcome you as a charge account customer of the Valley Department Store. Enclosed are your two charge account plates some information outlining our charge plan and a circular describing our special sale items for this month.

You may be interested Mrs. Smith in the special dress sale now in progress. In fact this sale is one of the best we have had this year. You can for example purchase many of our designer clothes at half price. We hope that you will be able to take advantage of these savings.

Sincerely yours,

*The answers to this exercise appear in the **Instructor's Manual and Key** for **HOW 8: A Handbook for Office Workers,** Eighth Edition.*

Comma Placement, Appositives (1-4)

Practice Sentences 4

1. This new budget was proposed by our accountant Stan Hughes last week.

2. John's sister the author of a best-seller has agreed to speak at one of our association meetings.

3. Senator Johnson a member of the finance committee favors our position.

4. John J. Lopez Jr. has requested our committee to provide new funds for his program.

5. Was your latest article "Skiing in California" accepted for publication?

6. Is it possible that they themselves are not confident of the outcome?

7. Janet Hodges our new assistant will be working in the office next to yours.

8. This book was written by Alice Porter and David Simms two prominent authorities on the subject of consumer finance.

9. Please refer any requests for further information to my assistant Bill Thompson.

10. One of our new clients Crutchfield Industries has recently been admitted to the New York Stock Exchange.

Check your answers with those given on page 314 before completing the following exercise.

Practice Paragraph 4

We have just learned that our president Mr. Black will retire next June. He has been president of Data Products Inc. for the past ten years. My assistant received the news yesterday and believes that Stephen Gold Ph.D. will be asked to fill the position. We will keep our employees informed of further developments through our monthly newsletter *Data Jottings.*

Check your answers with those given on page 314 before completing the following exercise.

Reinforcement Letter 4

Dear Mr. Ray:

Our newest project in the business communication area *Writing Résumés That Get Jobs* will be released within the next three months. Consequently we are in the process of preparing an advertising campaign for these materials. One of the authors James Martin Jr. will be contacting you shortly about the special features of this program.

The authors editors and reviewers all expect this book to be one of our best-sellers next year. There has been a need for a book of this type for some time. Hopefully our potential customers will recognize the considerable amount of effort that has gone into producing the kind of book for which they have indicated a need.

Mr. Sharp our advertising manager has asked his son Peter to work up some preliminary drawings for the artwork to advertise this new book. Peter has had considerable experience in this area and has done some other freelance work for our organization.

We will be able to meet with Peter as soon as he has had an opportunity to work up the preliminary drawings. He himself is not exactly sure when he can have them available. However I will contact you regarding a specific date time and place when we are ready for the initial conference.

Sincerely yours,

*The answers to this exercise appear in the **Instructor's Manual and Key** for **HOW 8: A Handbook for Office Workers,** Eighth Edition.*

Comma Placement, Dates and Time Zones (1-5)

Practice Sentences 5

1. The merger took place on February 28 1998.

2. On April 18 we will expect to receive your check for $720 to cover your overdue account.

3. Did you say that the president's address will be broadcast at 8 p.m. EST?

4. The contractor expects the shopping center to be completed by October 2000.

5. We have made arrangements for the conference to be held on Thursday June 12 1999.

6. By April 15 the bulk of our income tax work will have been completed.

7. Our records show that on November 4 1997 your association filed for tax-exempt status.

8. Your subscription to this vital magazine ends with the July 1999 issue.

9. American Airlines Flight 390 is scheduled to land in Chicago at 8:40 a.m. CST.

10. On Wednesday December 6 2001 the company will have been in business for a century.

Check your answers with those given on page 314 before completing the following exercise.

Practice Paragraph 5

We will meet on April 1 to plan the scheduled opening of two new branch offices on Tuesday May 3 and Thursday May 19. These offices are the first ones we have opened since August 22 1997. We will need to plan these openings carefully because we will be directly responsible for two additional openings in September 2000 and April 2001.

Check your answers with those given on page 314 before completing the following exercise.

Reinforcement Letter 5

Dear Charles:

We are pleased to announce that the next convention for hotel managers will be held from Tuesday September 30 1999 until Friday October 3 1999 at the West Hotel in Chicago.

The convention committee recognizes that the next convention was originally scheduled for September 2000. However the convention committee felt that the date should be moved forward since so many of our members had expressed an interest in meeting annually. We hope Charles that this change in convention plans will fit into your schedule.

We would very much like to have you speak at one of our morning meetings. Ed Bates our program chairman suggested that you might be interested in describing the new reservations plan you developed for the Holiday Hotels. Would you be able to address the membership on this topic on October 2?

Please let me know as soon as possible if you will be able to accept this invitation.

Sincerely,

*The answers to this exercise appear in the **Instructor's Manual and Key** for **HOW 8: A Handbook for Office Workers,** Eighth Edition.*

Comma Placement, Addresses (1-6)

Practice Sentences 6

1. Please return this application to Los Angeles Pierce College 6201 Winnetka Avenue Woodland Hills California 91371.

2. Mrs. Harvey presently resides at 98 Spring Lane Los Angeles California 90041-2027.

3. We will tour London England and Paris France during our travels.

4. Our company owns a number of condominium complexes in Honolulu Hawaii.

5. The tour agent sold us tickets to Albuquerque New Mexico in error

6. The closest branch office is located at 2150 Madison Avenue Knoxville Tennessee 37912-5821.

7. Please complete this form and send it to Mrs. Alice Stocker Office Manager Smythe & Ryan Investment Counselors 3370 Ravenwood Avenue Suite 120 Baltimore Maryland 21213-1648.

8. This customer's new address is Box 360 Rural Route 2 Bangor Maine 04401-9802.

9. Dallas Texas has been selected as the site for our next convention.

10. All these articles are imported from Madrid Spain.

Check your answers with those given on pages 314–315 before completing the following exercise.

Practice Paragraph 6

We sent the information to Mr. David Hope Manager Larry's Clothing Store 2001 Adams Street S.W. Atlanta Georgia 30315-5901. The information should have been sent to Mr. Hope's new address in Columbus Ohio. It is 2970 Olive Avenue Columbus Ohio 43204-2535.

Check your answers with those given on page 315 before completing the following exercise.

Reinforcement Letter 6

Ladies and Gentlemen:

Please reserve for me two gift subscriptions under your special holiday plan. These subscriptions are for one year and should begin with your January 1999 issue.

One gift subscription should be sent to Mrs. Alice Daily 65 Martha Road Apt 11A Boston Massachusetts 02114-1210. The other one should be sent to Mrs. Ann Green 421 30th Street Pittsburgh Pennsylvania 15219-3728.

I would appreciate your sending the bill for these subscriptions to my office. The address is Tower Building 500 Washington Street Suite 201 San Francisco California 94111-2919.

Please acknowledge receipt of this order. In addition I would appreciate your sending gift cards to both Mrs. Daily and Mrs. Green telling them of their gift subscriptions that are to begin on January 1 1999.

Sincerely yours,

*The answers to this exercise appear in the **Instructor's Manual and Key** for **HOW 8: A Handbook for Office Workers,** Eighth Edition.*

Comma Placement, Coordinating Conjunctions (1-7)

Practice Sentences 7

1. Three major accounting reports are due in January and two of them must be prepared for presentation to the Board of Directors.

2. The meeting was scheduled to adjourn at 3 p.m. but we had not finished all the business by then.

3. You may transfer to our Chicago office or you may remain here in Cincinnati.

4. Most of the applicants cannot keyboard well nor can they use our word processing program.

5. Marie was offered a promotion last week but did not accept it.

6. A new edition of this textbook is in the process of publication and it will be available for the spring semester.

7. We hope that Mr. Moore will be able to attend the convention and that he will be our guest for the banquet on May 5.

8. Tom will finish the project himself or he will arrange for his assistant to complete it.

9. Bob will no longer have to travel to Akron nor will he have to move out of this district.

10. Janet has been promoted twice and is now eligible for a third advancement.

Check your answers with those given on page 315 before completing the following exercise.

Practice Paragraph 7

We have checked our records and find that you are correct. Our deposit was mailed to your branch office but no record of this deposit was entered into our check record. Our records have been corrected and we appreciate your help in solving this problem. We hope that we have not caused you any inconvenience and that we may rely upon your help in the future.

Check your answers with those given on page 315 before completing the following exercise.

Reinforcement Letter 7

Dear Mr. Harris:

We are pleased to announce that in the near future we will be opening several new branch offices. The first one is scheduled to open in Tacoma Washington on June 1 1999. Other offices are planned for Indianapolis Indiana and Tampa Florida.

You may mail all future orders to the Tacoma office and we will fill these orders from there. Just fill out one of the enclosed order blanks and your order will be processed immediately upon receipt. We plan to serve our customers more rapidly and efficiently in this way.

Mr. Parks the former manager of our Portland branch will be in charge of the Tacoma office. He will be able to assist you with future orders and follow through on their delivery. We cannot promise you a three-day delivery date for regular orders but I can assure you that most orders will reach you within a week. Of course we will continue to provide our express overnight service for an additional shipping fee.

We hope that you will take advantage of ordering from our Tacoma office and that this new development in our company will expedite deliveries to your store.

Sincerely yours,

*The answers to this exercise appear in the **Instructor's Manual and Key** for **HOW 8: A Handbook for Office Workers,** Eighth Edition.*

Comma Placement, Independent Adjectives (1-8)

Practice Sentences 8

1. Mr. Sommers is known to be a pleasant patient supervisor.

2. Was your real estate agent able to locate an affordable five-bedroom home for the Lopezes?

3. The red brick building on the corner of Main and Third Streets is scheduled to be demolished next week.

4. The Hardys own an elegant cocluded restaurant in the Berkshires.

5. This afternoon one of the customers broke an expensive crystal vase.

6. Ms. Rice's ambitious greedy attitude made the other agents uneasy.

7. Our new filing system has caused considerable confusion.

8. Your outgoing cheerful manner has brought you many friends.

9. One of our wealthy well-known alumni has donated $1 million for the new library wing.

10. We still need to purchase an oak secretarial desk for the reception area.

Check your answers with those given on page 315 before completing the following exercise.

Practice Paragraph 8

Your informative well-written report was submitted to the board of education yesterday. You will certainly be permitted to purchase some inexpensive modern equipment on the basis of the facts presented. I am sure the board will agree that the present facilities do not reflect a realistic practical learning environment for business students.

Check your answers with those given on page 315 before completing the following exercise.

Reinforcement Letter 8

Dear Mr. Winters:

I am pleased to recommend John Davis for a position with your accounting firm. He has been in our employ for three years and we are sorry to see him leave our company.

Mr. Davis is an intelligent hardworking young man. His pleasant congenial manner has also contributed to our organization. Unfortunately our small company is unable to offer him the opportunities for advancement to which a person of his ability is entitled.

Mr. Davis has been in charge of accounts receivable for the last year. His duties included posting purchases to individual accounts entering customer payments and making appropriate journal entries in our computerized accounting program. Our accounting supervisor Mr. Long has often remarked about his prompt efficient handling of the duties that were assigned to him. Mr. Davis has contributed greatly to the smooth operation of the entire department.

I am pleased to be able to recommend such a capable young man to you. Do not hesitate to let me know if you should require any additional information about Mr. Davis.

Sincerely yours,

*The answers to this exercise appear in the **Instructor's Manual and Key** for **HOW 8: A Handbook for Office Workers,** Eighth Edition.*

Comma Placement, Introductory Clauses (1-9)

Practice Sentences 9

1. When you see John please ask him to call me.

2. While you were in New York the committee published its findings.

3. Before you leave for Denver will you finish the financial reports?

4. As stated previously we plan to renew our contracts with you next month.

5. Because Mr. Logan wishes to move to Indianapolis he has requested a transfer to our plant there.

6. If so may we count on you to ship the merchandise by November 14?

7. While Ms. Smith was conferring with her attorney her car was stolen.

8. Provided we have an adequate budget you may add one additional person to your staff next year.

9. If you cannot make an appointment at this time please let us know.

10. As explained above this refrigerator has a one-year warranty on all parts and labor.

Check your answers with those given on pages 315–316 before completing the following exercise.

Practice Paragraph 9

When you receive the material please review it carefully and return it to our office within two weeks. If possible note all changes in red. As soon as we receive your corrections we will be able to submit the manuscript to the printer. We expect that if the current production schedule is maintained the book will be released early in March.

Check your answers with those given on page 316 before completing the following exercise.

Reinforcement Letter 9

To: Henry Small

I recommend that we network the microcomputer stations in our Sales Department. Although expensive a network will save money and improve efficiency over a period of time.

I believe that if the present number of customer orders and inquiries continues we will have to modify update and streamline our current procedures to maintain our reputation for good service. If we network our equipment our sales staff will become more productive. They will have access to information processed by other employees and they will be able to keep up more easily with the increasing workload in this department. Where possible I myself would be willing to assist the staff in making any necessary changes.

May I have your approval to investigate further the possibility of installing a network to link our microcomputers? As soon as I hear from you I will be able to contact the various equipment vendors for specific price quotations.

*The answers to this exercise appear in the **Instructor's Manual and Key** for **HOW 8: A Handbook for Office Workers,** Eighth Edition.*

Comma Placement, Introductory Phrases (1-10)

Practice Sentences 10

1. To continue with this project we will need $2 million in additional funding.

2. Seeing that John had made a mistake Kate corrected his calculations.

3. After viewing the offices in the Hudson Building Dr. Ruston agreed that they were suitable.

4. Near the top of the new listings you will find the Hills' home.

5. Tired of her usual routine Jan took a three-week vacation.

6. During the next month we must decrease our inventory by at least 30 percent.

7. After the meeting a number of us plan to have dinner together at a nearby restaurant.

8. To be interviewed for this position an applicant must be fully qualified.

9. Until the end of the month no one may take additional vacation timo.

10. Encouraged by recent sales increases our buyer has expanded the number of product lines carried by our suburban stores.

Check your answers with those given on page 316 before completing the following exercise.

Practice Paragraph 10

For the past one hundred years our bank has served the needs of the people of Hartford. At the present time we wish to attract more depositors to our institution. To attract new customers to the Bank of Connecticut we have established a premium plan. Hoping that such an incentive will draw a large group of new depositors we have provided a number of gift items to be given away with the opening of new accounts for $1,000 or more.

Check your answers with those given on page 316 before completing the following exercise.

Reinforcement Letter 10

To: Karen Hill

With the purchase of additional computing equipment we will need to compile a series of form letters to answer our routine correspondence. I recommend that when Mr. Black returns from vacation he should be assigned the responsibility of analyzing our previous corre-spondence and composing a series of form letters to handle routine matters. If possible Mrs. Day should be requested to assist him.

Once the form letters have been compiled they can be stored on the computer. Then when the need for a certain kind of letter arises the secretary may retrieve and personalize the message. This method of answering routine correspondence will save a great deal of time and we will be able to cut costs by eliminating a considerable amount of repetitive typing.

The most prominent office systems magazine *Office Systems and Procedures* has been running a series of articles on word processing programs. In this series the authors describe the many different uses for word processing programs. They also describe the advantages and disadvantages of the various programs marketed by major software manufacturers. Attached are reprints of this series and I hope that you will have an opportunity to read them before our meeting.

I look forward to meeting with you on Monday August 4 to discuss the specific steps we should take to improve our handling of correspondence and reports. As you suggested I will be in your office at 10 a.m.

*The answers to this exercise appear in the **Instructor's Manual and Key** for **HOW 8: A Handbook for Office Workers,** Eighth Edition.*

Comma Placement, Nonrestrictive Phrases and Clauses (1-11)

Practice Sentences 11

1. Mr. Sims who has responsibility for reviewing all appeals will make the final decision.

2. Each person who has enrolled at the college will receive a schedule of classes.

3. Her latest article which appeared in last Sunday's local paper discussed family budgeting.

4. All students applying for a scholarship must attend the meeting on Wednesday.

5. Your order has already been shipped even though I tried to cancel it.

6. May I have copies of the materials that were distributed at the last meeting.

7. Mr. Davis who has attended many of our seminars is a licensed real estate broker.

8. May I have a copy of our latest financial report which was distributed at the last meeting of department heads.

9. We have decided to hold our conference at the Shadow Oaks Inn regardless of its expensive meals and remote location.

10. Our new company president planning to make major organizational changes first fired three of the top executives.

Check your answers with those given on page 316 before completing the following exercise.

Practice Paragraph 11

The new community library which is located on South Main Street is presently recruiting employees to serve the public during the evening hours. Mr. Davis is looking for staff members who would be willing to work from 5 to 9 p.m. on weekday evenings. He would be pleased to receive your recommendations if you know of any qualified individuals who would be interested in such a position. We would appreciate receiving your recommendations within the next few days since Mr. Davis must hire the evening staff by May 10 before the library opens on May 13.

Check your answers with those given on pages 316–317 before completing the following exercise.

Reinforcement Letter 11

Dear Mr. Little:

Now is the time to obtain the necessary protection for your family protection in terms of providing them with the life insurance needed by American families today.

We have several insurance plans that may be of interest to you. One of our most popular ones for young people is our home mortgage insurance. This plan which has been in existence for over forty years provides families with home insurance protection in the form of life insurance.

Our regular life insurance program as you can see from the enclosed brochure has been designed for the family that wishes to receive protection as well as provide for future savings and investment. During the lifetime of the policy it accumulates a cash value which may be withdrawn upon the expiration of the policy or may be used for extended life insurance coverage. Also you may borrow at a low interest rate against the value of your policy should you need to do so.

Another one of our plans provides term insurance coverage. This plan allows you Mr. Little to purchase the greatest amount of protection for your family during the time that it is most needed. By selecting this plan you will be able to obtain higher benefits at less cost when your family is young and its needs are greater.

Mr. Mills who has been one of our agents for more than ten years would be able to discuss further with you the advantages of our various programs. Please call Mr. Mills at 347-0881 and he will set up an appointment to meet with you.

Sincerely yours,

*The answers to this exercise appear in the **Instructor's Manual and Key** for **HOW 8: A Handbook for Office Workers,** Eighth Edition.*

Comma Placement, Contrasting and Contingent Expressions (1-12)
Comma Placement, Omitted Words (1-13)

Practice Sentences 12

1. The format not the content of the report made it unacceptable.

2. The sooner we receive your completed application forms the sooner we can process you for employment.

3. Tickets will be made available July 1 but only to members of the homeowners' association.

4. The more often you access and explore Internet sites the more adept you will become in using the Internet as a source of information.

5. I intend to write a full report not just a short memo outlining all the circumstances involved in this transaction.

6. Tom will leave for vacation on June 9; Mary June 15; Tod June 22; and Rosa June 30.

7. Just today we sold six of these advertised living room suites; yesterday three; and the day before two.

8. The Sales Department received 18 copies of the report; the Personnel Department 12; and the other departments 8.

9. Last month we received two orders of supplies; this month only one.

10. Four new expressways will be completed in 2000; three in 2001; two in 2002.

Check your answers with those given on page 317 before completing the following exercise.

Practice Paragraph 12

Last week our agent sold six homes this week just four. Mr. Stevens maintains that our construction site is not appealing to home buyers. His argument is plausible yet weak. Other builders in the area have been more successful in their marketing efforts. The more competition Mr. Stevens encounters the more his sales efforts seem to decline.

Check your answers with those given on page 317 before completing the following exercise.

Reinforcement Letter 12

Dear Ms. Stadthaus:

We appreciate receiving your order for 12 dozen of our Model 18 frying pan sets.

Because the Model 18 set has been so popular as a summer sale specialty we have not been able to keep up with the demand for this item. We have a number of these sets on hand but not 12 dozen. At the present time we would be able to supply you with 4 dozen.

Mr. Jones who is in charge of our Production Department promises us an additional supply of these pans within the next two weeks. He realizes that the more of these sets that we can manufacture during the next month the more of them we can sell during the summer sales.

The 4 dozen sets on hand can be shipped to you immediately; the remaining 8 dozen by April 18. Please let us know by returning the enclosed card or faxing us your response whether or not you wish us to make this partial shipment. We look forward to hearing from you within the next few days.

Sincerely yours,

The answers to this exercise appear in the **Instructor's Manual and Key** *for* **HOW 8: A Handbook for Office Workers,** *Eighth Edition.*

Comma Placement, Clarity (1-14)

Practice Sentences 13

1. We have dealt with this company for many many years.

2. A long time before she had spoken with the company president.

3. Whoever wins wins a $2,000 jackpot and a trip to Hawaii.

4. Ever since Mr. Salazar has kept a careful record of his expenses.

5. We were very very disappointed with the final recommendations given by the consultant.

6. Students who cheat cheat only themselves.

7. Three months before our sales manager had been offered a position by one of the leading manufacturers on the East Coast.

8. Whoever begins begins without our approval.

9. Even before he had shown an interest in that area.

10. After this time will seem to pass more quickly.

Check your answers with those given on page 317 before completing the following exercise.

Practice Paragraph 13

All the meeting was was a discussion of Mr. Green's plan to move the plant. Mr. Green has presented this same plan many many times. A few weeks before another committee totally rejected his proposal. Ever since he has looked for another group to endorse his ideas.

Check your answers with those given on page 317 before completing the following exercise.

Reinforcement Letter 13

To: Mr. John Allen

We were very disappointed to learn that you will not be able to deliver the main address at our sales conference in January. As you know the staff was extremely impressed with your last speech in Dallas. Ever since many of them have requested that we ask you to conduct the general session in January.

I understand Mr. Allen why you cannot attend our meeting. As national sales manager you must visit other regional sales meetings also. What it is is too great of a demand on one person's time.

We appreciate the many times in the past when you have addressed our Southern Region and we look forward to the time when you will be able to do so again.

*The answers to this exercise appear in the **Instructor's Manual and Key** for **HOW 8: A Handbook for Office Workers,** Eighth Edition.*

Comma Placement, Short Quotations (1-15)

Practice Sentences 14

1. "Please be sure to remove that sign" said Mr. Grey.

2. "How long" asked Ms. Foster "will it take to repair the monitor?"

3. The receptionist answered "no" very sharply and rudely.

4. Mr. Hughes said "Everyone must agree to sign his or her own contract."

5. "Not this time" was the answer given by many of our past donors.

6. "Are you finished" asked Scott "with that ledger?"

7. The witness reaffirmed "That man is the one who stole my car."

8. "Please finish this report by Friday, May 5" said Dr. Reynolds.

9. All the union members agreed "to abide by the judgment of the union leaders throughout the negotiations."

10. "Mr. David Brown" said Ms. Burns, the Department of Human Resources head "has been hired for the vacancy in your department."

Check your answers with those given on page 317 before completing the following exercise.

Practice Paragraph 14

Mr. Dallas answered the reporter's question with a simple "yes." His philosophy appeared to be "A bird in hand is worth two in the bush." The reporter then asked "Do you believe this labor problem will be settled within the next week?" Mr. Dallas answered confidently "I believe the terms of the contract will be accepted by a clear majority." "I am sure" added Ms. Hill "that the employees will be especially pleased with the additional insurance benefits offered."

Check your answers with those given on page 318 before completing the following exercise.

Reinforcement Letter 14

Dear Mr. Ryan:

Ask yourself "Did the Wilson Paper Company fill my last order accurately and promptly?" The answer is "yes." Ask yourself again "Did the Wilson Paper Company provide us with the promotional material we requested?" Again you must reply "yes."

We have carried out our part of the bargain Mr. Ryan. We have supplied you with the merchandise you ordered and the brochures you requested. Now in turn won't you be fair with us?

Your account is presently 60 days past due. We have sent you two reminders but have not received a check for $435 to cover our last statement. We can perhaps understand why you have not made payment but we cannot understand why you have not answered our letters. If there is some reason why you cannot make payment at the present time please let us know.

We have asked ourselves "Is this the way Ryan's Stationers has done business in the past?" "Not according to our previous records" our accountant said. So won't you be fair to both your credit record and to us by mailing your check for $435 in the enclosed envelope.

Sincerely yours,

The answers to this exercise appear in the **Instructor's Manual and Key** *for* **HOW 8: A Handbook for Office Workers,** *Eighth Edition.*

Semicolon Placement, No Conjunction (1-17)

Practice Sentences 15

1. Our company has released a new series of products we feel that the present market will receive these products favorably.

2. Ms. Stephens will file the rewritten reports she wishes to cross-reference some of them.

3. Andrea collated Kim stapled.

4. Place the instructions on the table I will review them later.

5. Steve has begun work on a new project he will be out of the office for the next three weeks.

6. I dusted furniture John cleaned the showcase Mary vacuumed—all just before the store opened.

7. Bill has not finished his sales report for Thursday's meeting he will work late tonight to complete it.

8. We received your application today the committee will make its decision regarding your loan within two weeks.

9. The thief entered he grabbed the jewels he exited swiftly.

10. Sales for July and August hit an all-time low they increased somewhat during September November recorded the highest sales for 1999.

Check your answers with those given on page 318 before completing the following exercise.

Practice Paragraph 15

We need someone to meet with the Atlas Corporation representatives. Please call Mr. Green ask him to be in my office by 10 a.m. tomorrow morning. He knows Piedmont he knows commercial real estate he knows prices. Mr. Green would be my first choice for the job Ms. Jones would be my second choice my final choice would be Mr. Bruce.

Check your answers with those given on page 318 before completing the following exercise.

Reinforcement Letter 15

To: Carol Smith

We are pleased with the results of the new commission plan that was initiated this year we hope that you will endorse it also.

During the past year our sales have increased 40 percent and this increase is reflected in the salaries earned by our staff. As our sales manager stated at last year's stockholders' meeting "By offering our sales force the opportunity for higher salaries through commissions we will be able to increase substantially our sales during the next year."

I believe our sales manager John Black was correct this sales increase appears to be related directly to our placing the staff on a commission basis. We do realize too that our economy has experienced favorable conditions during this past year.

I recommend that we continue our present commission plan it appears to provide the proper incentive for our staff. Please let me know Ms. Smith if you agree with this recommendation.

*The answers to this exercise appear in the **Instructor's Manual and Key** for **HOW 8: A Handbook for Office Workers,** Eighth Edition.*

Semicolon Placement, With Conjunction (1-18)

Practice Sentences 16

1. James Hogan who is originally from Nevada has written a book about tourist sights in Las Vegas and he plans to have it translated into several languages for purchase by foreign visitors.

2. Cliff Lightfoot our supervisor has been ill for several weeks but he plans to return to the office next Wednesday November 19 in time for our committee meeting.

3. We have purchased new carpeting and furniture for all the offices and we expect to have them completely redecorated this month.

4. We cannot Ms. Baron repair the clock radio under the terms of the warranty nor can we under the circumstances refund the purchase price.

5. Nevertheless the committee must meet again next Friday but today we will cut short the agenda.

6. Many of our employees live nearby and they often ride bicycles to work.

7. Unfortunately three of our large moving vans have developed engine problems but according to the latest information we have received they will be back in service next Monday morning.

8. I believe Ms. Edwards that the contract will expire next week and that it has been scheduled for renewal.

9. You may of course wish to keep your original appointment or you may reschedule it for another time during March.

10. Our last investment program was so successful that it netted a 16 percent return but we cannot guarantee that our next program or any other programs planned for the future will do as well.

Check your answers with those given on page 318 before completing the following exercise.

Practice Paragraph 16

We were pleased to learn Mr. Bell that you have opened a new store on West Main Street and you may be sure that we look forward to establishing a mutually profitable business relationship. Our new line of stationery greeting cards and other paper products should be of interest to you and we will have our sales representative in your area Jack Dale phone you for an appointment to view them. He can leave a catalog with you or he can take you personally to our showroom which is located only three miles from your store.

Check your answers with those given on page 318 before completing the following exercise.

Reinforcement Letter 16

Dear Mr. Mason:

We have written you three letters requesting payment of our last invoice 187365 for $98.84 but as of the close of business today we have not yet received your check or an explanation why this invoice has not been paid.

During the past year we have appreciated your business we cannot understand though why you have not made payment on this invoice. You as a businessman realize the importance of maintaining a high credit rating and the damage that nonpayment can do to your credit reputation.

We now find it necessary to place your account in the hands of a collection agency. Save yourself the embarrassment of a damaged credit rating mail your check in the enclosed envelope today. If we receive your payment by Friday May 11 there is still time to avoid legal action.

Sincerely yours,

*The answers to this exercise appear in the **Instructor's Manual and Key** for **HOW 8: A Handbook for Office Workers,** Eighth Edition.*

Semicolon Placement, With Transitional Expressions (1-19)

Practice Sentences 17

1. Our profits have declined drastically this year therefore we are planning a new promotional series.

2. Ms. Lee is in the process of arranging next week's schedule however your hours will remain the same.

3. We will not close our store for remodeling on the contrary we will be open longer hours to accommodate our clientele.

4. The foundation built a large new hospital wing consequently we will have new office space for this community project.

5. All the sixth-grade classes will need new math textbooks moreover they will need workbooks to accompany them.

6. Send us an outline and three chapters of your proposed novel then we will let you know if we will be able to publish it.

7. Our company no longer manufactures pencil sharpeners however we are enclosing the names and addresses of several companies that do.

8. Mr. Cooper vice president of Western Bank will not be able to attend our meeting consequently we will need to find a replacement speaker.

9. Our computer broke down yesterday for about eight hours thus all our payroll checks will

   be delayed until tomorrow.

10. Several of our salespersons are being transferred to the Chicago area therefore they will need your assistance in locating homes and apartments.

Check your answers with those given on page 319 before completing the following exercise.

Practice Paragraph 17

Our order for 24 sets of china arrived yesterday however more than half the sets have broken pieces. These china sets are a featured item for our May sale thus we would appreciate your sending an additional 14 sets to replace the broken ones. Please ship these replacements immediately so that they will arrive in time for our sale.

Check your answers with those given on page 319 before completing the following exercise.

Reinforcement Letter 17

To: Kristin Harris

We have received letters from two of our retailers they are complaining about our service in the Boston area. These retailers have not seen our salesperson for several months therefore their supply of our products has become depleted.

During our special discount sale neither of these retailers was contacted. They were unable to take advantage of our reduced prices consequently they are considering dropping our line unless some specific action is taken.

I have checked into this matter and found that our salesperson in this area has had a declining sales record during the past two years. His supervisor believes that he is not devoting the time necessary to cover all the accounts in his territory in fact his supervisor suspects that this salesperson is in the process of establishing his own business while at the same time retaining his position with our company.

As you know Kristin our sales in Boston have been declining steadily and as a result we cannot afford to lose any dealers in this area. I suggest therefore that you contact the two dealers personally and work out a procedure to retain their business. Also I suggest that you work closely with the supervisor in this area to establish a procedure for restoring our sales efforts.

Please let me know the outcome of your actions I am eagerly awaiting your reply.

The answers to this exercise appear in the **Instructor's Manual and Key** *for* **HOW 8: A Handbook for Office Workers,** *Eighth Edition.*

Semicolon Placement, Series and Enumerations (1-20 and 1-21)

Practice Sentences 18

1. Our family has lived in Miami Florida Houston Texas and Portland Oregon.

2. Attending the meeting were David Stevens president North Hills Academy Agnes Moore

   assistant principal Rhodes School and Vera Caruso director Flintridge Preparatory School.

3. We plan to initiate a new sales campaign for example we will flood the local media with advertisements offering discounts on several items in our product line.

4. Several factors have contributed to this problem namely labor shortages wage increases and frequent strikes.

5. Esther has done all the fact-finding for this case Jim has verified her findings and Paul will take the case into court next Wednesday morning.

6. Members from San Fernando California Phoenix Arizona and Reno Nevada plan to attend the Western Regional meeting.

7. The quiz cards asked the contestants to tell what important events occurred on July 4 1776 October 24 1929 and November 22 1963.

8. We have changed a number of our former procedures for example we no longer approve

   requisitions in this office.

9. Several of our agents have already exceeded the $1 million mark in real estate sales this

   year namely Charles Brubaker Dana Walters Phillip Gordon and Lisa Stanzell.

10. Corporate offices will be moved to Dayton Ohio sales territories will be expanded from eight to ten and the position of sales manager will be elevated to vice president.

Check your answers with those given on page 319 before completing the following exercise.

Practice Paragraph 18

Our next student travel tour will include visits to London England Madrid Spain and Frankfurt Germany. Two years ago we received 200 applications for our European tour last year we received nearly 400 and this year we expect over 700 students to apply for this tour.

This tour is one of the most popular ones we offer because the Smith Foundation underwrites many of the costs namely hotel accommodations meals and surface transportation.

Check your answers with those given on page 319 before completing the following exercise.

Reinforcement Letter 18

Dear Jason:

In 1996 our convention was held in Philadelphia Pennsylvania in 1997 it was held in Atlanta Georgia and in 1998 it was held in Dallas Texas. The selection of our 1999 convention site has been narrowed down to three cities namely Los Angeles San Francisco and Denver.

The majority of the planning committee favors Denver however hotel accommodations appear to be more favorable in the other two locations. As soon as the committee has had an opportunity to look into the matter further I will let you know the specific location for the 1999 convention.

For one of the program sessions we have been able to obtain four excellent speakers to serve on a resource panel but before we can publicize the names of our resource panel we must yet receive written confirmation from one of them. So far Ms. Ann Jones vice president of First National Bank Mr. Richard Lee treasurer of Security Savings Federal Bank and Dr. David Long professor of management at Illinois State College have formally accepted our invitation. Our fourth resource person Mr. James Fountain president of Investment Enterprises has tentatively accepted our invitation also.

As you can see plans are well under way for the 1999 convention. We are very close to selecting a site I am sure that we will have a decision within the next two weeks. Many of our speakers have been confirmed and I believe we will be able to provide a tentative program by the end of July. In the meantime if you have any comments or suggestions for the convention committee please let me know.

Sincerely yours,

*The answers to this exercise appear in the **Instructor's Manual and Key** for **HOW 8: A Handbook for Office Workers**, Eighth Edition.*

Colon Placement, Formally Enumerated or Listed Items (1-23)
Colon Placement, Explanatory Sentences (1-24)

Practice Sentences 19

1. Please order the following supplies bond paper pencils pens and writing pads.

2. Several people called while you were out Marguerite Rodriguez from Atlas Corporation Robert Wong from the Accounting Department Lynne Hale from Thompson Industries and Jerry Horowitz from the home office.

3. Carmen has thoroughly examined this case from every viewpoint she has studied all the evidence gathered by the investigators and the court decisions in similar cases

4. Included with this statement are bills for January 4 January 8 February 1 and February 7.

5. You may select merchandise from either of these catalogs Spring 1999 or Summer 1999.

6. Employees with the highest rating for the month of February were Naomi Chahinian Bertha Granados and Kelly Crockett.

7. Our buyer ordered the following items last week from your spring line shirts shoes belts skirts and hats.

8. Two of our subsidiaries have shown considerable growth during the last year Belmont Industries and Feldson Manufacturing Company.

9. Four of our products in this series are being discontinued we have had too many difficulties servicing them.

10. You will need to hire 14 temporary employees for our spring sale namely 3 cashiers 5 salespersons and 6 inventory clerks.

Check your answers with those given on pages 319–320 before completing the following exercise.

Practice Paragraph 19

New offices were opened in the following cities last year Albany Billings Dayton and Fresno. We had planned to add additional offices in Portland and San Antonio the high cost of financing has delayed the openings of these offices until next year. Both the planning and development of the new offices have been handled by five persons in our home office Bill Collins Brad Morgan Susan Smith Carol White and David Williams.

Check your answers with those given on page 320 before completing the following exercise.

Reinforcement Letter 19

Dear Mrs. Farmer:

We appreciate receiving your order. As you requested we are shipping the following items immediately

      1 carton bond copy paper, 8.5" x 11"

      1 carton laser printer paper, 8.5" x 11"

      1 print cartridge for HP LaserJet 5 printer

      2 dozen No. 2 pencils

You may place any future orders by telephone just call our toll-free number (800) 618-4932. Ask for one of the following salespersons Mary Small Bill Green or Ann Smith. If the items you order are in our current catalog they will be sent to you the same day you place your order. On the other hand allow at least ten days for delivery of noncatalog items namely odd-sized printer ribbons adding machine forms and supplies for equipment manufactured prior to 1992.

We are enclosing a copy of our latest catalog it may be helpful to you in placing future orders. We look forward to doing business with you and toward developing a successful business relationship.

                Sincerely yours,

*The answers to this exercise appear in the **Instructor's Manual and Key** for **HOW 8: A Handbook for Office Workers,** Eighth Edition.*

Dash Placement—Parenthetical Elements, Appositives, and Summaries (1-29)

Practice Sentences 20

1. Former employers and teachers these are the only names you should supply to prospective employers as references.

2. A number of urgent E-mail messages one from Mary Thompson two from Laura Woo and two from Michael Benton still need to be answered.

3. Several major factors increased interest rates higher property values and a general business slowdown have caused a real estate decline in this area.

4. The administrative staff hoping to boost employee morale increase sales and raise profit levels instituted a bonus-commission program.

5. Sunburst Apollo Courtyard and Terrace Blossom these four china patterns will be featured during our August sale.

6. Any number of private delivery services Airborne Express Federal Express United Parcel Service etc. can provide you with overnight service to Cincinnati.

7. All our staff members with possibly only one or two exceptions are Certified Public Accountants.

8. You may choose from a variety of colors black navy gray white bone red pink yellow brown taupe emerald and sky blue.

9. Three commercial on-line service providers America Online CompuServe and Prodigy are being evaluated by our manager.

10. Word processing spreadsheet and database any applicant we interview must have recent training or experience in these kinds of software programs.

Check your answers with those given on page 320 before completing the following exercise.

Practice Paragraph 20

Crestview Wood Finishing manufacturers of French doors and windows main entrance doors and window boxes has been serving our community for more than twenty-five years. Our quality workmanship which can be seen in the lustrous wood finish elegant hardware and precision fit of our doors and windows is guaranteed for five years. Stop by our showroom to view our new display of French doors and windows. Single pane double panes beveled or frosted you may choose any of these glass types for your French doors or windows.

Check your answers with those given on page 320 before completing the following exercise.

Reinforcement Letter 20

To: Susan Brady

This morning our bank president Herbert V. Hoover announced that Continental Bank will merge with United Federal Bank. The merger will become effective on January 1 and all Continental Bank offices will officially become part of United Federal Bank. At that time Continental Bank will cease to exist however every effort will be made to make this transition as smooth as possible for both our customers and our employees.

The Devonshire branch the Mission Hills Branch and the Chatsworth Branch these three Sun Valley branches will be closed as a result of the merger with United Federal Bank. Because United Federal Bank has existing branches in these areas the Continental Bank branch offices are no longer needed.

Between January 1 and February 28 the branches designated to close will maintain normal operations for all customers. All three branch managers Gail Davis Tony Garcia and Chris Ellis will begin transfer and shutdown operations on March 1. These managers besides notifying customers transferring accounts to other branches and vacating the premises will need to reduce their staffs by 50 percent and give proper notice to those employees who will no longer have positions with the bank. All displaced personnel who remain with the bank through March 31 the target date for the branch office closings will be awarded an attractive severance pay package.

As vice president of real estate and development you will need to determine the disposition of the furniture equipment and facilities for these three offices. Please keep me informed Susan of the progress you make in this regard.

*The answers to this exercise appear in the **Instructor's Manual and Key** for **HOW 8: A Handbook for Office Workers,** Eighth Edition.*

Section 2   Hyphenating and Dividing Words

Compound Adjectives (2-2)

Practice Guide 1

Instructions: Make any necessary corrections in the underlined words in the following sentences. Write your answers in the blank provided at the right of each sentence. If the underlined words are written correctly, write *OK* in the blank line.

1. Please have all applicants for the administrative assistant position take a <u>five minute</u> keyboarding test.   _____

2. We must bring our customer records <u>up-to-date</u> by the end of this month.   _____

3. At the present time our company uses three different <u>word-processing</u> programs.   _____

4. The <u>Boston-Miami</u> flight is scheduled twice daily on weekdays.   _____

5. An <u>alarmingly-toxic</u> gas was feared to have been dispersed by the factory's exhaust system.   _____

6. Next month we are scheduled to replace the two <u>slowest-printing</u> printers in our department.   _____

7. The contractor plans to build <u>three and four-bedroom</u> houses on this piece of land.   _____

8. Only <u>Oklahoma-University</u> students were issued tickets to the musical production.   _____

9. All the company's <u>newly-acquired</u> land holdings are in Marin County.   _____

10. Our manager, Mr. Allen, is one of the most <u>kind-hearted</u> people I have ever met.   _____

11. Were you able to obtain a <u>thirty year</u> loan on this property?   _____

12. Most of our <u>charge-account</u> customers have already received advance notice of our July linen sale.   _____

13. Tourists can view the <u>snow white</u> hills against the sky from the floor of the valley.   _____

14. Too many <u>long-winded</u> speakers at this banquet could cause a low attendance at tomorrow night's banquet.   _____

15. My present job is only <u>part time.</u>   _____

16. The First Lady's recent visit to England bolstered <u>British-American</u> relations.

_____

17. At least 300 students from our college have applied for <u>interest free</u> loans.

_____

18. Three of these programs are <u>government-sponsored</u> and will expire at the end of 2001.

_____

19. The daughter Mildred is the <u>least-known</u> member of the prominent Kensington family.

_____

20. The <u>air conditioning</u> equipment in our building broke down yesterday.

_____

21. Did you show the <u>high and low-selling prices</u> of this stock in the report?

_____

22. Please see that these dresses are shipped to our <u>Main-Street</u> store.

_____

23. Our sales manager received a <u>well-deserved</u> promotion last week to vice president of sales.

_____

24. John's advertising campaigns seem to take on a <u>hit and miss</u> nature.

_____

25. Our company bids on both <u>large and small-scale</u> construction projects.

_____

26. Be sure to include at least three <u>redeemable-store</u> coupons in the ad.

_____

27. Each year our store sponsors a local <u>Little-League</u> team.

_____

28. Please use <u>larger-size</u> poster board for the displays.

_____

29. How many <u>basic-accounting</u> classes are being offered this fall?

_____

30. This semester we plan to offer several <u>home study</u> courses through our local television station.

_____

Check your answers with those given on page 321 before completing the following exercise.

Name _____   Date _____

Practice Guide 2

Instructions: Make any necessary corrections in the following sentences by hyphenating any compound adjectives that require hyphens. Write your answers in the blank provided at the right of each sentence. If the sentence is correct, write *OK* in the blank line.

1. Use the electric shredder to dispose of these out of date files.

   _____

2. Please use a sans serif typeface for all headings in this report.

   _____

3. Most on line service providers offer unlimited Internet usage for a monthly flat fee.

   _____

4. Several delays in yesterday's New York Los Angeles flight caused Mr. Reynolds to be late for the meeting.

   _____

5. Many of the out of town visitors did not bring enough warm clothing for our cold weather.

   _____

6. After reading your run of the mill E-mail messages, delete them from your mailbox.

   _____

7. While working at the computer, maintain an erect position so that you do not become round shouldered.

   _____

8. Only Florida University students with tickets are to be admitted to the football game.

   _____

9. Most of these million dollar homes have been on the market for at least six months.

   _____

10. Begin shut down procedures on this equipment about a half an hour before closing time.

    _____

11. For our back to school sale, we will need to order additional notebooks, pens, erasers, and other such stationery supplies.

    _____

12. When your money market account matures, do you wish to have it roll over?

    _____

13. You will need to order an additional supply of 12 inch rulers for our sale.

    _____

14. Encourage television viewers to hurry in to our nearest location to take advantage of our rock bottom prices.

    _____

15. Someone left a pair of dark rimmed glasses in the reception area.

    _____

16. Fees for regularly scheduled classes at our college are only $13 per unit.

    _____

17. Cinco de Mayo is a holiday that is celebrated in the United States by many Mexican American people.

_____

18. Remind the conference speakers to allow enough time for a question and answer period at the end of their sessions.

_____

19. We may need to reduce even further the price of the least desirable lots in this housing tract.

_____

20. Many of our callers still do not use push button telephones.

_____

21. Stop by sometime soon to see our new line of high quality carpets.

_____

22. Ask the technicians to set up the public address system by 9 a.m. Tuesday.

_____

23. Locating this information on the Internet should not become an all day task.

_____

24. After six months a new employee is eligible to participate in the company's profit sharing plan.

_____

25. Present day communication systems, such as E-mail and fax transmissions, enable written messages to be exchanged within minutes.

_____

26. Our automobile loans are set up for three, four, and five year contracts.

_____

27. Arrangements we have purchased from The Flower Gallery have always been picture perfect.

_____

28. Do you have any smaller size note paper?

_____

29. If you spend money from the petty cash fund, please provide me with a receipt for your purchases.

_____

30. Most of our part time employees are students at a nearby college.

_____

31. Our brokerage firm does not handle over the counter securities.

_____

32. For this flight all seats in coach class have been sold, but some first class seats are still available.

_____

33. Since the downtown area consists of a series of one way streets, include a map for each applicant.

_____

34. The developers of this shopping mall have applied for an open end mortgage.

_____

35. For your convenience our management oriented training programs are offered evenings and on Saturdays.

_____

36. Atlas Software Corporation has developed several computer based accounting programs for small businesses.

   _____

37. Please purchase from the post office a roll of one hundred 32 cent stamps.

   _____

38. These independently sponsored Web sites provide career services for persons in a wide variety of occupations.

   _____

39. On the city freeways you will need to stay within the 65 mile an hour speed limit.

   _____

40. Our management consulting firm specializes in assisting medium and large size businesses.

   _____

*The answers to this exercise appear in the **Instructor's Manual and Key** for **HOW 8: A Handbook for Office Workers,** Eighth Edition.*

Name _____ Date _____

Practice Guide 3

Instructions: Make any necessary corrections in the following paragraphs. Delete any unnecessary hyphens and insert hyphens where they should be placed.

Last week we received several hundred letters from our readers. These letters dealt mostly with the hotly-controversial articles we published on Mexican American citizens in our community. This four week series caused considerable interest among our readers. In fact, it resulted in our receiving a record breaking number of responses.

These articles also comprise the highest-income producing series we have ever published. Circulation rose to a peak-point, one we had not experienced for at least a five year period. Increased circulation was not only in single copy purchases but also in the number of home delivery subscriptions.

The amazingly-large number of responses received from the series was not all one sided. Although some readers may have had a highly-critical response to one part of the article, they often then praised the high quality reporting in another section. Many other readers thought the entire series was thought-provoking and well-written; a few readers did express displeasure with all aspects of the series. As a whole, though, our readers did praise these well-researched and thoroughly-documented pieces of writing. Only the highest level newspaper-reporting techniques were used in these articles.

The long term goals of our newspaper should include more such feature articles that deal with the pulse of our community. These articles should rely on factually based reporting that can withstand controversially-provoked criticism.

*The answers to this exercise appear in the **Instructor's Manual and Key** for **HOW 8: A Handbook for Office Workers,** Eighth Edition.*

Name _____   Date _____

End-of-Line Divisions (2-5 Through 2-8)

Practice Guide 4

Instructions: Rewrite the following words or word groups in the blanks provided. Use a diagonal line to indicate the *preferable* line-ending divisions for the word or word group. If the word or word group may not be divided or word division should be avoided, write *ND* in the blank provided.

Ex. *corporation*   _____ *cor/pora/tion* _____

1. novelty   _____

2. undesirable   _____

3. January 14   _____

4. 4397 Halstead Street   _____

5. stripped   _____

6. letter   _____

7. Mary N. Gomez   _____

8. response   _____

9. 25 percent   _____

10. Columbus, Ohio 43210   _____

11. readers   _____

12. critical   _____

13. techniques   _____

14. San Francisco   _____

15. Agriculture   _____

16. Ms. Darlene Jackson   _____

17. 3942 East 21st Street   _____

18. December 17, 1999   _____

19. possible   _____

20. connection   _____

21. brother-in-law _____

22. thoroughly _____

23. Massachusetts _____

24. self-reliance _____

25. couldn't _____

Check your answers with those given on page 321 before completing the following exercise.

Practice Guide 5

Instructions: If a line-ending word or word group is divided correctly, write *OK* in the blank at the right. However, if the word or word group is divided incorrectly or the word division shown is not preferred, rewrite the correct answer in the blank. Show all preferred word divisions with a diagonal. Follow the style shown in the example exercise.

Ex. *be/ginning*   *begin/ning*

1. pos/itive   _____

2. congra/tulations   _____

3. Dr. Nicholas / R. Montesano   _____

4. careful/ly   _____

5. March 10, / 1999   _____

6. sup/ply   _____

7. 6721 West / 83rd Street   _____

8. necess/ary   _____

9. ob/jective   _____

10. gui/dance   _____

11. Norcross, Georgia / 30093   _____

12. supervi/sor   _____

13. Vir/ginia   _____

14. Ms. / Schmidt   _____

15. acknow/ledge   _____

16. exec/utive   _____

17. November / 10   _____

18. tent/ative   _____

19. 42 / Pontiac Road   _____

20. cus/tom   _____

21. KRAC-/TV   _____

22. brevi/ty _____

23. infor/mation _____

24. 1,350,/000 _____

25. abbrevia/tion _____

*The answers to this exercise appear in the **Instructor's Manual and Key** for **HOW 8: A Handbook for Office Workers,** Eighth Edition.*

Section 3 Capitalization

Practice Sentences, Practice Paragraphs, and Reinforcement Letters

The following materials contain five sets of exercises for the major principles governing the capitalization of nouns. These sets include *Practice Sentences,* a *Practice Paragraph,* and a *Reinforcement Letter.*

Each principle under consideration is labeled by name at the beginning of the exercise series. The section in *HOW* that explains the use of the principle is shown in parentheses.

For *Practice Sentences* use the revision mark for capitalization under each letter to be capitalized; that is, place three short underscores below the letter to be capitalized. Follow the procedure shown in the following example:

Mary richter ordered a model 5879 calculator for each member of the staff in our accounting department.

For those sentences requiring quotation marks, italics, or underscores, use revision marks to show these marks of punctuation directly on the copy. See the following illustration:

I read with interest your article more vacation for less money that appeared In the march issue of arizona highways.

Practice Sentences deal only with the principle or principles under consideration. After you have completed each exercise, check your answers on pages 322–323.

Practice Paragraphs illustrate further the capitalization principle or principles under consideration. Use the procedures described for *Practice Sentences* to complete the exercises. Check your answers on pages 322–323.

Reinforcement Letters are cumulative; that is, once a capitalization principle has been covered in a previous exercise, it may appear in the *Reinforcement Letters.* Use the same procedures outlined for the *Practice Sentences* and the *Practice Paragraphs* to edit the *Reinforcement Letters.* Check your answers with your instructor.

Practice Guides

Seven additional sets of exercises on capitalization follow the *Practice Sentence-Practice Paragraph-Reinforcement Letter* series. These *Practice Guides* correspond to the previous exercises and are designed to give additional, more intensive practice in the application of the capitalization principles under consideration.

Specific instructions for the completion of each *Practice Guide* are given at the beginning of the exercise material. For solutions to these exercises, check with your instructor.

Capitalization, Proper Nouns and Adjectives (3-2)

Practice Sentences 1

1. Did you know that dr. chu's new offices are located in the medical arts building?

2. Are there any stores in the promenade shopping mall that sell franciscan china?

3. We will visit the caribbean on the cruise ship the viking queen.

4. During the storm the green tree bridge collapsed into the suwannee river.

5. All our sharp calculators are being replaced by dorsey memocalcs.

6. Did you order caesar salad to accompany the beef stroganoff?

7. Our next convention will be held at the montclair hotel in the city of angels.

8. Miniblinds are a new version of the old-fashioned venetian blinds.

9. This year the dakota county fair will be held in norfolk.

10. All these sketches by john sreveskl are done in india ink.

Check your answers with those given on page 322 before completing the following exercise.

Practice Paragraph 1

In april we will meet in the islands to discuss the reorganization of territories in alaska, california, hawaii, oregon, and washington. Reservations have been made for april 7 on a united airlines flight to honolulu. Either american motors or ford motor company cars may be rented from budget car rental for those agents attending the meeting.

Check your answers with those given on page 322 before completing the following exercise.

Reinforcement Letter 1

Dear ms. harris:

We were sorry to learn that you were disappointed with the performance of your travelwell luggage during your recent trip to the far east.

We agree that the locks on your suitcases should not have broken. If you will take the cases and this letter to white's department store, the manager will have the locks on your travelwell luggage repaired free of charge.

We are sorry for the inconvenience you have been caused. As a token of our appreciation for your patience and to reaffirm your confidence in travelwell products, we are enclosing a $50 gift certificate that may be used toward your next purchase of any piece of travelwell luggage.

May we suggest you view our newest product, the travel-lite briefcase. Its lightweight feature and durability have made this briefcase one of our most popular products. See it for yourself at white's department store.

sincerely yours,

*The answers to this exercise appear in the **Instructor's Manual and Key** for **HOW 8: A Handbook for Office Workers,** Eighth Edition.*

Capitalization, Abbreviations (3-3)
Capitalization, Numbered or Lettered Items (3-4)

Practice Sentences 2

1. Please deliver this c.o.d. order before 2 p.m.

2. The cpa examination will be given at usc next month.

3. Unfortunately, twa flight 82 has been delayed several hours.

4. Enclosed is payment for invoice 578391, which covers all the merchandise we purchased from you last month.

5. Please refer to page 28 of our current catalog to see an illustration of our model 1738 vcr.

6. I believe the check I issued you, no. 347, was returned by the bank in error.

7. Notice that figure 3 on page 23 illustrates the decline in foreign car sales during the past two years.

8. I believe that paragraph 4 may be deleted from this report.

9. Have you notified the insured that policy no. 6429518-C will lapse in June?

10. Next week we will place our model no. 17 desk on sale.

Check your answers with those given on page 322 before completing the following exercise.

Practice Paragraph 2

The cost of damages resulting from your accident is covered by your policy, no. 846821. However, as stated in section B, paragraph 3, the company will cover medical costs only after the $100 deductible stipulation has been satisfied. If your medical expenses since January 1 have exceeded the deductible amount, please have your doctor fill out form 6B and return it in the enclosed envelope. If you have any questions, call me at 759-6382 any weekday between 9 a.m. and 4 p.m.

Check your answers with those given on page 322 before completing the following exercise.

Reinforcement Letter 2

Dear mrs. rice:

We have made reservations for you on american airlines flight 980 to new york city on march 18. Your flight will leave denver at 9:30 a.m., mst, and arrive in new york at 3:10 p.m., est. As shown on page 2 of the enclosed brochure, the tour will leave for europe the following day.

Please limit the weight of your luggage to 70 pounds. According to the enclosed policy, no. 48613, your luggage is insured up to $3,000 against loss or damage.

Once you arrive in new york, you will be met at jfk by a representative from our travel agency. She will take you to the wilson hotel where room 422 has been reserved for your overnight stay. Your tour guide will contact you there.

Do have a wonderful stay in europe. We appreciate your allowing us to make the arrangements for you.

sincerely yours,

*The answers to this exercise appear in the **Instructor's Manual and Key** for **HOW 8: A Handbook for Office Workers,** Eighth Edition.*

Capitalization, Personal and Professional Titles (3-5)

Practice Sentences 3

1. When does the governor wish to schedule the conference?

2. We have sent all the extra copies of this book to professor Carlos Rodriguez.

3. The announcement was made by Mark Swenson, president of Georgetown Steel.

4. Please submit this application to our vice president, Joshua Wooldridge.

5. We request, professor, that all grade reports be returned by the end of next week.

6. Tomorrow mayor-elect Ann Brown will take office.

7. Each semester Byron Teague, assistant dean of instruction, must visit at least once the classes of all probationary instructors.

8. Only our personnel director was invited to attend the meeting.

9. These orders are to be delivered to lieutenant colonel Bruno Furtado.

10. We hope that Bill Clinton, the president, will accept the key to our city during his visit here.

Check your answers with those given on page 322 before completing the following exercise.

Practice Paragraph 3

The purchasing agents' convention in miami was well attended this year. After a welcoming speech by mayor frank barnes, john lang, the president of williams manufacturing company, spoke on how inflation is affecting the inventories of many companies throughout the country. Also speaking on the same subject was professor roberta holt.

Check your answers with those given on page 323 before completing the following exercise.

Reinforcement Letter 3

Dear mr. ross:

As secretary for councilman john rogers, I, as one of my duties, schedule his appointments. On the day you wish to meet with him, he has an all-day meeting with alice day, auditor for los angeles county. Following his meeting with ms. day, he will fly to washington, d.c., to meet with george davis, senator from florida.

I expect councilman rogers to return on october 15. He is scheduled to arrive at lax on united flight 76 at 9:15 a.m.

I know that as chairperson of his reelection campaign, you are quite eager to meet with him. Would you be able to meet in room 117 of the broadway building at 2 p.m. on october 15? Please call me at 793-9461, ext. 523, to confirm this appointment or to set up a time for another one.

sincerely yours,

*The answers to this exercise appear in the **Instructor's Manual and Key** for **HOW 8: A Handbook for Office Workers,** Eighth Edition.*

Capitalization, Literary or Artistic Works (3-6 Through 3-9) Capitalization—Academic Subjects, Courses, and Degrees (3-13 and 3-14)

Practice Sentences 4

Note: The words appearing in brackets are titles of literary or artistic works.

1. We must purchase the book [a history of the americas] for our history 12 class.

2. Did you know that your subscription to [music world of wonder] will expire with the next issue?

3. Theresa Flores, ph.d., has agreed to teach a conversational spanish class during the next semester.

4. Walt Disney's movie [the lion king] is available on videocassette for your children's continual enjoyment.

5. Make an appointment to see Lisa Gartlan, m.d., for a physical examination.

6. Did you read [a look at teenage life in these united states] that appeared in the April issue of [outlook magazine]?

7. In June Mr. Magnuson will be awarded his master of science degree in engineering.

8. The group sang [singing in the rain] for its last number.

9. We are presently running ads in [the new york times] and [the wall street journal].

10. All the students in our theater arts 23 class went to see [fiddler on the roof].

Check your answers with those given on page 323 before completing the following exercise.

Practice Paragraph 4

I plan to interview fred case, ph.d., the author of the book [it's easy to make a million dollars]. This interview will be the basis for a feature article that will appear in the [people today] section of the sunday [chronicle]. I am interested to learn whether the ideas outlined in his book came from actual experience, research, or both. I understand, too, that the newly released movie, [how to make a million without really trying], is based on dr. case's book.

Check your answers with those given on page 323 before completing the following exercise.

Reinforcement Letter 4

Dear dr. carnes:

It was a pleasure to be able to meet with you to discuss the editorial problems we experienced with the manuscript for your latest book, [economics for the consumer]. Your production editor, mary jones, agrees with me that all the changes you suggested can be made easily so that the book will be applicable for use in consumer education classes.

As far as publicity for the book is concerned, charles singer, director of advertising, suggested that we advertise the book in [consumer reports], a periodical for teachers of home economics, distributive education, and consumer education.

I am enclosing a copy of an article entitled [the consumer revolt—is it really here?] that appeared in the last issue of [new yorker] magazine. The author's ideas seem to be quite similar to yours, so I thought you might be interested in seeing it.

If I can be of any further editorial help to you, please let me know.

sincerely,

The answers to this exercise appear in the **Instructor's Manual and Key** *for* **HOW 8: A Handbook for Office Workers,** *Eighth Edition.*

Capitalization, Organizations (3-15)

Practice Sentences 5

1. Please make your tax-deductible check payable to the national fund for the protection of american wildlife.

2. This bill was passed by the senate during its last session. (United States Senate)

3. All persons employed by the company and their families are ineligible to participate in the contest.

4. These forms must be approved by the accounting department before they can be forwarded to the payroll department.

5. Please ask our advertising department to make the changes shown on the enclosed copy.

6. Yesterday we learned that all county employees will receive an 8 percent pay increase.

7. Contact the department of human resources to assist you in finding a position.

8. Only government employees are eligible to receive this discount.

9. The contracts must be ready for members of the board of directors to sign by June 4.

10. Are you a member of the national council of teachers of english?

Check your answers with those given on page 323 before completing the following exercise.

Practice Paragraph 5

Bill hughes has recently been promoted to head our public relations department. As a former president of both the chamber of commerce and the rotary club, he is well acquainted with many members of the business community. One of his main responsibilities in his new position at fairchild enterprises will be to promote the company among his business contacts.

Check your answers with those given on page 323 before completing the following exercise.

Reinforcement Letter 5

Dear mr. smith:

Thank you for your time and cooperation in helping us conduct the yearly audit of watson corporation. Your accounting department is among the most efficient and well-organized ones I have ever visited.

Hopefully your loan application to the small business administration will be approved. If you would like some advice or assistance in completing the loan application, you may wish to contact john jones, vice president of ryan corporation. He is quite knowledgeable in dealing with sba matters and would be able to answer any questions you may have. I have informed john that you may be calling him.

Please give my regards to your controller, peter swift. We appreciated his efforts during the audit to make our stay at watson corporation a pleasant one.

sincerely yours,

The answers to this exercise appear in the **Instructor's Manual and Key** *for* **HOW 8: A Handbook for Office Workers,** *Eighth Edition.*

Practice Guide 1: Capitalization—Proper Nouns and Adjectives (3-2)

Instructions: Proofread the following sentences for errors in capitalization of proper nouns or adjectives. Underline any errors, and supply the correct answer in the blank at the right. If a sentence is correct, write *OK* in the blank.

Ex. *Our offices are located in the Union Bank <u>building</u> on the corner of Broadway and State Street.*   _____*Building*_____

1. One of our most popular cruises takes travelers through the Panama canal.   _____

2. Within the Springfield area we have at least four Italian Restaurants.   _____

3. Use this CD to locate the 9-digit ZIP Codes for the enclosed list of addresses.   _____

4. Your out-of-warranty Emerson Computer can be repaired by one of our local authorized dealers.   _____

5. You will need to cross the San Francisco Bay bridge to reach our offices.   _____

6. All these american corporations have been in existence for at least fifty years.   _____

7. Please order an additional supply of letter-size Manila file folders.   _____

8. Prices for this year's models of Sony Digital Cameras have dropped considerably.   _____

9. Since our company has a number of clients in Chicago, I often visit the windy city.   _____

10. Alfredo's is best known for its delicious Chili con carne.   _____

11. A number of our clients have expressed an interest in taking a tour of the Mississippi river.   _____

12. Our design center features scandinavian furniture and modern art.   _____

13. This new fast-food chain serves only hamburgers, French fries, and an assortment of beverages.   _____

14. Clients may enjoy a cup of starbucks coffee during their appointment with one of our investment counselors.   _____

15. The camarillo fashion mall is scheduled to open on October 1.   _____

16. Although they appear to be made of wood, all these statues are made of Plaster of Paris.   _____

17. Our deluxe mixture consists of almonds, walnuts, cashews, and Brazil nuts.

_____

18. Dr. Lee has moved her offices to the Desert medical center.

_____

19. Salad dressing choices for our customers include Italian, French, Ranch, and Blue Cheese.

_____

20. Heavy storms over the Rockies have delayed most flights.

_____

21. With each entrée you have a choice of broccoli soup, caesar salad, or a visit to our salad bar.

_____

22. The Pasadena rose parade is televised each year on national television.

_____

23. We import only european-made clothing, shoes, and handbags.

_____

24. At our department store you may obtain all available patterns of Lenox China.

_____

25. The xerox in our office needs to be serviced before I can make these copies.

_____

The answers to this exercise appear in the **Instructor's Manual and Key** for **HOW 8: A Handbook for Office Workers,** Eighth Edition.

Practice Guide 2: Capitalization—Abbreviations (3-3), Numbered or Lettered Items (3-4)

Instructions: Proofread the following sentences for errors in capitalization of abbreviations and numbered or lettered items. Underline any errors, and supply the correct answer in the blank at the right. If a sentence is correct, write *OK* in the blank.

1. Our store hours are from 9 A.M. to 5 P.M. daily. _____

2. All our scanners are fully illustrated and described on pages 78–86 of the enclosed catalog. _____

3. Your check number 382 was returned by the bank for insufficient funds. _____

4. We are moving our offices from suite 340 to suite 200 next month. _____

5. Several people in our office are taking courses toward earning a b.a. degree. _____

6. Do we have any additional Size 8 dresses in Style 4328? _____

7. The Premium on your fire insurance policy, number 18754BVN834, is due on March 1. _____

8. You will be flying to Atlanta on Delta Flight 1074, which is scheduled to depart on time. _____

9. This E-mail message was sent today at 12 noon, est. _____

10. One of our computers, serial no. 18754390, will not boot up. _____

11. The cpa examination is given biannually in Tampa. _____

12. We have been rescheduled to meet in room 570 instead of room 420. _____

13. Two of these orders are to be sent COD. _____

14. Is the monthly rental fee correct as stipulated in paragraph 5,

    line 3, of the enclosed lease agreement? _____

15. No. 440 in our wheelchair line will be discontinued as soon as the current stock is sold. _____

16. Enclosed is a check to cover your invoice 8321 for $3,687. _____

17. The Hewlett Packard Deskjet printer, model 855C, uses separate cartridges for printing in black and other colors. _____

18. Because of the dense fog, many planes have been rerouted to lax. _____

19. Please refer to figure 4 on page 17 of the annual report for net earnings during the last quarter of the year. _____

20. If you are interested in part-time employment, fill out and return only form B in the enclosed envelope. _____

21. This invoice was paid for by check no. 472 last week. _____

22. Because flight 1054 was overbooked, we were rerouted on flight 1283. _____

23. These records belong to employee No. 576827, who is a supervisor at our Springfield plant. _____

24. A summary of grammar rules appears in appendix A of this business communications text. _____

25. John R. Jones, Soc. Sec. #576-41-9031, has signed the consent form for us to authorize a credit check. _____

*The answers to this exercise appear in the **Instructor's Manual and Key** for **HOW 8: A Handbook for Office Workers,** Eighth Edition.*

Practice Guide 3: Capitalization—Personal and Professional Titles (3-5)

Instructions: Proofread the following sentences for errors in capitalization of personal or professional titles. Underline any errors, and supply the correct answer in the blank at the right. If a sentence is correct, write *OK* in the blank.

1. When you complete the report, please forward a copy to Doctor Jeffrey Weisel.   _____

2. Such a decision will have to be made by the Vice President of Marketing.   _____

3. You will need to speak to sergeant Chris Nelson, the police officer who took the report.   _____

4. We expect, professor, to receive additional copies of this text by August 3.   _____

5. Bill Clinton, president of the United States, will visit our city next month.   _____

6. Our new Vice President, Cameron Bentley, has arranged to visit all our branch offices during the next three months.   _____

7. Will rabbi Goldman be conducting the marriage ceremony?   _____

8. Our Director of Human Resources has announced that she will retire on June 30.   _____

9. This bill was initiated by the Senator from Indiana, John Simpson.   _____

10. Our schedule shows, captain, that your next assignment is Flight 1042, on Tuesday, March 3, departing at 10:43 a.m.   _____

11. Copies of these reports should be sent to Governor-Elect Aaron Wagner before the end of the week.   _____

12. If you need additional information about our operations, just contact our general manager, Alice Duffy.   _____

13. At the next board meeting, our President, Gordon Hampton, will present plans to open branch offices in Bogotá and Buenos Aires.   _____

14. All requests for grade changes must be reviewed by Ms. Rodriguez, the Dean of Academic Affairs.   _____

15. Please forward all this mail to major Morgan at his new address.   _____

16. Mark W. Couleter, the Reverend at St. Luke's Trinity Church, is the beneficiary of this insurance policy.   _____

17. Ms. Foster's Grandmother, Estella Carter, named Ms. Foster executrix of her estate.   _____

18. We will be meeting with the mayor on this issue next week.   _____

19. Anita E. Gould, Professor of English, has been elected chairperson of the English Department.   _____

20. Charles E. Young, President of American Banking Services, has agreed to deliver the keynote address at the bankers' convention.   _____

21. You may, Mister Evans, wish to consult one of our attorneys about this matter.   _____

22. The dean of students has suggested we invite Senator Peter Goodwin to deliver this year's commencement address.   _____

23. When did queen Elizabeth make her last public appearance in London?   _____

24. Since Former Mayor Clarence Chapman left office, he has had several offers from prestigious law firms in our city.   _____

25. The Academy Award-winning Actress, Heather Starr, has agreed to make a guest appearance on our show.   _____

The answers to this exercise appear in the **Instructor's Manual and Key** *for* **HOW 8: A Handbook for Office Workers,** *Eighth Edition.*

Practice Guide 4: Capitalization—Literary or Artistic Works (3-6 Through 3-9)

Instructions: From the answers given below, select the correct one or ones. Write the corresponding letter or letters in the blank provided.

1. Which of the following are correct to express the name of a newspaper?
   a. The Evening Outlook
   b. The Evening Outlook
   c. The evening outlook
   d. "The Evening Outlook"
   e. The Evening Outlook   1. _____

2. How would you express the name of the following song?
   a. A Paradise of Happiness
   b. *A Paradise of Happiness*
   c. A Paradise of Happiness
   d. "A Paradise Of Happiness"
   e. "A Paradise of Happiness"   2. _____

3. When referring to the appendix of a specific book, how would you express this reference?
   a. *Appendix*
   b. Appendix
   c. "Appendix"
   d. Appendix
   e. appendix   3. _____

4. According to *HOW,* which of the following parts of speech are not capitalized in titles unless they (a) contain four or more letters or (b) appear as the first or last word?
   a. Nouns, pronouns, verbs
   b. Articles, conjunctions, prepositions
   c. Verbs, prepositions, conjunctions
   d. Interjections, pronouns, conjunctions
   e. Prepositions, verbs, articles   4. _____

5. Which of the following titles follow correctly the rules of capitalization for literary and artistic works?
   a. In this World of Music
   b. Learning through Proper Study Habits
   c. How to Learn What is Important in Looking for a Job
   d. So you Think You're In?
   e. A Guide to Understanding Literature   5. _____

6. Which of the following titles follow correctly the rules of capitalization for literary and artistic works?
   a. A Guide to Successful Lawn Care
   b. The Beginning of a New Era is Approaching
   c. What is Word Processing all About?
   d. The Computer Age: an Analysis of Today's Society
   e. Problems Of Urban Living   6. _____

7. How would you express correctly the name of the following chapter in a textbook?
   a. The Office Environment and Its Effect on Performance
   b. "The Office Environment and Its Effect on Performance"
   c. "The Office Environment and its Effect on Performance"
   d. The Office Environment and Its Effect on Performance
   e. *The Office Environment and its Effect on Performance*   7. _____

8. How would you express correctly the name of the following book?
   a. The World Dictionary Of the German Language
   b. *The World Dictionary of the German Language*
   c. "The World Dictionary of the German Language"
   d. The World Dictionary of the German Language
   e. *The World Dictionary Of The German Language*   8. _____

9. Which of the following is written correctly to express the names of these famous paintings?
   a. PINK LADY and BLUE BOY
   b. Pink Lady and Blue Boy
   c. "Pink Lady" and "Blue Boy"
   d. Pink Lady and Blue Boy
   e. *Pink Lady* and *Blue Boy*   9. _____

10. How would you properly express the title of the following unpublished report?
    a. Report on the Reconstruction of the Innercity
    b. Report on the Reconstruction of the Innercity
    c. REPORT ON THE RECONSTRUCTION OF THE INNERCITY
    d. "Report on the Reconstruction of the Innercity"
    e. "Report On The Reconstruction Of The Innercity"   10. _____

*The answers to this exercise appear in the **Instructor's Manual and Key** for **HOW 8: A Handbook for Office Workers,** Eighth Edition.*

Practice Guide 5: Capitalization—Literary or Artistic Works (3-6 Through 3-9 and 3-12)

Instructions: Proofread the following sentences. In the blank lines provided, rewrite each sentence, making any necessary changes in *punctuation* and *capitalization.* The names of literary or artistic works are shown in brackets.

1. Professor Schwartz requested the class to read the book [a short history of the roman empire] by March 21.

   _____

   _____

2. The new newspaper column [to and from] that appears in the Sunday issue of the [springfield tribune] has been an unexpected success.

   _____

   _____

3. Did you see the movie [an american werewolf in london].

   _____

   _____

4. When will we receive a copy of Professor Clybourne's lecture entitled [how long can interest rates go up].

   _____

   _____

5. In the [preface] the author explains how to use the textbook.

   _____

   _____

6. I read with interest your most recent article [changing trends in the housing industry] that appeared in last month's issue of [contractors' world].

   _____

   _____

   _____

7. The artist has called this painting [mood for a midnight dream].

   _____

   _____

8. His thesis [a statistical analysis of two approaches for analyzing consumer responses to newspaper advertising] was accepted by the committee last week.

_____

_____

_____

9. We hope that our new television series [for the love of law] will be as great a success as [l.a. law].

_____

_____

10. When will you revise the pamphlet [can you hold a job].

_____

_____

11. Be sure to read the chapter [economic declines and depressions] that appears in the latest edition of our economics textbook [modern economic theories and philosophies].

_____

_____

_____

12. If you have any difficulty locating the information, be sure to consult the [index].

_____

_____

13. Last Sunday's sermon [it is up to you] left the congregation with a challenge.

_____

_____

14. When will our class view the movie classic [who's afraid of virginia woolf].

_____

_____

15. The column [brian williams reports] no longer appears in our local newspaper [the daily news].

_____

_____

The answers to this exercise appear in the **Instructor's Manual and Key** for **HOW 8: A Handbook for Office Workers,** Eighth Edition.

Practice Guide 6: Capitalization—Academic Subjects, Courses, and Degrees (3-13 and 3-14)

Instructions: Proofread the following sentences for errors in capitalization of academic subjects, courses, and degrees. Underline any errors, and supply the correct answer in the blank at the right. If a sentence is correct, write *OK* in the blank.

1. Most of our english classes for nonnative speakers are offered in the evening hours. _____

2. The instructor for our European history class is Paul D. Whalen, ph.d. _____

3. Unfortunately, speech 31 is offered only during the spring semesters. _____

4. You will be eligible for your bachelor of science degree next June provided that you complete the courses listed below. _____

5. All our Conversational Spanish classes are usually filled during the first two weeks of registration. _____

6. Before you may enroll in Accounting 1, you must take a Mathematics proficiency test. _____

7. Two of our instructors have just been accepted into the Master's program at Loyola University. _____

8. Business 8, introduction to business, will be offered Tuesdays and Thursdays from 8:30–10 a.m. _____

9. You may wish to take a Music Appreciation class to fulfill this requirement. _____

10. Two-year colleges offer only associate in arts degrees or associate in science degrees. _____

11. A course in Business English will give you a better understanding of language principles. _____

12. William J. Clark, m.d., will be the surgeon operating on your son next week. _____

13. Our English Department offers several american literature courses. _____

14. Business 85, Excel 7 for Windows 95, was inadvertently omitted in the listing of classes for the current class schedule. _____

15. Our Nursing program was established at the college in 1980. _____

16. You may fulfill the language requirement by taking any course in french, german, japanese, or spanish. _____

17. Professor Taylor teaches three sections of principles of marketing each semester.

_____

18. Darryl's research topic deals with the origin and development of Greek mythology.

_____

19. Marian's Bachelor's degree is in marketing and management.

_____

20. Kevin Dickinson, D.d.S., has rented all this space for his new dental offices.

_____

21. The student wishes to know if her Greek Literature classes will satisfy any general education requirements.

_____

22. As a student of history, Robert has read most of the books listed in the professor's suggested reading list.

_____

23. Bryton College, a private career college, is the only college in this area that offers courses in Medical Office Procedures.

_____

24. History 12, history of the Americas, will be offered each semester and during the summer session.

_____

25. To complete the requirements for the Associate in Arts degree, you will need to complete at least 60 units in a prescribed program.

_____

*The answers to this exercise appear in the **Instructor's Manual and Key** for **HOW 8: A Handbook for Office Workers,** Eighth Edition.*

Practice Guide 7: Capitalization—Organizations (3-15)

Instructions: Proofread the following sentences for errors in capitalization of organizational names and divisions. Underline any errors, and supply the correct answer in the blank at the right. If a sentence is correct, write *OK* in the blank.

1. Elizabeth Hoover obtained her master's degree from the Fisher school of accounting at the University of Florida. _____

2. All contributions to the muscular dystrophy foundation are tax deductible. _____

3. Our customer service department is open from 8 a.m. to 5 p.m., EST. _____

4. All City offices will be closed on January 17, so you must file these papers before that date. _____

5. Please make your check payable to the Arizona Association For The Preservation of National Forests. _____

6. Under this program the federal government will guarantee the loan. _____

7. Revisions in the tax laws regarding capital gains should come before congress during this session. _____

8. When you have projected the costs of this advertising campaign, please report your findings to the manager of the sales and marketing department. _____

9. All these federal housing projects are under the jurisdiction of the department of housing and urban development. _____

10. You will need to submit this petition for a grade change to the office of academic affairs. _____

11. Employees are eligible for health insurance benefits after six months of continuous employment with the Company. _____

12. The board of directors meeting has been rescheduled for March 4. _____

13. Our survey included the Accounting Departments of over 50 major United States corporations. _____

14. When did the Supreme Court render a decision on this issue? _____

15. All state employees were granted a 4 percent pay increase, retroactive to July 1. _____

16. Members of the City Council have been unable to agree upon a plan to revitalize the downtown area.

   _____

17. On Thursdays you may pick up your check in the payroll department between 2 and 3 p.m.

   _____

18. Up-to-date population figures should soon be available from the bureau of the census.

   _____

19. Please contact the school of engineering and computer science for more information about this major.

   _____

20. Many Research Departments throughout the nation have used this software successfully to obtain long-term grants.

   _____

21. Contact the department of highways for its construction plans in this area during the next five years.

   _____

22. Students from high school and postsecondary music departments will be participating in this concert on May 1.

   _____

23. You may obtain an application for employment from our human resources department.

   _____

24. Ms. Donohue's latest experience is in the Product Development Department of Microsoft corporation.

   _____

25. Our Service department stands ready to serve you every day of the week from 8 a.m. to 6 p.m.

   _____

*The answers to this exercise appear in the **Instructor's Manual and Key** for **HOW 8: A Handbook for Office Workers,** Eighth Edition.*

Section 4 Numbers

Practice Sentences, Practice Paragraphs, and Reinforcement Letters

The following materials contain four sets of exercises for several major principles governing the expression of numbers. These sets include *Practice Sentences,* a *Practice Paragraph,* and a *Reinforcement Letter.*

Each principle under consideration is labeled by name at the beginning of the exercise series. The section in *HOW* that explains the use of the principle is shown in parentheses.

For *Practice Sentences* select from the alternatives in parentheses the correct choice for the expression of numbers. Underline your answers. Sentences deal only with the principle under consideration. After you have completed the exercise, check your answers on pages 324–325.

Practice Paragraphs Illustrate further the number-usage principle under consideration. From the alternatives given in parentheses, select and underline the correct one. Check your answers on pages 324–325.

Reinforcement Letters are cumulative; that is, once a number-usage principle has been covered in a previous exercise, it may appear in the *Reinforcement Letters.* For the *Reinforcement Letters* select the correct alternative in parentheses and underline your answer. Check your answers with your instructor.

Practice Guides

Two additional sets of exercises on numbers follow the *Practice Sentence-Practice Paragraph-Reinforcement Letter* series. The first *Practice Guide* corresponds to the previous exercises and is designed to give additional, more intensive practice in the application of principles governing figure and word style. The second *Practice Guide* contains a series of number application exercises related to business calculations.

Specific instructions for the completion of each *Practice Guide* are given at the beginning of the exercise material. For solutions to these exercises, check with your instructor.

Numbers, General Rules (4-1)

Practice Sentences 1

1. Mrs. Hayes invited (27, twenty-seven) people to her reception.

2. The committee will sponsor (6, six) candidates.

3. (36, Thirty-six) students will attend the competition.

4. Mr. Lucas will hire (10, ten) new clerks.

5. Dr. Francis will lecture on (5, five) symptoms of the common cold.

6. There are (38, thirty-eight) signatures on the roll sheet.

7. (86, Eighty-six) members of the club attended the convention.

8. Ms. Brown has flown (three million; 3 million; 3,000,000) miles since 1994.

9. The department has received (25, twenty-five) applications.

10. There are only (12, twelve) of these radio-stereo combinations left in stock.

Check your answers with those given on page 324 before completing the following exercise.

Practice Paragraph 1

Mr. Wells requested that we send him (seventy-five, 75) copies of our latest catalog He is conducting (three, 3) separate workshops at Eastern Business College and believes that over (twenty, 20) business teachers will sign up for each course. So that the business teachers can become acquainted with the materials we have available, Mr. Wells would like to give each teacher a copy of our catalog.

Check your answers with those given on page 324 before completing the following exercise.

Reinforcement Letter 1

Ladies and Gentlemen:

We appreciate your filling our order for (two hundred twenty-five, 225) Johnson serving tables. (Twenty-three, 23) pieces, however, were damaged in transit and cannot be sold in their present condition. Since (two, 2) separate transit companies handled the shipment of the tables, we cannot determine who is responsible for the damage.

We expect that over (two hundred, 200) of our charge account customers will purchase the Johnson tables during our presale, which is scheduled to begin next week. Therefore, we would appreciate your rushing us an additional (twenty-three, 23) tables to replace the ones that were damaged. Also, please let us know what should be done with the damaged merchandise.

Sincerely yours,

*The answers to this exercise appear in the **Instructor's Manual and Key** for **HOW 8: A Handbook for Office Workers,** Eighth Edition.*

Numbers, Related Numbers (4-2)

Practice Sentences 2

1. We have 26 computers, but (3, three) need to be repaired.

2. The number of visitors to this national park has increased from 980,000 last year to (1 million; 1,000,000) this year.

3. We have requested 23 books, 15 workbooks, and (10, ten) teacher's manuals from the publisher.

4. Each of the (11, eleven) applicants gave (4, four) references.

5. Pat found 21 examples of this feature, but only (7, seven) were applicable to our company's needs.

6. There are (382, three hundred eighty-two) active members in this organization, but only (9, nine) are willing to be officers.

7. The prizes—5 television sets, 10 bicycles, and 20 gift certificates—will be awarded during the (2, two) days of our official opening.

8. The produce truck delivered 18 cartons of lettuce, 11 cartons of apples, and (8, eight) cartons of oranges.

9. Our company will manufacture between (1 million; 1,000,000) and (1.5 million; 1,500,000) of these pills.

10. Mrs. Hooper has requested 13 new employees for the (4, four) departments.

Check your answers with those given on page 324 before completing the following exercise.

Practice Paragraph 2

We appreciate your order for (eight, 8) pocket radios, (twenty-two, 22) cassette tape recorders, and (six, 6) portable television sets. At the present time we have only (nine, 9) cassette tape recorders in our Dallas warehouse. We will check with our (three, 3) branch offices and our (two, 2) retail stores to determine whether they have available the remaining (thirteen, 13). In the meantime, we are shipping you (eight, 8) pocket radios, (nine, 9) cassette tape recorders, and (six, 6) portable television sets.

Check your answers with those given on page 324 before completing the following exercise.

Reinforcement Letter 2

Dear Bob:

We are expecting at least (one hundred, 100) people to attend our banquet planned for next Friday. Would you please have the hotel set up (fourteen, 14) circular tables, each one to accommodate (eight, 8) people. Although the total seating capacity will result in (one hundred twelve, 112), I would prefer to have the extra (twelve, 12) seats available in case the attendance rises to this level.

(Ninety-eight, 98) paid reservations have been received so far. I am especially pleased with the enthusiastic response we have received from people who are not members of our organization. In addition to the (seventy-three, 73) reservations received from our membership, we have received (nineteen, 19) reservations from business executives throughout the region and (six, 6) reservations from professors at nearby colleges.

I appreciate your handling the arrangements for the banquet and look forward to seeing you on Friday.

Cordially,

*The answers to this exercise appear in the **Instructor's Manual and Key** for **HOW 8: A Handbook for Office Workers,** Eighth Edition.*

Numbers, Money and Percentages (4-4 and 4-5)
Numbers, With Nouns and Abbreviations (4-8)

Practice Sentences 3

1. The new listings may be found on (Page seven, Page 7, page 7).

2. Our insurance agent sent me a rider to (policy 83478, Policy 83478, Policy 83,478) in error.

3. Please refer to the restrictions; (Number three, Number 3, No. 3) is the most important one.

4. (Number 1880, No. 1880) battery chargers are no longer manufactured by our company.

5. The names of all participating dealers are listed in (Paragraph Eight, paragraph eight, paragraph 8, Paragraph 8).

6. The cash register receipt listed items for $1.98, $2.03, $3.01, and ($4, $4.00).

7. Enrollment figures for this year show a (6%, 6 percent, six per cent) increase over last year.

8. These supplies vary in cost from (20 cents, $.20) to $2.35.

9. Our employer has given all workers an (8%, eight percent, 8 percent) pay increase.

10. The new price for these rulers will be (85 cents, eighty-five cents, $.85) each.

11. The highway repairs will cost between $980,000 and ($1 million; $1,000,000).

12. The city council has allotted (four million dollars, $4 million) for the housing project.

13. Ms. Lloyd has a (22%, 22 percent, 22 per cent) interest in the earnings of this company.

14. The wholesale price of these new pencils will be (30 cents, thirty cents, $.30).

15. There has been a (.4, 0.4) percent decrease in the current interest rate since last week.

Check your answers with those given on page 324 before completing the following exercise.

Practice Paragraph 3

A copy of your homeowner's policy, (policy 7832146, Policy 7832146), is enclosed. As you will note on (page 1, Page 1), (line 6, Line 6), the total company liability under this policy cannot exceed (Forty-seven Thousand Dollars; $47,000; $47,000.00). Please submit this year's premium of (One Hundred Sixty-eight Dollars, $168.00, $168). Because increasing costs have forced us to raise our premium rates, this premium reflects an increase of (eight, 8) percent over last year's premium.

Check your answers with those given on page 324 before completing the following exercise.

Reinforcement Letter 3

Dear Mr. Black:

Although the (twelve, 12) batteries and (two, 2) drills arrived in good condition, we were sorry to learn that (three, 3) of our (Number 114, number 114, No. 114, no. 114) electric motors arrived in damaged condition. According to our records, we shipped you (Serial Numbers, serial numbers, Serial Nos., serial nos.) 832961, 832962, 832963, and 832964. Would you please let us know the serial numbers of the (three, 3) damaged motors.

We have credited your account for (Six Hundred Thirty Dollars, $630, $630.00) plus (Forty-three Dollars and Fifty Cents, $43.50) shipping for the damaged motors. Please keep in mind that you are eligible for a (ten, 10) percent discount on the price of the remaining motor. Also, should you wish us to replace the damaged motors, the (ten, 10) percent discount is still applicable on your reorder.

We were pleased to learn that the remainder of your order arrived in good condition. We are especially proud of the results the (no. 118, No. 118, Number 118, number 118) drill has achieved. Nearly (one hundred, 100) customers have written to tell us of its superiority over other drills on the market.

Please return the damaged electric motors to our Chicago office. A prepaid shipping authorization is enclosed. If you wish us to replace the electric motors, just return the enclosed postcard and we will do so.

Sincerely yours,

*The answers to this exercise appear in the **Instructor's Manual and Key** for **HOW 8: A Handbook for Office Workers,** Eighth Edition.*

Numbers, Weights and Measures (4-6 and 4-7)
Numbers, Dates and Periods of Time (4-9 Through 4-12)

Practice Sentences 4

1. The Johnsons' new baby weighed (9 pounds, 12 ounces; 9 pounds 12 ounces; nine pounds, twelve ounces; 9 lbs. 12 oz.).

2. The engineers' report stated that the boulder weighed at least (three, 3) tons.

3. We will celebrate the fifth anniversary of our company on (June 3, June third, June 3rd).

4. Mrs. Lopez will arrive at (6 P.M., 6 p. m., 6 p.m.).

5. Mr. Hodges will trim (8 inches, eight inches, 8") from each edge.

6. The package weighed (4 pounds, 2 ounces; 4 pounds 2 ounces; 4 pounds, two ounces; 4 lbs. 2 oz.).

7. (October 25, October 25th) has been set as the date for the next board meeting.

8. The orientation meeting was held at (9 o'clock a.m., 9 o'clock in the morning).

9. The flight will leave on the (1st of January, 1 of January, first of January) as scheduled.

10. During the last (18, eighteen) months, we have had two serious fires in our Toledo warehouse.

11. This invoice must be paid within (30, thirty) days to avoid interest charges.

12. In our state no one under (18, eighteen) may work in restaurants that serve alcoholic beverages.

13. Ms. Ige will be (33, thirty-three, thirty three) on her next birthday.

14. Our city will celebrate its (125th, one hundred twenty-fifth) birthday in 2001.

15. Bob Sarafian, (63, sixty-three, sixty three), announced that he plans to take an early retirement at the end of this year.

Check your answers with those given on page 325 before completing the following exercise.

Practice Paragraph 4

When we were in Phoenix from (August 13, August 13th) until (August 24, August 24th), the average high temperature reading was (one hundred sixteen degrees, 116 deg., 116°, 116 degrees). On the (25 of August, 25th of August), the temperature reading dropped to (one hundred ten degrees, 110 deg., 110°, 110 degrees). We did enjoy our (twelve-day, 12-day) vacation but wished our stay had been a cooler one.

Check your answers with those given on page 325 before completing the following exercise.

Reinforcement Letter 4

Dear Mr. and Mrs. Reed:

We know that you will be pleased with your new home. With its (two thousand one hundred; 2,100; 2100) square feet of living space, you will find enjoyment and conveniences that will make it a real pleasure.

As you know, within your unit we have built (sixteen, 16) town houses; at present (nine, 9) of them have been sold. We expect that within the next (eleven, 11) months, the remaining units will be occupied.

We are now in a position to offer you a special furniture value. At prices (thirty, 30) percent below retail value, you may purchase furniture you need for your new home. For example, you may purchase a (model 17, Model 17) Johnson dining room set, which retails for (Eight Hundred Seventy Dollars, $870, $870.00), for only (Six Hundred Dollars, $600, $600.00).

To purchase your new furniture, you need place only a (twenty, 20) percent down payment on your selections. The balance is due (thirty, 30) days after delivery of the furniture, or you may use one of our convenient financing plans. If you are interested in taking advantage of this offer and wish to have one of our decorators call, please return the enclosed postcard.

Sincerely yours,

*The answers to this exercise appear in the **Instructor's Manual and Key** for **HOW 8: A Handbook for Office Workers,** Eighth Edition.*

Practice Guide 1: Numbers—Figure and Word Style (4-1 Through 4-16)

Instructions: Proofread the following sentences for errors in figure or word format. Underline any errors, and supply the correct answer in the blank at the right. If a sentence is correct, write *OK* in the blank.

Ex. *Since we posted this opening at our Web site Career Center, we have received* <u>twenty-three</u> *résumés.*   *23*

1. Members of the staff are making plans to celebrate the 50th anniversary of the college next year. _____

2. Your request for a thirty-day loan for $1,500 at 12 percent interest has been granted. _____

3. Our company has occupied this suite of offices for the past 17 years. _____

4. If the meeting is still in session at 2 this afternoon, I will need to leave early to catch my flight. _____

5. Would you please ensure that this proposal reaches the FedEx office by four p.m. _____

6. If you wish to use these travel vouchers, you must book your flight before the 31st of March. _____

7. Please send us a duplicate of Invoice #36583. _____

8. Be sure to write the customer's check no. on the sales invoice. _____

9. Our office is approximately 30 km. outside London. _____

10. Priority Mail packets weighing up to two pounds may be sent for a standard flat fee. _____

11. Although we suffered a 6% sales decline during the last quarter, we showed a 2% increase in profits. _____

12. Damage to the city block area is estimated to be in excess of $17,500,000. _____

13. Candy bars usually sell for 55 cents each, but The 99¢ Store is selling them at three for $.99. _____

14. The twins' birth weights were recorded as 4 pounds, 14 ounces, and 5 pounds, 2 ounces. _____

15. 43 orders are still waiting to be processed before we close today. _____

16. Golden Star Realty's residential listings include 62 single-family residences, 18 condominium units, and three apartment complexes. _____

17. This week I processed checks to Eagle Software for $657.85, $250, and $187.59. _____

18. In the large banquet room, we can fit up to 30 60-inch round tables, which will each seat ten people.   _____

19. Homes planned for this new residential housing tract will have from 3600 to 4850 square feet of living space.   _____

20. You will need to send 7 original copies of the proposal to the client.   _____

21. Nearly one hundred of these mailers were returned because of insufficient postage.   _____

22. Fifty two reservations are still needed to meet our guarantee for the president's retirement banquet.   _____

23. We will need an additional 78 55-cent stamps to send out the remainder of these invitations.   _____

24. For the additional 14 Model AR110 wall air-conditioning units, please check our other 3 warehouses.   _____

25. There are too many 0's in this total for the spreadsheet formula to be correct.   _____

*The answers to this exercise appear in the **Instructor's Manual and Key** for **HOW 8: A Handbook for Office Workers,** Eighth Edition.*

Practice Guide 2: Numbers—Number Applications (4-18 Through 4-28)

1. Round the following figures to the number of decimal places specified. Write your answers in the answer column.

Figure	Number of Decimal Places	Answer
12.26876	3	
41.81408	2	
0.05498	4	
6.35812	1	
83.47062	0	

2. Convert the following fractions to decimal equivalents. For uneven amounts round the answer to four decimal places and write your answers in the answer column.

Fraction	Decimal Equivalent	Fraction	Decimal Equivalent
1/3		2/5	
1/2		1/6	
3/8		5/12	
5/16		3/10	
3/4		5/8	

3. Convert the following decimal numbers to percent form. For uneven amounts round the answer to two decimal places and write your answers in the answer column.

Decimal	Percent	Decimal	Percent
0.66667		0.4	
1.5		0.83333	
0.875		0.41667	
0.5625		0.7	
2.25		0.625	

4. Convert the following percentages to decimal form. Write your answers in the answer column.

Percent	Decimal	Percent	Decimal
40%		6.5%	
83.9%		2.833%	
120%		4 1/2 %	
0.1%		8 1/4 %	
9%		3 5/8 %	

5. In the following two exercises, calculate the totals. Then determine the percent each figure represents of the total. Round the percent answer to one decimal place. Show your formula in the column titled *Calculation.*

Investment Analysis John Doe				
Type	Value	Calculation	Decimal	Percent
Cash	$39,386			
Real estate	$273,500			
Securities	$127,357			
Total				

ABC Shirt Company Number of Shirts Sold				
Shirt Type	Number	Calculation	Decimal	Percent
Dress shirts	10,833			
Golf shirts	3,476			
T-shirts	12,946			
Sweatshirts	7,210			
Total				

6. Calculate the amount of sales tax and the total cost for each of the purchases shown in the following table. Round the answer to two decimal places. Show your formula in the column titled *Calculation*.

State and Local Sales Taxes				
Purchase	Sales Tax Rate	Calculation	Amount of Sales Tax	Total Cost
$7.95	6%			
$87.50	6 1/2%			
$187.99	7 3/4%			
$2,380.00	7 1/2%			
$14,721.83	5 1/4%			

7. Calculate the number of miles traveled and the mileage expense for each trip listed in the following table. Round the expense calculation to two decimal places.

Mileage Expense Calculations					
Trip	Beginning Mileage	Ending Mileage	Miles Traveled	Per Mile Allowance	Total Expense
A	32,496	32,612		$.35	
B	46,856	47,158		$.28	
C	58,657	59,208		$.22	

8. Calculate the discount amount and resulting cost of the purchases in the following table. Round the answers to two decimal places. Show your formula in the column titled *Calculation*.

Simple Discount Calculations				
Regular Price	Discount	Calculation	Amount of Discount	Cost of Purchase
$45.99	25%			
$137.83	40%			
$1,084.63	2%			
$219.99	15%			
$784.50	1/3 off			

9. In 1996 AAA Manufacturing Company showed a net profit of $437,982. For 1997 the company had a net profit of $486,080. What percent increase in profit over 1996 did AAA manufacturing experience? Show your calculations in the space provided below, and round the answer to one decimal place.

Percent increase _____

10. January sales for Miller's Stationery Store totaled $89,396; in February sales totaled $98,973. What percent increase did Miller's Stationery Store experience in February sales over January sales? Show your calculations in the space provided below, and round the answer to one decimal place.

Percent increase _____

11. Kelly Paper Company purchased from the manufacturer rolls of gift wrapping paper for $16.50 each. The company is selling the gift wrapping paper to retail outlets for $29 each. Determine the percent of markup. Show your calculations in the space provided below, and round the answer to one decimal place.

Percent of markup _____

12. Shaw Jewelers purchased from Gold Craft Jewelry Manufacturing gold chains for $127 each. The jewelry store is featuring these chains during their May sale for $299.95 each. Determine the percent of markup. Show your calculations in the space provided below, and round the answer to one decimal place.

Percent of markup _____

13. In 1996 Balway Air-Conditioning Company showed a net profit of $1,378,903. For 1997 the company had a net profit of $998,380. What percent decrease in profit did Balway Air-Conditioning experience in 1997? Show your calculations in the space provided below, and round the answer to one decimal place.

Percent decrease _____

14. September sales for Jerome's Auto Supplies stores totaled $387,692; in October sales totaled $328,904. What percent decrease in sales did Jerome's Auto Supply stores experience in October? Show your calculations in the space provided below, and round the answer to one decimal place.

Percent decrease _____

15. Party World was selling gift wrapping paper from rolls for 30 cents a foot. For its weekend sale Party World is offering this same paper for 22 cents a foot. Determine the percent of markdown. Show your calculations in the space provided below, and round the answer to one decimal place.

Percent of markdown _____

16. Broadway Department Store was selling famous-brand sweaters for $88. Since the sweaters did not sell, Broadway reduced the price to $49.99. The price was reduced further to $29.99 when the bulk of the sweaters were still not sold at the end of the season. Determine the percent of both markdowns from the original selling price. Show your calculations in the space provided below, and round the answers to one decimal place.

Percent of markdown _____

Percent of markdown _____

17. Calculate the amount of simple interest to be paid for the loan amounts, interest rates, and time periods shown in the following table.

Simple Interest Calculations				
Amount Borrowed	Rate	Time	Calculation	Interest
$2,500	6%	3 years		
$13,800	9 1/2%	5 years		
$2,800	7%	18 months		
$11,200	8 1/4%	30 months		
$1,250	9%	60 days		
$14,400	8 3/4%	45 days		

*The answers to this exercise appear in the **Instructor's Manual and Key** for **HOW 8: A Handbook for Office Workers,** Eighth Edition.*

Section 5 Abbreviated Forms

Abbreviations (5-1 Through 5-13)

Practice Guide 1

Instructions: In the following sentences underline those words or phrases that *may* or *must be* abbreviated in business correspondence. Place the correct form of the abbreviated word or phrase in the blank that appears to the right of each sentence. If no word or phrase in a sentence may be abbreviated, write *OK* in the blank at the right.

Ex. *One of our leading citizens, <u>Mister</u> Darryl Holtzgang, has consented to donate $1 million for the construction of a new art center.*   *Mr.*

1. Please book me on a flight to Chicago that will arrive by 2 p.m., Central Standard Time.   _____

2. Some of the artifacts in this museum date back to the year 900 before Christ.   _____

3. Eleanor Clen, Chartered Life Underwriter, was promoted to head the Claims Department.   _____

4. We have written Senator Lauder several letters about this problem, but so far we have had no response from his office.   _____

5. This show will be broadcast on National Broadcasting Company television next month.   _____

6. A copy of these materials should be sent to Doctor Carol Larson Jones.   _____

7. Only Professor Thomas Propes was unable to accept our invitation.   _____

8. Please purchase three 2-liter containers of 7 Up for the reception.   _____

9. We no longer manufacture our Model Number 1417 cassette recorder.   _____

10. Your order will be sent collect on delivery by next Thursday.   _____

11. The mailing address we have for Ann Knight is 1147 West 118th Street.   _____

12. When you call our office, ask for Extension 327.   _____

13. Our imports from the United Kingdom have declined during the past five years.   _____

14. Send these contracts to the client's attorney at 4700 Bell Avenue, Northeast, Portland, Oregon 97206-1054.   _____

15. The reception will be given in honor of Brigadier General Retired Foster L. Klein.   _____

16. Existing fixtures, carpeting, draperies, and so forth, are included in the price of this condominium. _____

17. The length of all packages must be limited to 36 inches. _____

18. Make your check payable to Yung Yum, Doctor of Medicine. _____

19. Last week Ralph T. Drengson Senior announced that the company would be moving its headquarters to Albuquerque. _____

20. Have you already made arrangements to purchase an International Business Machines Aptiva to replace our IBM Personal System 2? _____

21. I believe Allen R. Benson, Esquire, drew up the majority of these contracts. _____

22. Our offices close at 5 post meridiem on weekdays; on Saturdays they close at noon. _____

23. Number 456B heating units are temporarily out of stock; therefore, please notify these customers of the shipping delay. _____

24. Stanley F. Hubbard, Doctor of Philosophy, has been selected to receive this year's Outstanding College Professor of the Year Award. _____

25. The Merriam-Webster on-line dictionary is stored on a single compact disk-read only memory. _____

Check your answers with those given on page 325 before completing the following exercise.

Practice Guide 2

Instructions: In the following paragraphs some words or word groups that should be written in full are abbreviated; in other cases words or word groups that should be abbreviated are written in their entirety. Please make any necessary corrections: underline the word or word group that is expressed incorrectly and write the correct form directly above it.

Last week Mister Walter Tessier notified us that three universities have already invited

Gov. Evans to speak at their commencement ceremonies: UCLA, University of Southern

California, and UCSB.

The new chancellor of UCLA, Victor Mallory, Doctor of Philosophy, and the governor's

personal friend, Aaron Weiss Junior, both extended invitations to Gov. Evans for the UCLA

commencement. This ceremony is scheduled for Thurs., June 2, at 4 P.M. Since the governor

will leave New York City at 10 A.M., Eastern Standard Time, he should be able to arrive in

Los Angeles in time for the commencement ceremony. Therefore, please phone the

chancellor's assistant, Ms. Dixie Slater, at 469-8282, extension 113, to inform her that the

governor will accept the university's invitation for June 2.

The University of Southern California and UCSB have scheduled their graduations for the

same day—Fri., June 10. Since the invitation from Prof. James Wrigley arrived first, the

governor has agreed to accept the invitation from UCSB. Please write Prof. Wrigley at

800 W. College Dr., Santa Barbara, CA 93107, to let him know that the governor can accept

his invitation. Also, please send the governor's regrets to Pres. Vern Tuppering at the

University of Southern California. Explain carefully the circumstances, and indicate that the

lt. governor would be willing to substitute for Gov. Evans.

*The answers to this exercise appear in the **Instructor's Manual and Key** for **HOW 8: A Handbook for Office Workers,** Eighth Edition.*

Contractions (5-14)

Practice Guide 3

Instructions: Make any necessary corrections in the following sentences. If a contraction is written incorrectly, underline it and place the correct form in the blank to the right of the sentence. If a contraction is written correctly, write *OK* in the blank.

Ex. *We <u>have'nt</u> received your last payment for May.*   *haven't*

1. It won't be necessary for you to call in person to order your
    new SMA television set.   _____

2. I amn't convinced that a strike can be prevented before the 1st
    of the year   _____

3. This is'nt the same grade of material I ordered from your sales
    representative.   _____

4. Our company doesn't sell directly to retail customers.   _____

5. Your one of the youngest students in this class.   _____

6. Mr. Riley has'nt arrived at work on time once this week.   _____

7. We'll be sure to credit your account for the full amount.   _____

8. This movie has not been able to recover it's production costs. _____

9. Yes, their usually able to meet all production schedules.   _____

10. Who's in charge of ordering the office supplies?   _____

Check your answers with those given on page 325.

Section 6 Grammar and Usage

Noun Plurals (6-4)

Practice Guide 1

Instructions: Write the plural form for each item given below. Use the blank provided at the right of each item.

1. policy	_____	26. alumnus	_____
2. church	_____	27. per diem	_____
3. radio	_____	28. county	_____
4. life	_____	29. box	_____
5. Montgomery	_____	30. Koltz	_____
6. tomato	_____	31. A	_____
7. curriculum	_____	32. bronchus	_____
8. statistics	_____	33. lessee	_____
9. mumps	_____	34. father figure	_____
10. brigadier general	_____	35. father-in-law	_____
11. yes and no	_____	36. valley	_____
12. cupful	_____	37. R.N.	_____
13. bookshelf	_____	38. Ms. Ross	_____
14. brother-In-law	_____	39. datum	_____
15. basis	_____	40. Mickey Mouse	_____
16. pants	_____	41. going-over	_____
17. 9	_____	42. t	_____
18. roof	_____	43. jockey	_____
19. attorney	_____	44. Japanese	_____
20. waltz	_____	45. Mr. Ramirez	_____
21. alto	_____	46. embargo	_____
22. cargo	_____	47. yourself	_____
23. this and that	_____	48. chassis	_____
24. monkey	_____	49. half	_____
25. analysis	_____	50. German	_____

Check your answers with those given on page 326 before completing the following exercise.

Practice Guide 2

Instructions: In the following sentences underline any errors in the use of noun plurals. Write the correct form in the blank at the right. If a sentence is correct, write *OK* in the blank.

1. Flood control construction projects are scheduled to begin in both vallies on May 1.

1. _____

2. Have the cargos been loaded on the two ships scheduled to sail today?

2. _____

3. Did you find both halfs of the torn $100 bill?

3. _____

4. Be sure to call a pest control company to rid our warehouse of all these mouses.

4. _____

5. We have not yet received bill of ladings for any of these shipments.

5. _____

6. We no longer accept trade-ins on any computer purchases.

6. _____

7. Please write your 2's more legibly.

7. _____

8. Several major financial crisises have forced the company to file bankruptcy.

8. _____

9. We are not permitted to accept IOUs from any of our customers.

9. _____

10. Disregard any of the information contained in parenthesis.

10. _____

11. What percent of incoming freshman this semester have qualified to enroll in College English?

11. _____

12. Make sure that all new employees fill out W-4's.

12. _____

13. The two companys have yet to agree on the terms of the merger.

13. _____

14. Each year we issue new picture ID's to all our employees.

14. _____

15. The Hillarys have purchased the home we had listed on Elm Street.

15. _____

16. The mosquitos in this meadow prohibit our using this area for outdoor weddings and other events.

16. _____

17. There are too many zeroes in this number for it to be correct.

17. _____

18. Yesterday the city council members unanimously voted themselfs pay increases.

18. _____

19. Many of our college alumnuses have made substantial contributions to the scholarship fund.

19. _____

20. All our economicses classes are offered through the School of Business.

20. _____

Check your answers with those given on page 326 before completing the following exercise.

Name _____ Date _____

Practice Guide 3

Instructions: Based on the context of the following letter, first underline all those nouns that should be written in plural form. Then write the correct spellings in the blank lines given below.

Dear Mr. Washington:

    According to our staff of analyst, there are several basis on which your tax were determined. Separate analysis from three of our staff member are enclosed.

    As your attorney, we advise you to appeal individually the assessed valuation of two property; the other seven property appear to have been assessed correctly. If we can assist you with these proceeding, please call one of our secretary to set up an appointment within the next two week.

    In order to protest the two assessment, we will have to collect sufficient datum to show the value of other duplex in the area. Both Mr. Avery would be able to help us gather this information. One of the major criterion will be the average price of comparable real estate turnover during the last six month. Another factor will be the assessed valuation of other such property in both the Borden and Simi Valley. Survey of three or four real estate agency should provide the appropriate information to assist us with these two case.

    We believe there is an excellent opportunity to have the tax assessment on both these duplex reduced considerably. Please let us know if we may be of assistance to you.

                 Sincerely yours,

1. _____

2. _____

3. _____

4. _____

5. _____

6. _____

7. _____

8. _____

9. _____

10. _____

11. _____

12. _____

13. _____

14. _____

15. _____

16. _____

17. _____

18. _____

19. _____

20. _____

21. _____

22. _____

23. _____

24. _____

25. _____

*The answers to this exercise appear in the **Instructor's Manual and Key** for **HOW 8: A Handbook for Office Workers,** Eighth Edition.*

Noun Possessives (6-5)

Practice Guide 4

Instructions: So that each of the following sentences will read correctly, write in the blank at the right the proper form of the word(s) shown in parentheses.

1. Our (son-in-law) business went bankrupt last month.

2. The (child) bicycles were stolen from the garage.

3. (Everyone else) room was locked.

4. Yesterday Ms. Purdy gave the boss a (week) notice.

5. Three members of the (personnel manager) association agreed to speak to our class

6. The (Ross) and (Lopez) mountain cabin was damaged severely during the snowstorm.

7. The (girl) softball team will participate in the championship playoffs.

8. A file of delinquent accounts is kept in (Mr. Beaty) office.

9. (Bob) and (Phil) offices are located in Suite 454.

10. This (company) stock declined sharply during the last six months.

11. The store manager moved (lady) apparel from the second floor to the third floor.

12. You are still responsible for four (month) interest on this loan.

13. (Mary) receiving the scholarship was no surprise to me.

14. (Mrs. Jones) car was parked illegally.

15. The (chief of police) answer did not satisfy the reporters.

16. (Alumnus) children receive preferential consideration for admission to our college.

17. (ITT) investment in new equipment this year amounted to $18 million.

18. The (lease) expiration date is July 30.

19. Do you carry (man) and (boy) clothing?

20. (Martha) and (Don) house was sold yesterday.

1. _____

2. _____

3. _____

4. _____

5. _____

6. _____

7. _____

8. _____

9. _____

10. _____

11. _____

12. _____

13. _____

14. _____

15. _____

16. _____

17. _____

18. _____

19. _____

20. _____

Check your answers with those given on page 326 before completing the following exercise.

Practice Guide 5

Instructions: In the following sentences underline any errors in the use of noun possessives. Write the correct form in the blank at the right. If a sentence is correct, write *OK* in the blank.

1. All womens' wearing apparel has been moved to the first floor.

   1. _____

2. This computer's floppy disk drive needs to be replaced.

   2. _____

3. Julie's and Brad's E-mail address is jbstevens@aol.com.

   3. _____

4. During the last year our companys profits increased 17 percent.

   4. _____

5. If the tenant does not pay his rent by July 15, give him a 30 days' notice to move.

   5. _____

6. Our new office is scarcely a stones throw from the old one.

   6. _____

7. Bob hesitating to accept our offer leads me to believe he may be negotiating with other firms.

   7. _____

8. All these students term papers have been graded.

   8. _____

9. What percent of this company stock is your brother-in-laws?

   9. _____

10. Be sure to send Ms. Jones commission checks to her new address.

    10. _____

11. Adams and Barbaras offices are located on the second floor.

    11. _____

12. All our fire stations are ready to respond on a moments notice.

    12. _____

13. We spent the entire afternoon at our attorneys giving depositions.

    13. _____

14. Mr. Stevens appointment with Dr. Rose has been scheduled for Tuesday, June 2, at 2 p.m.

    14. _____

15. Both your companys and our companys downsizing has caused major unemployment in our community.

    15. _____

16. Who witnessed Mr. Smith's signing the contract?

    16. _____

17. Most of the editor in chief suggestions related to the design of the book.

    17. _____

18. Because of manufacturing difficulties, we are experiencing a weeks delay in shipping all orders.

    18. _____

19. Only three of our regional managers' have submitted their reports.

    19. _____

20. Already six of these truck's engines have been rebuilt.

    20. _____

Check your answers with those given on page 326 before completing the following exercise.

Practice Guide 6

Instructions: Based on the context of the following letter, first underline all those nouns that should be written in the possessive form. Then write the correct spelling of each in the blank lines given below.

Dear Ms. Huffman:

Because of your companys outstanding payment record, we are extending an invitation to you to increase your credit limit. This months charges on your account reached $5,600, $600 beyond your present limit. If you wish to extend your credit line to $7,500, all we need is your Purchasing Departments approval and Mrs. Kellys signature on the enclosed application.

Next month we will be distributing our holiday sales catalog. This seasons merchandise is even more exciting than last seasons. You will see by your salespeoples enthusiasm that we have the best product line in our history. Childrens toys are more advanced than ever before with electronic game toys promising to be best-sellers. Also, for this year the number of items in boys and girls wearing apparel has nearly doubled.

By distributing our catalog early in August, we hope to get a two months head start on the season. With everyones cooperation we can have record-breaking sales this year. Our managers new shipping program can have any of the catalog merchandise at your door with only seven working days notice.

To encourage buyers early orders, we are offering a 25 percent discount on all babys clothing and furniture ordered during September. Similar discounts are being offered on mens clothing and ladys lingerie. Take advantage of Septembers savings; place your order when the holiday catalog arrives. Turn todays savings into future profits.

1. _____
2. _____
3. _____
4. _____
5. _____
6. _____
7. _____
8. _____
9. _____
10. _____
11. _____
12. _____
13. _____
14. _____
15. _____
16. _____
17. _____
18. _____
19. _____
20. _____

*The answers to this exercise appear in the **Instructor's Manual and Key** for **HOW 8: A Handbook for Office Workers,** Eighth Edition.*

Pronouns (6-6 Through 6-8, 6-18)

Practice Guide 7

Part 1. Subjective- and objective-case pronouns. From the choices given in parentheses, select the correct pronoun form. Write your answer in the blank line given at the right of each sentence.

1. (We, Us) secretaries are planning a surprise party for Ms. Phillips.   1. _____

2. Be sure to give a copy of the sales receipt to Ron or (I, me, myself).   2. _____

3. Speaking of Mr. Reynolds, that was (he, him) on the telephone.   3. _____

4. Mr. Ryan is more likely to receive the appointment than (I, me).   4. _____

5. I would not want to be (she, her) when our sales manager discovers the error.   5. _____

6. Dr. Boyer asked (we, us) nurses to work overtime during the epidemic.   6. _____

7. The person at the end of the hall could not have been (he, him).   7. _____

8. The receptionist mistook my brother to be (I, me).   8. _____

9. I would prefer to send the letter to Ms. Cook rather than (she, her).   9. _____

10. We, John and (I, me), plan to attend the convention.   10. _____

Check your answers with those given on page 327 before completing the following exercise.

Part 2. Subjective- and objective-case pronouns. If a pronoun is used correctly in the following sentences, write *OK* in the blank line. If a pronoun is used incorrectly, underline the error and write the correction in the blank line.

1. Between you and I, I believe this new microchip will revolutionize the industry.   1. _____

2. Did you say that the top salesperson was her?   2. _____

3. I was taken to be her at the company Halloween party.   3. _____

4. The person who ordered the new equipment must have been him.   4. _____

5. Copies of the announcement were sent to us, Paul and myself.   5. _____

6. Dr. Rich asked Teri and I to cancel his appointments for the remainder of the day.   6. _____

7. Ms. Allison knows as much about this contract as I.   7. _____

8. Three accountants—Bob, Arlene, and me—attended the convention in Chicago.   8. _____

9. If you were me, what decision would you have made?

9. _____

10. I would not want to be he under these circumstances.

10. _____

Check your answers with those given on page 327 before completing the following exercise.

Part 3. *Who* and *whom* pronouns. From the choices given in parentheses, select the correct form. Write your answer in the blank line given at the end of each sentence.

1. Our company needs an engineer (who, whom) understands construction design.

1. _____

2. Do you know (who, whom) Mr. Reece selected to serve as his assistant?

2. _____

3. We do not know (who, whom) the real estate agent could have been.

3. _____

4. John is a person (who, whom) I believe will perform well under pressure.

4. _____

5. (Whoever, Whomever) acts as chairman of the committee will have an advantage.

5. _____

6. Elizabeth Jones is the person (who, whom) we believe will be elected.

6. _____

7. (Who, Whom) did John recommend for the position?

7. _____

8. Ms. Hill is courteous to (whoever, whomever) enters the office.

8. _____

9. Please list the names of the staff members (who, whom) you think will participate in the contest.

9. _____

10. My supervisor, (who, whom) you met yesterday, will retire next year.

10. _____

11. (Whoever, Whomever) arrives at the airport first should check on our reservations.

11. _____

12. Call me as soon as you learn (who, whom) has been awarded the contract.

12. _____

13. Mr. Dorman may have been the agent (who, whom) we contracted originally.

13. _____

14. I cannot imagine (who, whom) you thought him to be.

14. _____

15. I do not know (who, whom) the newest member of the board could be.

15. _____

Check your answers with those given on page 327 before completing the following exercise.

Practice Guide 8

Instructions: In the following sentences underline any errors in pronoun usage. Write the correct form in the blank at the right. If a sentence is correct, write *OK* in the blank line.

1. The judge assigned to the case could be her.

   1. _____

2. None of we stockholders were interested in purchasing additional shares.

   2. _____

3. Please ask all patients to check in with either Jessica or me.

   3. _____

4. Yes, two of our employees, Steve and her, have requested transfers to our Orange County office.

   4. _____

5. You may give a copy of this brochure to whomever requests one.

   5. _____

6. John is a person that always seems to have a complaint about any change in procedures.

   6. _____

7. On the telephone Alice is often thought to be me.

   7. _____

8. Between you and I, I believe the price of this stock will drop even further.

   8. _____

9. When will the company issue it's next dividend to stockholders?

   9. _____

10. Several other instructors asked Mark and me to help them create Web sites on the Internet.

    10. _____

11. Donna always takes longer lunch breaks than me.

    11. _____

12. The vice president has requested we managers to attend an emergency meeting tomorrow morning.

    12. _____

13. You may obtain this information from either one of our investment counselors, Ms. Wong or he.

    13. _____

14. Ms. Lloyd delivered the signed contracts to the attorney herself.

    14. _____

15. Call for return interviews only those applicants whom you believe would be willing to travel.

    15. _____

16. The company is giving new hires the same benefit package as we.

    16. _____

17. Be sure to ask all patients for there insurance cards.

    17. _____

18. Only two of the applicants who we interviewed seemed
    qualified for the position.   18. _____

19. Alan Whitman, Melanie Lipmann, and myself have been
    selected to serve on the interview committee.   19. _____

20. I work for a company which deals exclusively with recycling
    preowned computers.   20. _____

Check your answers with those given on page 327 before completing the following exercise.

Name _____ Date _____

Practice Guide 9

Instructions: In the following sentences underline any errors in pronoun agreement. Write the correct form in the blank at the right. If a sentence is correct, write *OK* in the blank line.

1. Some members of the production team had not completed its assignment from the previous meeting.

   1. _____

2. Each of the council members involved in the fraud has been asked to submit their resignation.

   2. _____

3. Shari Thomas, who recently earned her master's of accounting, has applied for a position with Ernst & Young.

   3. _____

4. Please ask everybody to clear their table before leaving the lunchroom.

   4. _____

5. Robert is one of those computer enthusiasts who spend much of his free time browsing the Internet.

   5. _____

6. Since Ellen is chair of the editorial committee, please give your suggestions to them.

   6. _____

7. If somebody requests more information about our products, refer them to me.

   7. _____

8. Dylan Investment Company has already sent us copies of their annual report.

   8. _____

9. Only one of the bidding companies will guarantee their work beyond one year.

   9. _____

10. Meredith is one of those persons who are always willing to help others solve his or her problems.

    10. _____

11. Speak-Eze Corporation plans to introduce their new voice-activated software for home computer users next week.

    11. _____

12. Either Marissa or Andrea will take her vacation the first week in June.

    12. _____

13. Toy sales, which are usually at its high during the holiday season, have dropped nearly 10 percent

    13. _____

14. If anything is missing from this gem collection, please list them on this form.

    14. _____

15. Our president is one of those executives who believe in praising his employees for a job well done.

    15. _____

16. Since neither company guaranteed their work, the county refused to accept either bid.

    16. _____

17. Will everyone please return their car pool forms by May 15.   17. _____

18. Anyone who has completed their assignments may take the final examination early.   18. _____

19. My assistants will be able to help you with this report, so please provide him and her with appropriate instructions.   19. _____

20. Neither Ms. Hastings nor Ms. Carson has read their E-mail messages today.   20. _____

Check your answers with those given on page 327 before completing the following exercise.

Practice Guide 10

Instructions: Based on the context of the following letter, first underline all those pronouns that are used incorrectly. Then write the correct pronouns in the blank lines given below.

To the Staff:

During the next month us nurses must renew our parking

permits. Be sure to bring your permit to either Mr. Feinberg or

myself before April 30. Mr. Feinberg is in the office longer

hours than me, so perhaps you may find leaving your parking

permit with him more convenient than leaving it with me. The

person issuing the new parking permits will be him.

All of us—you, the other nurses, and I—will be prohibited

from parking in the visitors' parking lot. The hospital security

staff has been instructed to issue tickets to whoever they find

illegally parked. This restriction will be implemented because

our chief administrator, Ms. Takagi, has received numerous

complaints about the crowded condition of this lot. It was her

who decided that this lot would be closed to all staff members,

no matter whom the individual may be or what his or her

position may entail. I realize that a number of the staff may

be annoyed with Ms. Takagi's decision. Under these

circumstances I would not want to be her. Between you and I,

though, I believe that our chief administrator had no other

alternative.

Ms. Takagi has asked we employees to park in Lot C, which

is located in our high-rise parking facility. An additional security

guard, who Mr. Feinberg recently employed, will patrol this

employee parking area during the evening hours. The new

security officer, Ian Davis, has asked Mr. Feinberg and I to inform

you of his presence. He will be pleased to help whomever needs

1. _____

2. _____

3. _____

4. _____

5. _____

6. _____

7. _____

8. _____

9. _____

10. _____

11. _____

12. _____

13. _____

14. _____

15. _____

his assistance with any parking problems. Ian is a person whom I believe will be an excellent addition to our hospital staff.

If you have any questions about the new parking regulations, please be sure to consult me personally.

The answers to this exercise appear in the **Instructor's Manual and Key** *for* **HOW 8: A Handbook for Office Workers,** *Eighth Edition.*

Verbs (6-10 Through 6-18)

Practice Guide 11

Instructions: In the following sentences underline any errors in the use of verb parts or tenses. Write the correct form in the blank at the right. If a sentence is correct, write *OK* in the blank line.

1. The client payed his bill yesterday.
1. _____

2. Susan has called all the patients this morning.
2. _____

3. As soon as we receive your payment, we are shipping your order.
3. _____

4. Dr. Warner also teachs courses at the regional occupational center.
4. _____

5. We received your revised order after we already shipped your original one.
5. _____

6. If home sales continue at the same rate, we will have sold all the homes in this construction phase before ground is even broken.
6. _____

7. Sales in the northern region increased steadily since we opened our new office in Billings.
7. _____

8. This baggage claim area has laid idle for the last 48 hours.
8. _____

9. More and more, small companies are useing computerized accounting programs.
9. _____

10. Neither applicant has yet submitted his résumé.
10. _____

11. During the last year our sales in this county have growed from $1.2 million to $1.8 million.
11. _____

12. Do you know when the city council will chose a new chief of police?
12. _____

13. Our spring sale has begun on March 21 and will continue until March 31.
13. _____

14. During the past few months, representatives from both sides have lain the groundwork for the new labor contract.
14. _____

15. Yesterday the workers hanged draperies in all the model homes.
15. _____

16. Our credit union loans money to its members at low interest rates.
16. _____

17. We cannot afford to loose any more of the market share.   17. _____

18. I have spoke personally to several of our employees about
    applying for the management opening.   18. _____

19. Do not leave any papers or litter laying around in the
    conference room after the meeting.   19. _____

20. Has anyone verifyed the accuracy of these figures?   20. _____

Check your answers with those given on page 327 before completing the following exercise.

Practice Guide 12

Instructions: In the following sentences underline any errors in subject-verb agreement. Write the correct form in the blank at the right. If a sentence is correct, write *OK* in the blank line.

1. Pork and beans are a favorite dish among our customers. 1. _____

2. Our supply of new 3.5-inch floppy disks are rapidly diminishing. 2. _____

3. Every student, instructor, and administrator is expected to evacuate the building when the fire alarm sounds. 3. _____

4. The administrative staff and the president is planning to attend the board meeting this afternoon. 4. _____

5. Someone in our Human Resources Department need to resolve this issue 5. _____

6. A check for the first night's stay or a credit card number are all you need to hold this reservation. 6. _____

7. Most of the salespersons in our Portland office has been with the company for over five years. 7. _____

8. Either you or Alex has won the sales contest. 8. _____

9. There is at least four candidates on this list whom we should interview. 9. _____

10. The committee were arguing continually throughout the entire meeting. 10. _____

11. The number of business people who communicate through E-mail are rising rapidly. 11. _____

12. If I was you, I would certainly apply for the promotional position. 12. _____

13. Nearly 60 percent of the students enrolled in our college needs to take some kind of computer literacy course. 13. _____

14. The secretary and treasurer of our small company approve all purchases over $1,000. 14. _____

15. Everything in these boxes need to be placed on the shelves by tomorrow morning. 15. _____

16. Whenever our supervisor leaves the office, Danielle acts as if she were in charge. 16. _____

17. Each of the applicants have been notified that additional scholarships have been made available through the grant program. 17. _____

18. A detailed description of possible side effects are included with each filled prescription. 18. _____

19. Neither of them have submitted an application. 19. _____

20. An unusually large number of stockholders has requested extra copies of our annual report. 20. _____

Check your answers with those given on page 328 before completing the following exercise.

Practice Guide 13

Instructions: If the verb is used correctly in the following sentences, write *OK* in the blank line following the sentence. If the verb is used incorrectly, underline the error and write the correct form in the blank line.

1. Have you wrote letters to the two agencies?

   1. _____

2. The tract of new homes were laid out to attract buyers with growing families.

   2. _____

3. Our client has already spoke to several agents in your firm.

   3. _____

4. The patient asked if he could lay down on the cot.

   4. _____

5. Has the criteria been ranked in the order of their importance?

   5. _____

6. There is several alternatives you may wish to consider.

   6. _____

7. Neither of them wish to postpone his vacation.

   7. _____

8. One fourth of the light bulbs in this shipment were broken.

   8. _____

9. Dr. Sanders is one of those doctors who knows a great deal about law.

   9. _____

10. Our stock of felt-tip pens have disappeared from the supply cabinet.

    10. _____

11. He had forgot about this appointment until his secretary reminded him.

    11. _____

12. Until last Wednesday the book had laid on top of the counter.

    12. _____

13. All the juice in these bottles have been drunk.

    13. _____

14. Between the two bookcases was a locked cabinet.

    14. _____

15. Neither you nor the other accountant have been absent this year.

    15. _____

16. Each sofa, chair, and table needs to be replaced.

    16. _____

17. The staff was arguing loudly about their duties.

    17. _____

18. One of the mothers have consented to bring donuts for the class.

    18. _____

19. All our bills for this month have been payed.

    19. _____

20. Either Allen or Nanette is to receive the commission for this sale.

20. _____

21. Have the Board of Directors approved this purchase?

21. _____

22. There is still a number of options we need to explore before we can institute a new loan-tracking system.

22. _____

23. Michael has drove nearly 15,000 miles this month visiting all the doctors in his territory.

23. _____

24. Either you or I am responsible for closing the store each afternoon.

24. _____

25. The stock market has sank 107 points within the last two days.

25. _____

26. I sent you this information after the 1998 financial information was compiled.

26. _____

27. Bob worked in our Research Department since 1991.

27. _____

28. Have the committee submitted their report?

28. _____

29. None of the antiques was damaged during the earthquake.

29. _____

30. By the opening of the fall semester, we will have provided Internet access to all our classroom computers.

30. _____

Check your answers with those given on page 328 before completing the following exercise.

Practice Guide 14

Instructions: As you read the following paragraphs, first underline all the verb forms that are used incorrectly. Then write the correct answers in the blanks provided at the right.

To: Mr. Pflum

In national medical journals we have ran several ads

describing our new disposable thermometers. Although the

number of responses we have received to these ads have

been great, the staff is in disagreement as to whether this

advertising mode should be continued. One of the officers feel

strongly that we have exhausted the market reached by the

medical journals. She believes local distribution channels or

direct mail advertising are more effective than national

advertising.

Hospitals is the main users of our disposable thermometers.

Our supply of these thermometers are almost depleted because

one of the clerks in our main office had forgot to notify the

factory to manufacture an additional supply. We have spoke

to him about this matter, and he has took steps to prevent

this error from occurring again. In the clerk's defense, however,

we must consider that a large number of these disposable

thermometers had laid in our warehouse for over four months

without our filling any orders from this supply. All the orders

was filled directly from the factory.

Dr. Maedke is one of those doctors who has supported the

use of disposable thermometers since their introduction. He

believes that every doctor's office, medical clinic, and hospital

need to use this kind of thermometer; it is more sanitary and

economical than the conventional thermometer. Dr. Maedke

has brung out this concept in a number of the speeches he has

1. _____

2. _____

3. _____

4. _____

5. _____

6. _____

7. _____

8. _____

9. _____

10. _____

11. _____

12. _____

13. _____

14. _____

15. _____

16. _____

17. _____

18. _____

19. _____

20. _____

given at national medical conventions. We are fortunate to have the support of a person who are so well-known in the profession.

We are looking forward to this product becoming a top seller. Although advertising in medical journals has payed for itself, two members of the staff prefers alternate methods of advertising. Neither of them, though, have yet offered specific advertising plans. When the media for future advertising has been selected, we will let you know.

*The answers to this exercise appear in the **Instructor's Manual and Key** for **HOW 8: A Handbook for Office Workers,** Eighth Edition.*

Adjectives (6-19 Through 6-24)

Practice Guide 15

Instructions: In the following sentences underline any errors in the use of adjectives. Write the correct form in the blank at the right. If a sentence is correct, write *OK* in the blank line.

1. Our client wishes to lease an one-bedroom apartment in the area before buying a home.

   1. _____

2. We wish to have a more lighter oak finish for these cabinets.

   2. _____

3. The programmer we hired recently is less knowledgeable than any programmer in the department.

   3. _____

4. This month's sales quotas seem more impossible to reach than last month's.

   4. _____

5. Although Lynn did not feel good all week, she did not miss a day's work.

   5. _____

6. The starting rate for nursing assistants at Bayview Hospital is $9.50 a hour.

   6. _____

7. Of all the contestants Carl seems to be the least confident.

   7. _____

8. Amy felt worser this afternoon than she did this morning, so she left early today.

   8. _____

9. I feel badly that you did not receive information about this scholarship before the filing deadline date.

   9. _____

10. Andrea keyboards faster than anyone in the office.

    10. _____

11. Although this new musical has an historical perspective, it is definitely a modern production.

    11. _____

12. The most prompt response to our inquiries came from the Baltimore Chamber of Commerce.

    12. _____

13. We have found that E-mail is a more better way to communicate with our clients in the East.

    13. _____

14. License fees in this state for reregistering out of state cars are prohibitive.

    14. _____

15. For this construction project we must erect a 12 foot fence around the site.

    15. _____

16. Our office just listed a eight-unit apartment house on Superior Street.

16. _____

17. Probably the most sturdy cribs on the market today are manufactured by Baby Town.

17. _____

18. If we are to compete in this market, we must create more unique television commercials.

18. _____

19. The dissension among the partners is becoming noticeabler every day.

19. _____

20. In this condominium complex the two-bedroom unit has more square footage than any unit.

20. _____

Check your answers with those given on page 328 before completing the following exercise.

Adverbs (6-25 Through 6-29)

Practice Guide 16

Instructions: In the following sentences underline any errors in the use of adverbs. Write the correct form in the blank at the right. If a sentence is correct, write *OK* in the blank line.

1. Kevin checked these sales figures less careful than he should have.

1. _____

2. Our fund-raiser for the new library has nearly netted $2.3 million.

2. _____

3. Both agents certainly should receive some compensation for their assistance with the sale.

3. _____

4. The red-and-white letters looked well against the black background.

4. _____

5. Who has been with the company longer—Barry, Claudia, or Matthew?

5. _____

6. Do not discuss the proposed merger with nobody.

6. _____

7. Our department expects to shortly receive the two color printers we ordered.

7. _____

8. I have scarcely had an opportunity to review this report.

8. _____

9. Fresh fruits and vegetables are delivered regular to our restaurants throughout the city.

9. _____

10. Most of the students who graduate from our law school do good on the state bar examination.

10. _____

11. Your computer processes more slower than mine.

11. _____

12. This team's research findings have scratched the surface barely.

12. _____

13. We cannot hardly believe that the company is moving all its operations to another state.

13. _____

14. You shouldn't feel badly about not reaching your sales quota this month.

14. _____

15. Is the air-conditioning system in our building working good?

15. _____

16. This news commentator claims to be the more widely
    listened to of all.

16. _____

17. Most of us were real disappointed to learn of our
    president's resignation.

17. _____

18. I haven't received no information about the new
    products we will be featuring.

18. _____

19. Let us hope that these contract negotiations will run
    smoothlier than the last ones.

19. _____

20. Please ask our attorneys to carefully evaluate all the
    clauses in this contract.

20. _____

Check your answers with those given on page 329 before completing the following exercise.

Prepositions (6-30 Through 6-33)

Practice Guide 17

Instructions: In the following sentences underline any errors in the use of prepositions. Write the correct form in the blank at the right. If a sentence is correct, write *OK* in the blank line.

1. Between the three of us, we should be able to complete the inventory by the end of this weekend.

1. _____

2. Has the committee finally agreed upon the location for the new warehouse site?

2. _____

3. The plans for this new medical building are quite different than what I had expected.

3. _____

4. There seems to be a discrepancy among the expense report and the receipts submitted.

4. _____

5. Most of these suggested policy changes are identical to the recommendations we have already submitted to the executive committee

5. _____

6. Does the company plan on expanding its operations internationally?

6. _____

7. According to the new contract, all salary increases are retroactive from January 1.

7. _____

8. All of the computers in our department have on-line access to the Internet.

8. _____

9. Our offices are located in the building directly opposite of Westlake Square.

9. _____

10. Pick up your visitor's badge at the booth just inside of the main entrance to the building.

10. _____

11. Do you know who removed the dictionary off of this counter?

11. _____

12. With all the loud shouting, we could hardly help from hearing the customer's angry remarks.

12. _____

13. Did you receive the fax message from Marie?

13. _____

14. Is the date and time set for the meeting convenient to you?

14. _____

15. Both of these recommendations have been submitted to the board of education for approval.

15. _____

16. Before beginning the final draft, please ensure that these
grant proposals are in compliance to the specifications
prescribed in the instructions.   16. _____

17. If you become angry at one of the clerks, do not display your
feelings in front of the other employees.   17. _____

18. Between themselves the committee members agreed to limit
their meetings to no longer than two hours.   18. _____

19. All consultants in our employ are expected to conform to the
dress standards set by our organization.   19. _____

20. We were able to buy off of Midtown Office Supply all its
sale cartridges for our inkjet color printers.   20. _____

Check your answers with those given on page 329 before completing the following exercise.

Conjunctions (6-34 Through 6-37)

Practice Guide 18

Instructions: In the following sentences underline any errors in the use of conjunctions. Write the correct form in the blank at the right. If a sentence is correct, write *OK* in the blank line.

1. We can either send you this information by fax or E-mail.

1. _____

2. Talking about becoming a doctor is one thing, but to become one is quite another.

2. _____

3. This year's profits are not so high as last year's.

3. _____

4. Our company manufactures not only stand-alone home stereo systems but also installs stereo systems in new home construction.

4. _____

5. Neither Dana or Shannon has the combination to the vault.

5. _____

6. Before we can release the keys, we will need both a certified check and to have the tenants sign the lease.

6. _____

7. None of these new designs look like I thought they would.

7. _____

8. For the meeting I am responsible for reserving the conference room and to prepare the agenda.

8. _____

9. Our new low-priced desk model laser printer has become so popular as our standard model.

9. _____

10. We would appreciate your taking a few minutes to fill out the enclosed questionnaire and to return it in the enclosed envelope.

10. _____

11. Our organization not only provides assistance to physically handicapped children but also to emotionally disturbed children.

11. _____

12. You may either receive your dividends monthly or reinvest them in the bond fund.

12. _____

13. He felt he not only scored well on the written examination but also the interview.

13. _____

14. Unfortunately, the molds for these new figurines did not turn out like we had hoped.

14. _____

15. This professor has neither the patience nor has he the understanding to work well with students.

15. _____

16. We can either ship your order by Standard Mail (B) or United
    Parcel Service.   16. _____

17. If you need assistance with your financial affairs you may
    wish to contact one of our consultants.   17. _____

18. Providing information about our city and to assist visitors
    are the main functions of our bureau.   18. _____

19. Please cancel all appointments for next week, because the
    doctor will be out of the office.   19. _____

20. Replace the printer cartridges just like the diagram
    illustrates.   20. _____

Check your answers with those given on page 329 before completing the following exercise.

Section 7 Words Often Confused and Misused

Practice Exercises for Words from *A/An* Through *Aisle/Isle*

Practice Guide 1

Instructions: Select the correct word or a form of the word from each set of word confusions to complete the following sentences. Write your choice in the blank provided.

A/An

1. We have not yet received ___an___ application from Ms. Harris for this position.

2. Please ask ___a___ representative of your company to call me.

3. You may wish to discuss this situation with ___a___ union representative.

4. John will need at least ___an___ hour to review each file.

5. We must obtain from each patient ___a___ history of his or her medical conditions and treatments.

A lot/Allot/~~Alot~~

6. For the last few days, ___a lot___ of dust has been coming through the air vents on this floor.

7. We are unable to ___allot___ any additional funds for this project.

8. All members of the investment club have agreed to ___allot___ $100 a month for stock purchases.

9. Laura has been spending ___a lot___ of time on the Internet doing preliminary research for our survey.

10. How many hours have you ___alloted___ for us to complete this project?

A while/Awhile

11. We should receive this merchandise in ___a while___.

12. If you will read ___awhile___ each day, your comprehension and speed will improve.

13. ___A while___ ago I sent you information about our new home security system.

14. Although you have not placed an order with us for ___awhile___, we still consider you among our preferred customers.

15. Only by resting ___awhile___ each afternoon will you be able to regain your strength.

Accede/Exceed

16. Be careful not to _____exceed_____ your authority.

17. Has management agreed to _____accede_____ to the union demands?

18. If this budget is accepted, it will _____exceed_____ last year's by over 15 percent.

19. We cannot _____accede_____ to the landlord's request for a 30 percent rent increase.

20. Your commission on this sale may not _____exceed_____ $200.

Accelerate/Exhilarate

21. If we are to meet the deadline date, we must _____exhilarate_____ our progress.

22. Most accidents at this intersection are caused because drivers tend to _____accelerate_____ going down this hill.

23. The fresh air and an early morning walk will surely _____exhilarate_____ you.

24. There are a number of software programs available that can _____accelerate_____ the processing speed of your computer.

25. The executive staff was _____exhilarate_____ by the news that our company stock had risen 9 points during the past week.

Accept/Except

26. Our restaurant does not _____accept_____ dinner reservations on weekends.

27. Everyone in our department _____except_____ Mr. Fielding has requested a computer for his or her work station.

28. For money market checking accounts, all withdrawals are unlimited _____except_____ those made by check.

29. We _____accept_____ only cash or major credit cards—VISA, MasterCard, or American Express.

30. Applications for this position will be _____accepted_____ through June 30.

Access/Excess

31. Because of the floods, all the _____access_____ roads to the city were closed.

32. Building costs for the new offices were in _____excess_____ of $3.5 million.

33. Please ship all _____excess_____ supplies and materials to our Toledo warehouse.

34. Only the president and executive vice president have _____access_____ to the combination of this safe.

35. All our store locations have easy freeway _____excess_____.

Ad/Add

36. How many more salespeople do you plan to _____add_____ to our staff?

37. If you _____add_____ a security system to the building, you will be able to reduce your insurance costs.

38. By placing an _____ad_____ in our classified section, you will reach over 27,000 readers.

39. Students may not _____add_____ classes after the second week of the semester.

40. Our last _____ad_____ did not attract many new customers.

Adapt/Adept/Adopt

41. Do you believe the manager will _____adopt_____ our new supervisor's policy recommendations?

42. Too many of our employees do not _____adapt_____ readily to technological advancements.

43. Fortunately, Nicole is _____adept_____ at providing rapid and intelligent responses.

44. Will you be able to _____adapt_____ this new software to operate on other computers?

45. The instructor's manual, transparency masters, and a computer test bank are all given free of charge to instructors who _____adept_____ our book.

Addict/Edict

46. Too many of today's children are television _____addicts_____.

47. The general's _____edict_____ was not well received by the other officers.

48. Only a bare majority of the city council members support this _____edict_____.

49. Most of the drug _____addict_____ in our clinic are from the local area.

50. Bill manages by _____edict_____ rather than soliciting cooperative participation.

Addition/Edition

51. When will the new _____edition_____ of this book be available for purchase?

52. We anticipate several new _____addition_____ to our staff this year.

53. An _____addition_____ to our main dining room has been planned for next year.

54. These artists' prints are available in limited _____edition_____ only.

55. Please obtain for me a copy of *The New York Times* morning _____edition_____.

Adherence/Adherents

56. _____ to these policies will be strictly enforced.

57. The _____ of his many fans has kept alive the memory of Elvis Presley.

58. Football's many _____ have turned this sport into a multimillion-dollar industry.

59. The governor's _____ were disappointed when he withdrew his name as a contender for the presidential nomination.

60. Your _____ to these regulations is required as long as you occupy this apartment.

Adverse/Averse

61. I am not _____ to experimenting with new ideas and methods to improve communication within our organization.

62. Yesterday's _____ publicity has caused our stock to drop 3 points on the New York Stock Exchange.

63. Our manager appears to be _____ to any suggestions offered by the younger members of the staff.

64. _____ conditions in the building industry have resulted in substantial losses for many subcontractors.

65. The Board of Directors is _____ to expanding our operations at the present time.

Advice/Advise

66. Would you _____ us to contact an attorney for further information?

67. To select the correct courses, you should seek the _____ of a counselor.

68. I appreciate your _____ and will pursue the ideas you shared with me.

69. Upon the _____ of an investment counselor, we have purchased additional shares of CompuTab stock.

70. We _____ you to investigate this company carefully before purchasing any of its stock.

Affect/Effect

71. We have been unable to determine what _____ this advertising campaign has had on sales.

72. Did the unusual summer heat wave _____ your August sales?

73. Do you think the new manager will _____ many changes in our department?

74. How will this merger with General Computer Systems _____ our employees?

75. The changeover from a semester system to a quarter system has had no apparent _____ on enrollment at the college.

Aid/Aide

76. Our representatives are trained to _____ you in the selection of insurance policies that will fit your needs.

77. May we _____ you further by supplying information about our tax-free investments?

78. Please contact my _____ to obtain brochures about the leading companies in the computer industry.

79. Each department in our company has been supplied with a fully stocked first-_____ kit.

80. According to the news report, none of the presidential _____ could be reached for questioning.

Aisle/Isle

81. The carpet in the center ____aisle____ of the theater needs repair.

82. Please check the fire regulations to determine how much space must be left between the _____.

83. Catalina is an ____aisle____ approximately 23 miles from the Pacific coastline at Long Beach.

84. The ____Isle____ of Bermuda is a vacationer's paradise, often equated to Hawaii.

85. Before you take that "walk down the ____aisle____," be sure to visit our bridal gown showroom.

Check your answers with those given on pages 330–331 before completing the following exercise.

Reinforcement Guide 1

Instructions: Select one of the words (or a form of the word) shown below to complete each of the following sentences.

A/An
A lot/Allot/Alot
A while/Awhile
Accede/Exceed
Accelerate/Exhilarate
Accept/Except

Access/Excess
Ad/Add
Adapt/Adept/Adopt
Addict/Edict
Addition/Edition
Adherence/Adherents

Adverse/Averse
Advice/Advise
Affect/Effect
Aid/Aide
Aisle/Isle

1. On the _____ of his doctor, Mr. Reed has requested a three months' leave of absence.

2. According to the last _____ issued by our company president, no employees may park in the customer parking lot.

3. We will _____ applications for enrollment for the next academic year only through March 31.

4. You must separate each row of computer stations with a 42-inch _____.

5. Although I am not _____ to working overtime, I would prefer to work only my regularly assigned hours.

6. This firm specializes in seminars that help staff _____ to technological change and other modifications in the work environment.

7. Please do not permit this year's budget to _____ last year's.

8. Government _____ programs for the elderly have been curbed substantially during the past few years.

9. Strict _____ to outdated policies and procedures has been a major contributor to the company's present financial difficulties.

10. Student records are protected by law, and only certain authorized individuals may have _____ to their contents.

11. Everyone who visits the doctor nowadays expects to wait _____.

12. Large increases in raw material costs will _____ the prices of all our products.

13. This construction company specializes in house _____.

14. We have run this _____ in the *Daily Star* for the last three weeks but still have not found a qualified assistant to replace Ms. Chin.

15. Please have _____ union representative contact me as soon as possible.

16. These new personnel practices are certain to have a(n) _____ effect on employee morale.

17. Fortunately, most of our employees are _____ at upgrading their skills as new versions of word processing, spreadsheet, and database programs are released.

18. We wish it were possible to _____ to your request for an increased wage scale, but conditions within the industry forecast a profit decline during the next six months.

19. The new owners of the mall have already begun to _____ a number of changes.

20. Credit card purchases that _____ your account limit will not be approved for payment.

21. We have received _____ of customer complaints from the Orange County area.

22. You may obtain E-mail _____ through any of the Internet service providers listed on the enclosed sheet.

23. These _____ materials must be disposed of properly.

24. All union employees have been granted an 8 percent increase in pay _____ for those still on probationary status.

25. The Juvenile Division is recommending to the court that the Smiths' petition be accepted and that the Smiths be allowed to _____ the child named in the petition.

*The answers to this exercise appear in the **Instructor's Manual and Key** for **HOW 8: A Handbook for Office Workers,** Eighth Edition.*

Practice Exercises for Words From *All ready/Already* Through *Any Way/Anyway*

Practice Guide 2

Instructions: Select the correct word or a form of the word from each set of word confusions to complete the following sentences. Write your choice in the blank provided.

All ready/Already

1. The materials for these brochures are ___*all ready*___ to be taken to the printer's.

2. We have ___*alread*___ received over 50 orders as a result of the new advertising campaign initiated last week.

3. As you may ___*already*___ know, our division is being merged with another division in the company.

4. Most of our staff has ___*already*___ received training on using the spreadsheet aspects of Excel.

5. We were ___*all ready*___ to interview candidates when Mr. Graham informed us that the position was going to be abolished.

All right/Alright

6. Your test answers were ___*all right*___.

7. As far as I am concerned, it is ___*alright*___ for you to begin your vacation on July 15.

8. It is not ___*alright*___ to extend your lunch hour 15 minutes every day.

9. Our accountant agreed that Lisa's classifying the entries as she had done was ___*all right*___.

10. Unfortunately, the answers in this test key are not _____.

All together/Altogether

11. I believe we can expect _____ nearly 75 participants for this conference.

12. Please gather _____ the reports that have been written regarding this project.

13. If we work _____, we can finish this instructional manual by May 1.

14. We have collected _____ only $10,400 as a result of this charity function.

15. This year's holiday sales are _____ lower than last year's.

All ways/Always

16. You have _____ been a prompt-paying customer.

17. Our accountant has _____ notified us of any discrepancies in our accounts.

18. We have tried _____ possible to please you, but you still seem to be dissatisfied with our service.

19. Our employees are _____ paid on the 1st and 15th of each month.

20. Please note that _____ have been explored to expedite the manufacture and delivery of these airplane parts.

Allowed/Aloud

21. No minors under 21 years of age are _____ on the premises.

22. Federal law has not _____ major corporations to form industry monopolies since the last century.

23. Please read _____ the president's response to our inquiry.

24. We have always _____ students to petition for graduation until April 30 of the year of graduation.

25. You are requested not to speak _____ during the consultant's presentation.

Allude/Elude

26. Did the manager of human resources _____ to any possible openings in his department?

27. Dora seems to expend more effort to _____ work than she would need to accomplish her job.

28. In your opening address at our national sales meeting, you may wish to _____ to the projected market increase forecast by our sales analysts.

29. Mr. Roberts has managed to _____ answering my questions for the last week.

30. In our annual report please _____ to the technological advancements made by our company during the last year.

Allusion/Delusion/Illusion

31. Although Mr. Smith lives lavishly, his great wealth is a mere _____.

32. Too many people suffer from the _____ that technological advancements will lead to mass unemployment.

33. In order to promote sales, this investment firm promoted the _____ that all these properties were lakefront lots.

34. Did Mr. Martin make any _____ to our acquiring financial assistance from foreign investors?

35. For this perfume commercial we will want to create an _____ of intrigue and romance.

Almost/Most

36. ___Almost___ everyone in our department has been employed by the company for at least five years.

37. ___Most___ managers expect their employees to arrive at work on time.

38. These sales catalogs have already been sent to ___almost___ all our new customers.

39. We expected that ___almost___ every airline would have already been booked for this date.

40. I did not realize that we had sold ___almost___ all our stock of Hi-Tech video cassettes.

Altar/Alter

41. Please do not ___alter___ any dates on this delivery schedule.

42. We manufacture a variety of artifacts for church ___altar___.

43. As a result of the electrical fire, the ___altar___ was badly damaged.

44. If you wish to _____ your travel plans, please contact our agency rather than the airlines or hotels.

45. Our architect is reluctant to _____ the church plans any further.

Alternate/Alternative

46. Whom have you selected as an _____ delegate to the convention?

47. We have no other _____ but to issue additional stock and offer it for sale to the general public.

48. During the renovation please locate an _____ conference room for our weekly meetings.

49. Please _____ the responsibility for closing the store between Leslie and Dana.

50. Our goal is to offer employees several _____ in selecting a health plan to meet their needs.

Among/Between

51. Please distribute these brochures _____ all our agency managers.

52. There appeared to be major discrepancies _____ the two witnesses' testimonies.

53. The commission is to be divided equally _____ Ann and Phil.

54. We are unable to disclose this information because it is confidential _____ the client and our agent.

55. You may wish to have the office employees discuss this proposal _____ themselves before they make a decision.

Amount/Number

56. A large ___number___ of people gathered to hear the announcement of who had been awarded the contract.

57. During the next three years, we will reduce the _____ of employees in our Springfield plant.

58. Our company recently sold a large ___number___ of farm lands to independent growers.

59. Please check the ___amount___ of flour we have in stock.

60. Our store was understaffed to handle adequately the ___number___ of sales we had yesterday.

Anecdote/Antidote

61. Our manager seems never to miss the opportunity to relate an _____ about one of the employees.

62. Most speakers begin their presentation with an _____.

63. Is there an _____ for lead poisoning?

64. One of our community service seminars for new mothers discusses emergency procedures and _____ for common household poisons.

65. The entire audience was amused by Ms. Green's series of _____ regarding the recent election.

Annual/Annul

66. The agent was able to _____ the contract because it had been prepared incorrectly.

67. The _____ membership fee for the use of your Money-Bonus card is only $30.

68. Our audit is conducted on an _____ basis.

69. If the Board of Directors chooses to _____ this long-established policy, it may alienate a number of stockholders.

70. Both parties were eager to _____ the marriage.

Anxious/Eager

71. Our manager appears _____ about the forthcoming visit from our director of marketing.

72. I am _____ to see the page proof for our new sales brochure.

73. All the members of our staff are _____ to get started on the development of this new software version.

74. A number of students are _____ about accessing and using the Internet to gather information for their term report.

75. We are all _____ to learn who was chosen to fill the vacancy on the board of education.

Any one/Anyone
of

76. Hand a leaflet describing our sale prices to _____ who enters the store.

77. ___*any one*___ of our salespeople can help you select the refrigerator you will need.

78. Please notify _____ of the instructors in our Word Processing Center if you plan to drop the course.

79. _____ in our Counseling Department can give you this information.

80. We have not yet received an application from _____ who is qualified for the position.

Any time/Anytime

81. _____ you need assistance, please do not hesitate to call on me.

82. Please visit our showroom _____ within the next three weeks to pick up your free calendar appointment book.

83. Our auto body shop can repair your car _____ next week.

84. We cannot divert _____ from this project to review new manuscripts.

85. You may call our toll-free number _____ you need technical assistance with one of our software programs.

Any way/Anyway

86. We are not in a position to finance this project _____.

87. _____ you select to assign these tasks is acceptable to me.

88. We have not yet found _____ to bond these two surfaces permanently.

89. Our supplier cannot in _____ promise a May 1 delivery date.

90. _____, this model printer is no longer available.

Check your answers with those given on pages 331–332 before completing the following exercise.

Reinforcement Guide 2

Instructions: Select one of the words (or a form of the word) shown below to complete each of the following sentences.

All ready/Already
All right/Alright
All together/Altogether
All ways/Always
Allowed/Aloud
Allude/Elude

Allusion/Delusion/Illusion
Almost/Most
Altar/Alter
Alternate/Alternative
Among/Between
Amount/Number

Anecdote/Antidote
Annual/Annul
Anxious/Eager
Any one/Anyone
Any time/Anytime
Any way/Anyway

1. We have not yet found _____ to market our products outside the United States.

2. Unfortunately, I do not know an _____ for unmitigated greed and a compelling quest for power.

3. Because of the contract deadline, we have asked _____ everyone on our staff to work overtime next week.

4. Although Mr. Bryce was not selected, our staff was not _____ disappointed in the Board of Director's choice for executive vice president.

5. Please call on us _____ we can be of further service to you.

6. None of us could believe the _____ of errors that appeared in the sales letter written by the new manager.

7. The best way to solve a problem is not _____ readily apparent.

8. If your exchanging desks is _____ with your supervisor, I have no objection.

9. Are you able to recommend _____ for this position?

10. Please distribute these files _____ Peter, Diana, and Chris.

11. The manager's memo left us with the _____ that the in-service classes on computer applications were for supervisory personnel only.

12. Ms. Davis was _____ to leave for the airport when she learned that her flight had been canceled because of the weather.

13. Although neither party wished to _____ the contract, the court ruled the contract was invalid as written.

14. How many times have you been forced to _____ the plans for opening our new branch office?

15. In your progress report you may wish to _____ to the difficulties we have experienced because of the recent snowstorms.

16. No children are _____ in the pool area unless accompanied by an adult.

17. Heavy fines were imposed upon the school and its owners for promoting the _____ it was an entity of the federal government.

18. Companies that continue to dump waste into the harbor will no longer be able to _____ court action.

19. You may choose _____ of the items illustrated in the brochure as your free gift.

20. Please store this equipment in the closet _____ Room 14 and Room 16.

21. Most credit card companies charge an _____ fee to cardholders in addition to interest charges for unpaid balances.

22. After being housed in these temporary quarters for the last six months, everyone is _____ to move into the new offices in the Blackburn Building.

23. Please post a sign in the reading area requesting children and adults not to read _____.

24. If you were making the decision, which _____ would you choose?

25. _____ everyone in our group has agreed to ratify the proposed new union contract.

*The answers to this exercise appear in the **Instructor's Manual and Key** for **HOW 8: A Handbook for Office Workers,** Eighth Edition.*

Practice Exercises for Words From *Appraise/Apprise* Through *Bolder/Boulder*

Practice Guide 3

Instructions: Select the correct word or a form of the word from each set of word confusions to complete the following sentences. Write your choice in the blank provided.

Appraise/Apprise

1. Be sure to _____ Ms. Reynolds of any sudden changes in the price of our stock.

2. We have not been _____ of any offers to purchase our company.

3. According to our accountant, the property has been _____ for nearly $75,000 more than the prospective buyers offered.

4. Once you have had an opportunity to _____ the situation, please give us your candid opinion.

5. Have you _____ the parents of their daughter's belligerent behavior in the classroom?

As/Like

6. Ms. Harris manages the office _____ a conscientious and competent supervisor should.

7. We are striving to operate this charity boutique _____ a business.

8. You may be certain that we will deliver this order by July 15, just _____ we promised.

9. Although these sunglasses look _____ ours, they were produced and sold illegally by a manufacturing counterfeiter.

10. _____ I said in yesterday's staff meeting, we must create several innovative new toys to remain competitive in this market.

Ascent/Assent

11. The recent _____ of stock market prices has caused even more trading on the New York Stock Exchange.

12. Do you think the Board of Directors will _____ to the president's plan for expanding our operations?

13. Mr. Brooks rapid _____ to executive vice president has caused quite a stir among the other young executives.

14. The _____ of the plane to its cruising altitude was hindered by strong head winds.

15. Will management _____ to the union's request for an additional 1 percent pay increase?

Assistance/Assistants

16. Were you able to obtain any additional financial _____?

17. Please ask the receptionist for _____ in completing these forms.

18. Congress recently provided for additional _____ to the elderly and others on fixed-income programs.

19. Neither of the doctor's _____ could provide the information we need for this report.

20. If you are unable to attend the meeting, please have one of your _____ substitute for you.

Assume/Presume

21. We can no longer _____ any responsibility for pets without proper identification tags.

22. Unfortunately, Mr. Grant _____ that his direct flight to New York was also nonstop.

23. According to the newscasters' weather reports, we can _____ that the Rose Parade on New Year's Day will be favored with a beautiful sunny day.

24. Perhaps one of your assistants can _____ these duties temporarily?

25. I _____ you will notify all our clients of our new address and telephone number at least one month before our scheduled move.

Assure/Ensure/Insure

26. Can you _____ that this project will be completed by its deadline date, September 1?

27. You may wish to _____ your property against other losses besides fire.

28. If you can _____ that I will be able to see Dr. Norris, I will make an appointment for that time.

29. We can _____ you at this time that these dresses will be available in time for holiday purchases.

30. Please allow me to _____ you that we will do all we can to retrieve your stolen goods.

Attendance/Attendants

31. Your poor _____ record was the decisive factor in your dismissal.

32. How many members of the council must be in _____ to comprise a quorum?

33. Each of the bride's _____ will carry a bouquet of delicate pink rosebuds.

34. Before accepting each instructor's _____ roster, please make sure that it has been signed.

35. Please ask one of the ambulance _____ to sign the patient release form.

Bad/Badly

36. I feel _____ that we were unable to locate your lost briefcase.

37. The incumbent was defeated _____ by his young, energetic opponent.

38. I did not realize that I had done so _____ on this examination.

39. Why does the air in this office always smell _____?

40. Marie must certainly feel _____ that she did not receive the promotion to assistant sales manager.

Bail/Bale

41. How many _____ of hay did you order for the horses?

42. This defendant is being held without _____.

43. The judge has agreed to set _____ for our client tomorrow.

44. We cannot even begin to estimate the number of _____ of wheat destroyed by the fire.

45. Please tie all these newspapers in _____ for recycling.

Bare/Bear

46. Many successful businesses have emerged from _____ beginnings.

47. I do not know how much longer XYZ Corporation can _____ these exorbitant losses.

48. We only maintain the _____ minimum balance in our checking account; other liquid assets are deposited in higher interest-earning accounts.

49. The house had been allowed to deteriorate so badly that in many places the _____ wood was exposed.

50. The time allotted for my presentation enabled me to discuss only the _____ findings of the study.

Base/Bass

51. Do you still play the _____ violin in our community orchestra?

52. The _____ of this statue is filled with lead.

53. All the fillings in our candies have a chocolate _____.

54. If these conclusions do not stem from a solid _____ of data, then our sales efforts will be unsuccessful.

55. We are still looking for a _____ voice for the company "barber shop quartet."

Bazaar/Bizarre

56. Our new television series is based on documented eye-witness accounts of _____, peculiar, and curious events.

57. We manufacture gaming equipment for church _____ and other charity events.

58. Most of the proceeds from our annual _____ are used to provide clothing and toys for underprivileged children.

59. This witness's account of the event is so _____ that scarcely anyone else will believe it.

60. Fewer and fewer of our students are focusing on _____ hair styles and clothing trends.

Berth/Birth

61. We expect the Village Queen to _____ here tomorrow afternoon shortly after 3 p.m.

62. Mrs. Gilmore gave _____ to twin girls at Valley Hills Hospital yesterday.

63. Was the father present during the _____ of this child?

64. All the _____ on this train have already been sold.

65. Only three of the _____ at Island Harbor are presently occupied by cruise ships.

Beside/Besides

66. Who else _____ Don is entitled to a bonus this month?

67. Place one of these new copyholders _____ each computer.

68. Please move the file cabinet _____ the window in my new office.

69. Several distinguished government officials _____ the mayor were present for the opening session of our convention.

70. You should probably invite other clients _____ those with whom we have had business dealings for over ten years.

Bi-/Semi-

71. The _____ weekly issues of our local newspaper are published on Thursdays and Sundays.

72. All our employees are paid _____ monthly; checks are issued on the 1st and 15th each month.

73. _____ monthly meetings of our committee are held in February, April, June, August, October, and December.

74. Our company listing of employment opportunities on the Internet is updated _____ weekly; that is, every other Friday I add new listings and remove those that have been filled.

75. The _____ monthly meetings of the board of education are held on the second and fourth Tuesdays at 2 p.m.

Biannual/Biennial

76. Your _____ royalty checks are issued in March and August.

77. The first of this year's _____ reports to stockholders will be issued in February.

78. _____ elections of officers for our organization are held in even-numbered years.

79. These _____ reports must be submitted to the federal government by January 31 and July 31.

80. Unfortunately, this research digest is published only _____; the next issue will not appear for another year.

Bibliography/Biography

81. Be sure to include a _____ at the end of your report.

82. Did you place any Internet references in your _____?

83. The manuscript on your desk is a _____ of Ronald Reagan.

84. Use the format shown in Chapter 11 of *HOW 8* to prepare the entries in your _____.

85. You can probably find a copy of this book in the _____ section of the library.

Billed/Build

86. Have you _____ Ms. Davis for her last order?

87. How many homes has Hodge & Sons been contracted to _____?

88. We plan to _____ our new offices on this site within the next two years.

89. Our plan is to _____ a good relationship with the community before relocating our plant there.

90. Your company has not yet _____ us for the 36 dozen 3.5-inch disks we received last January.

Boarder/Border

91. The brochure will be more attractive if you remove the _____ around the graphic.

92. Did you advertise in the *Daily News* that you had a room available for a _____?

93. At the present time Oakley House has only 18 _____.

94. You may pick up the shipment at the _____ on August 2.

95. If you do not plan to frame this photograph, we can place an attractive
_____ around it.

Bolder/Boulder

96. Unless we adopt _____ merchandising policies, we will face even greater losses in this tough, competitive market.

97. Traffic was held up for over two hours because a loose _____ had blocked the tunnel entrance.

98. Our new store manager is somewhat _____ than I thought he would be.

99. You should perhaps be _____ in expressing your concerns to the management team.

100. The foundation for this eighteenth-century house is comprised of _____ from the local countryside held together by thin layers of cement.

Check your answers with those given on pages 332–333 before completing the following exercise.

Reinforcement Guide 3

Instructions: Select one of the words (or a form of the word) shown below to complete each of the following sentences.

Appraise/Apprise
As/Like
Ascent/Assent
Assistance/Assistants
Assume/Presume
Assure/Ensure/Insure
Attendance/Attendants

Bad/Badly
Bail/Bale
Bare/Bear
Base/Bass
Bazaar/Bizarre
Berth/Birth
Beside/Besides

Bi-/Semi-
Biannual/Biennial
Bibliography/Biography
Billed/Build
Boarder/Border
Bolder/Boulder

1. Place a fancy _____ around this flier.

2. Four other dignitaries _____ General Taylor were honored at the banquet.

3. All of us feel _____ that we were unable to complete the project by its initial deadline date.

4. _____ our receptionist told you, we are able to sell our products only to persons with resale licenses.

5. Our _____ conventions are held in odd-numbered years.

6. Please order the feed company to deliver an additional _____ of hay daily.

7. Your account balance has dropped below the _____ minimum to maintain an account free of service charges.

8. This month three of our clients were _____ for services they did not receive.

9. Be sure to _____ our company president of any news events that may affect our industry.

10. The sudden _____ of raw material prices will effect price increases throughout the automobile industry.

11. Without the _____ of you and your staff, we would have had great difficulty publishing this textbook.

12. Unless you _____ the arrival of our order in time for holiday sales, we will be unable to guarantee its acceptance.

13. Please explain to the manager that his _____ at this meeting is of prime importance.

14. The new shopping center will be located at the _____ of the Flintridge Foothills.

15. Within the last few months, the committee has adopted _____ policies regarding the collection of delinquent accounts.

16. Once you have had an opportunity to _____ the situation in our Chicago plant, please call me directly.

17. Unless the Board of Directors _____ unanimously to the merger, we will need to take your proposal to the stockholders.

18. To _____ that each payment has been credited to the proper account, please double-check each entry.

19. One sales representative behaved so _____ at the meeting that the sales manager had to ask him to leave.

20. Dividends on this stock are paid _____, once in January and then again in July.

21. We cannot _____ that all our present employees will move with us to the Montrose plant.

22. On this cruise our ship will _____ in Acapulco for two days.

23. News coverage concerning this _____ incident has been nationwide for the past week.

24. Issues of our _____ weekly campus newspaper are published and distributed to students on Mondays and Thursdays.

25. All references appearing in the footnotes of your report should be cited in the _____.

The answers to this exercise appear in the **Instructor's Manual and Key** *for* **HOW 8: A Handbook for Office Workers,** *Eighth Edition.*

Practice Exercises for Words From *Born/Borne* Through *Coarse/Course*

Practice Guide 4

Instructions: Select the correct word or a form of the word from each set of word confusions to complete the following sentences. Write your choice in the blank provided.

Born/Borne

1. His efforts have _____ great success within only a few months.

2. Our division in the company has _____ financial losses each quarter for the last two years because of poor management.

3. This industry was _____ scarcely three decades ago.

4. How many children has the patient _____?

5. According to our records, the child was _____ with this heart defect.

Bouillon/Bullion

6. We are completely out of stock on Hillsdale's _____ cubes.

7. The possession of gold _____ in this country was once illegal.

8. The safe was filled with ingots of gold and silver _____.

9. The addition of chicken _____ instead of boiling water will enhance considerably the flavor of this recipe.

10. We prefer to serve hearty cream soups instead of _____.

Breach/Breech

11. As the months wore on, the _____ between the two partners grew even wider.

12. The judge found difficulty in determining which of the parties had _____ the contract.

13. A crack in the _____ of the gun rendered it useless.

14. Does your client wish to sue ABC Corporation for _____ of contract?

15. Please pack the _____ between the two properties with clean fill dirt.

Bring/Take

16. For each session be sure to _____ your textbook and data disks to class.

17. Oftentimes patients will _____ with them magazines we have in the waiting area.

18. When you have your signature witnessed by a notary public, be sure to _____ with you a photo identification.

19. When you visit our store, be sure to _____ the pattern for the glass tabletop you wish cut.

20. Please _____ all these extra copies of our annual report to the storage room.

Calendar/Colander

21. The plastic _____ are considerably less expensive than the stainless steel ones.

22. Will we be sending new wall _____ for next year to each of our clients?

23. As soon as you check your _____, please let me know if Thursday, April 21, at 2 p.m. will be a convenient time for you to meet with me.

24. Have you received the _____ of events scheduled for the summer months in the Hollywood Bowl?

25. If the holes in the _____ are too large, some of the smaller food particles will fall through.

Callous/Callus

26. Caution our medical personnel not to become _____ in dealing with the needs of our patients.

27. Your _____ attitude toward the children forces us to dismiss you as a teacher's aide.

28. No _____ can form with the protection of our new Syntho-fiber gardening gloves.

29. Police officers soon learn to become _____ to the remarks of irate motorists.

30. My index finger has developed a _____ from using this punch.

Can/May

31. You _____ mail us your reply in the return envelope.

32. Only members of our personnel staff _____ have access to these employee records.

33. Most of our staff members _____ use word processing, spreadsheet, and database programs.

34. _____ you provide us with this information by May 1?

35. Of course, you _____ borrow these instructions to set up your accounts receivable program.

Canvas/Canvass

36. We are presently out of stock on _____ tents.

37. How many salespeople have been assigned to _____ the Springfield area?

38. Many athletes still prefer to wear _____ tennis shoes rather than leather tennis shoes.

39. Several of the people who work in our real estate office have volunteered to _____ the area.

40. If you were to _____ the shopping malls in this area, perhaps you could determine the buying patterns of residents here.

Capital/Capitol

41. How much _____ will you need to launch this program?

42. The Department of Education is located in Room 450 of the state _____ .

43. Our senior class will visit the _____ in May to tour the city and its surrounding area.

44. In most countries murder is considered to be a _____ crime.

45. When visiting Washington, D.C., you must be sure to visit the _____ to see where Congress convenes.

Carat/Caret/Carrot/Karat

46. One of our customers wishes to purchase a 5-_____ blue topaz pendant for her daughter.

47. We do carry a few chains in 18-_____ gold, but most of our jewelry is 14 _____ .

48. When using revision marks, please use a _____ to indicate where letters or words are to be inserted.

49. The customer wishes a piece of _____ cake with whipped cream frosting for dessert.

50. Many pieces of European jewelry are made with 10-_____ gold.

Cease/Seize

51. Our competitors have been ordered by the courts to _____ their false advertising.

52. When did Lenox _____ manufacturing this crystal pattern?

53. Young executives today must _____ every opportunity to move ahead, even if promotion means relocating to other parts of the country.

54. Was Drake Industries able to _____ control of Litchfield Petroleum Corporation?

55. We must _____ work on this project until after the rainy season.

Ceiling/Sealing

56. When will the work crews finish _____ the wooden floors in our offices?

57. Price _____ on many agricultural products have been lifted temporarily.

58. _____ these surfaces with Varathane-3 has kept them from cracking and peeling.

59. Many investment analysts believe the stock market has reached its _____ for this year.

60. All the walls and _____ in this building need to be repainted.

Censor/Censure

61. Many countries regularly _____ all mail directed outside their boundaries.

62. Senator Billings was subjected to public _____ once the press disclosed his questionable financial affiliations.

63. The board of education _____ the principal for negligence in not investigating the numerous parent complaints received about this hazardous situation.

64. The _____ have barred this film from television viewing.

65. Not all the _____ material had been removed from the script before filming.

Census/Senses

66. Which of the _____ are tested by this procedure?

67. Enrollment _____ figures are reported to the state monthly for each of our classes.

68. The latest _____ reports show that the population of our state has increased 5.7 percent during the last decade.

69. At the present time the _____ in this retirement home is 12 persons below capacity.

70. When one of the _____ becomes impaired, patients tell us that others seem to become keener and compensate somewhat for the loss.

Cent/Scent/Sent

71. Although Mr. Wilson is a millionaire, he acts as though he doesn't have a _____ to his name.

72. Last week you were _____ three copies of the signed contract for your files.

73. We are in the process of testing several new _____ for our fall perfume collection.

74. Before completing the arrangements, be sure to inquire if anyone in the wedding party is allergic to the _____ of gardenias.

75. Please do not include _____ amounts in this report; round each figure to the nearest dollar value.

Cereal/Serial

76. The _____ numbers of all our equipment have been recorded on individual cards and entered into our computer database.

77. This new breakfast food is made from 100 percent whole grain _____.

78. When advertising our new high-fiber _____, be sure to mention its crunchiness and tasty cinnamon-apple flavor.

79. Our company will not purchase advertising time on daytime _____ television programs.

80. You may upgrade your version of WordProcessor for only $90 by sending us payment and the _____ number of your current program.

Choose/Chose

81. Last year most of our employees _____ to receive their bonuses in stock issues.

82. Please _____ your vacation date for this year by April 15.

83. The committee will _____ the final Rose Queen contestants by December 1.

84. Although the manager _____ not to select an assistant at this time, she reserved the right to do so at a later date.

85. You may _____ any color shown in this chart for the exterior of your home.

Cite/Sight/Site

86. Within the next two weeks, we will select a _____ for our new warehouse facility.

87. Please _____ at least two authorities to substantiate your position.

88. Our travel agency can offer you _____-seeing tours in all parts of the world at reasonable prices.

89. The defendant was also _____ for driving without a license.

90. None of the _____ we have seen so far are suitable for the construction of the entertainment center we have in mind.

Close/Clothes/Cloths

91. We plan to _____ out this line of swimsuits at the end of the season.

92. Play Time, Inc., manufactures children's _____ and accessories.

93. Ask the building superintendent's assistant to order an additional supply of dust _____.

94. When you _____ the office at the end of the day, be sure the front door is fastened securely.

95. Several of our _____ racks are broken and need to be replaced.

Coarse/Course

96. You may wish to complete our beginning accounting _____ before taking any other business classes.

97. Before committing themselves to any specific _____ of action, the committee wanted to review more carefully the recommendations of the consultants.

98. The texture of this sand is too _____ for use in the manufacture of ceramic tile.

99. Both homes and luxury condominiums will be built around this new golf _____.

100. During the _____ of the conversation, neither party discussed the financial commitments that would be necessary from each of them.

Check your answers with those given on pages 334–335 before completing the following exercise.

Name _____ Date _____

Reinforcement Guide 4

Instructions: Select one of the words (or a form of the word) shown below to complete each of the following sentences.

Born/Borne Canvas/Canvass Cent/Scent/Sent
Bouillon/Bullion Capital/Capitol Cereal/Serial
Breach/Breech Carat/Caret/Carrot/Karat Choose/Chose
Bring/Take Cease/Seize Cite/Sight/Site
Calendar/Colander Ceiling/Sealing Close/Clothes/Cloths
Callous/Callus Censor/Censure Coarse/Course
Can/May Census/Senses

1. Be sure to record the _____ numbers of all the bonds in this issue before forwarding them to our New York office.

2. If you refuse to _____ these illegal practices, we will be forced to seek an injunction.

3. You _____ call our toll-free number, (800) 555-3783, any time you need information about current interest rates on the accounts we offer.

4. Too many customers have complained about the _____ grains in our new bran cereal.

5. Most nonallergenic cosmetics have no discernible _____ whatsoever.

6. Proofreaders and editors use a _____ to indicate where insertions should be placed in a document.

7. When elected officials become _____ and indifferent to the needs of their constituents, they should be replaced.

8. The _____ for the new hospital and medical center has not yet been selected.

9. None of these _____ figures support the mayor's claim that business investments in our city have doubled since he has been in office.

10. Our offices are located in Room 450 of the state _____.

11. Within the last few weeks, the _____ between the mayor and several city council members has become apparent to the public.

12. Whom did the Board of Directors _____ to replace our retiring treasurer?

13. Although the governor's personal business activities were not in direct violation of the law, he was _____ by the press for his inability to explain his connection with the Zorga Corporation.

14. Which of our employees has been assigned to _____ the area directly south of Wilshire Boulevard?

15. May I suggest that you select as the first course for the banquet a beef _____.

16. Franchises usually require their participants to invest a substantial amount of _____ before permitting them to operate under the company name.

17. To substantiate your proposal, please _____ the names of several companies that have used this plan successfully.

18. At the present time most of our housing projects are in the outlying areas adjacent to the Florida state _____.

19. After the convention you may wish to view some of the historic _____ in and around Boston.

20. You will need to _____ this movie substantially for television viewing.

21. The parent company, BTP Enterprises, has _____ the losses of its two subsidiaries for the past five years.

22. To ensure that your application will be processed quickly, _____ it in person to the Admissions Office.

23. Send E-mail messages to all our Midwestern sales representatives so they can mark their _____ for the regional sales meeting scheduled for January 15–19.

24. Real estate agents fear that this period of climbing interest rates has not yet reached its _____.

25. None of the _____ on these racks are on sale.

*The answers to this exercise appear in the **Instructor's Manual and Key** for **HOW 8: A Handbook for Office Workers,** Eighth Edition.*

Practice Exercises for Words From *Collision/Collusion* Through *Deference/Difference*

Practice Guide 5

Instructions: Select the correct word or a form of the word from each set of word confusions to complete the following sentences. Write your choice in the blank provided.

Collision/Collusion

1. The two executive officers had worked in _____ for several years embezzling funds steadily from their investors.

2. The impact of the _____ was heard over a block away.

3. Although the state official was suspected of being in _____ with the contract awardee, no one could produce sufficient evidence to substantiate the suspicion.

4. You can see from just observing the manager and his assistant, they are on a definite _____ course.

5. The evidence clearly indicated that the security guard was not in _____ with the bank robbers, as they had indicated.

Command/Commend

6. Please _____ Ms. Harris on her excellent sales performance during this quarter.

7. You are to be _____ for having the foresight to install this computer network when the division was reorganized.

8. To operate this computer program, you must first learn a series of _____.

9. The Navy's personnel department has assigned a new officer to _____ this ship.

10. Effective managers will always _____ employees under their supervision for a job well done.

Complement/Compliment

11. You may wish to _____ your tempura shrimp entrée selection with a mixture of Oriental vegetables.

12. None of the wall decorations in the outer office _____ the rest of the office decor.

13. Please select upholstered chairs to _____ the new gray carpeting that will be installed in our office next week.

14. These calendars will be given to all the conference participants with our
_____.

15. Did you remember to _____ the staff on its outstanding production
performance this month?

Complementary/Complimentary

16. All of us appreciate your _____ remarks about our products and service.

17. None of the colors selected by the decorator are _____ to the existing
wall paint.

18. The qualifications possessed by Ms. Lee are certainly _____ to those
possessed by other members of our staff.

19. To celebrate the opening of our new La Habra store, we will serve _____
coffee and cookies at all our stores on October 1.

20. In general, student evaluations of Mr. Reed have been quite _____.

Confidant/Confident

21. Mr. Burns has been the senator's _____ for many years.

22. When you feel more _____ about your skills, please return to our
Department of Human Resources to take the employment test.

23. I am _____ that we will have over 100 registrants for this conference.

24. The information was evidently passed on to the press through the president's assistant
and _____.

25. Our sales manager feels _____ that her staff members will reach their
quotas by the end of the fourth quarter.

Conscience/Conscious

26. In all good _____, I cannot permit you to take this equipment until we
have completed all the safety tests.

27. Are you _____ of the new marketing techniques launched by your
toughest competitor?

28. Obviously these publishers have little _____ if they are willing to publish
such obscene materials.

29. Two of the entrapped victims were still _____ when the police entered
the vault.

30. Are you _____ of the new developments that have occurred with laser
surgery within the last five years?

Console/Consul

31. This _____ unit may be purchased with either an oak or a walnut finish.

32. Only standard-size televisions will fit in these _____.

33. To receive a refund of the value-added tax, you must have the German
_____ witness your affidavit that the goods purchased were brought to
the United States.

34. Unfortunately, the right side of the _____ was damaged during shipment.

35. Did you invite the _____ to join us for dinner on May 24?

Continual/Continuous

36. Our receptionist's _____ talking irritates a number of our other staff
members.

37. We have experienced rainy weather here _____ for the last week.

38. Please place this roll of _____-form paper in the printer.

39. The water had run _____ for three days before the gardeners discovered
the leak in the pipe.

40. Customers are _____ complaining about our service in the southwest
area of the city.

Convince/Persuade

41. Were you able to _____ any stockholders to invest additional money in
the company?

42. No matter how hard we tried, we were unable to _____ Aaron to remain
with the company.

43. Were you able to _____ our manager that we should network the
computers in our division?

44. Before we move any further ahead with this project, we must _____ the
president of its profitability.

45. How can we _____ you to accompany us on this business trip to Orlando?

Cooperation/Corporation

46. We would appreciate your _____ in helping us complete this survey.

47. Several members of our _____ will be attending your seminar on local
area networks scheduled to be held in Chicago from April 22 through April 24.

48. Unless we have the _____ of the majority of our employees, this
incentive plan will fail.

49. Only through the _____ and hard work of all the committee members
were we able to plan and carry through this successful trade convention.

50. Several _____ have expressed an interest in acquiring our product.

Corespondent/Correspondence/Correspondents

51. Who was named as _____ in the divorce case?

52. Would you please direct to my attention all _____ relating to this matter.

53. None of our foreign _____ have yet responded with a story from this part of the world.

54. We have received _____ from all over the United States expressing concern over the complexity of the new tax laws.

55. Please have one of the _____ in our Customer Relations Department answer this inquiry.

Corps/Corpse

56. Authorities have still not been able to identify the _____ found yesterday in the desert near Palm Valley.

57. A _____ of reporters flocked around the winning pitcher as he left the dressing room.

58. A recruitment officer from the U.S. Marine _____ will visit our campus next week.

59. The _____ has already been moved to the downtown morgue.

60. A large _____ of government workers has petitioned the governor to reconsider his stand on proposed wage and salary cutbacks.

Council/Counsel

61. Three members of our city _____ are up for reelection this year.

62. I would suggest that you seek _____ from an attorney before taking any further action.

63. The _____ meeting was postponed because a quorum was not present.

64. You should write your city _____ member directly about the problem.

65. Each staff member _____ at least 12 to 15 students daily.

Credible/Creditable

66. We have received this information from several _____ sources.

67. Your sales record with our company is certainly _____.

68. Mr. Holmes' _____ service record with our organization indicates that he is a likely candidate for promotion.

69. The witness's testimony was hardly _____ in view of the evidence uncovered by the police laboratory.

70. Unless our candidate's statements are viewed as _____ in the public's eye, he will not have any chance to win this election.

Deceased/Diseased

71. Please notify the family of the _____ victim before releasing his name to the press.

WORDS OFTEN CONFUSED AND MISUSED

72. The surgeon was able to remove all the _____ tissue without amputating the limb.

73. All the _____ animals must be separated from the herd before they infect others.

74. What kind of fungicide should we use for these _____ plants?

75. One of the beneficiaries in this will has been _____ for six months.

Decent/Descent/Dissent

76. Most of the people who live in this area are of Irish _____.

77. People in this country are at least able to earn a _____ wage.

78. _____ among the workers is causing a major problem for our manager.

79. The company's profit picture began its _____ approximately four years ago.

80. Several major stockholders have sensed the _____ between the president and the chairman of the Board of Directors over this issue.

Defer/Differ

81. You may _____ payment of this invoice until the 1st of March.

82. Although I _____ with you on the media we should use, I agree we should increase our advertising efforts.

83. We can no longer _____ calling in these high-interest bonds.

84. All such retirement programs only _____ the payment of taxes until a later date.

85. The candidates seemed to _____ on each issue brought up for discussion.

Deference/Difference

86. We have expanded our business offerings in _____ to the many requests from the community.

87. I find little _____ between the new edition and the previous edition of this text.

88. Would you please explain the _____ between analog and digital signals.

89. Have you noticed any _____ in the quality of custodial services within the last month?

90. Most of our imported food products have been grouped according to country of origin in _____ to our customers' preferences.

Check your answers with those given on pages 335–336 before completing the following exercise.

Reinforcement Guide 5

Instructions: Select one of the words (or a form of the word) shown below to complete each of the following sentences.

Collision/Collusion	Console/Consul	Council/Counsel
Command/Commend	Convince/Persuade	Credible/Creditable
Complement/Compliment	Cooperation/Corporation	Deceased/Diseased
Complementary/Complimentary	Corespondent/Correspondence/	Decent/Descent/Dissent
Confidant/Confident	Correspondents	Defer/Differ
Conscience/Conscious	Corps/Corpse	Deference/Difference

1. One of the vendors will be serving _____ wine and cheese in the exhibit area from 5 to 7 p.m.

2. If Mr. Smith does not cease his _____ harassment of employees in the Sales Department, we will discontinue selling to him.

3. So far, only three of the _____ members have submitted their reports.

4. We will be subjecting all our new products to more stringent testing procedures in _____ to our customers' demands for higher-quality, longer-lasting electrical appliances.

5. At least two government officials were in _____ with the more than 50 individuals collecting welfare payments fraudulently.

6. Ms. Morris has been the president's assistant and _____ for nearly twenty years.

7. If no one else in the _____ is willing to assume this responsibility, I will gladly do so.

8. The Wilson Agency's many contributions to charitable organizations in the community are _____ to its present management and staff.

9. Be sure to _____ the cafeteria staff on the excellent luncheon it served for our seminar.

10. Are you _____ of the fact that nearly 10 percent of our employees are absent on a regular basis?

11. Please respond to any incoming _____ within three days of its receipt.

12. The recent _____ of interest rates has stimulated real estate sales in general and the home-buying market in particular.

13. For this particular china pattern, a _____ crystal selection would be either Rose Bud or Fontaine.

14. All the shelves in our _____ have mar-proof finishes.

15. Both the defendant and his attorney rushed past the _____ of reporters gathered outside the courtroom door.

16. We will _____ making a decision on this matter until next week.

17. Be sure that your floral selections _____ the tablecloths and the room decor.

18. The air purifiers in our office should run _____—24 hours a day, seven days a week.

19. Upon the advice of legal _____, we have decided not to pursue this case any further.

20. Although his reasons for late payment are always _____ and certainly understandable, we cannot waive the late-payment penalty.

21. We must _____ our sales manager to delay these price increases until after the 1st of the year.

22. Unless she remarries, lifetime benefits will continue for the widow of the _____ policyholder.

23. In _____ to the many requests from our employees with below-school-age children, the company will establish a child care center.

24. From the police report everyone could easily see that the defendant was responsible for the _____.

25. At first the child's accusation against the other children seemed _____, but upon investigation it was found to be only imaginary.

The answers to this exercise appear in the **Instructor's Manual and Key** *for* **HOW 8: A Handbook for Office Workers,** *Eighth Edition.*

Practice Exercises for Words From *Deprecate/Depreciate* Through *Executioner/Executor*

Practice Guide 6

Instructions: Select the correct word or a form of the word from each set of word confusions to complete the following sentences. Write your choice in the blank provided.

Deprecate/Depreciate

1. Please do not _____ any further management's attempt to introduce new technologies in our office.

2. Under the new tax laws, investors may still _____ rental properties.

3. The value of some cars _____ more rapidly than the value of others.

4. Employees who continually _____ their coworkers decrease employee morale and increase personnel problems.

5. Property owners are fearful that the proposed airport expansion will _____ property in this area.

Desert/Dessert

6. This project will bring water to many barren Arizona _____ areas.

7. Many of our retirement centers have been built in _____ areas surrounding major cities.

8. Our company specializes in creating, packaging, and marketing low-calorie _____ .

9. Pumpkin pie is our most popular _____ item during the Halloween-Thanksgiving holiday season.

10. Be sure not to bring the _____ tray to customers' tables until the entrée dishes have been cleared.

Device/Devise

11. Can you _____ a plan to prevent employees from copying for personal use company-purchased software packages?

12. Did you _____ an alternate plan for marketing these remote controls in case Video Industries refuses our offer?

13. A _____ within this switch reacts to sound and activates the light switch.

14. Because of snowstorms in the East, we must _____ an alternate route to Philadelphia.

15. By attaching this security _____ to expensive clothing, you can reduce your shoplifting losses.

Dew/Do/Due

16. Payments are _____ by the 15th of each month.

17. The early morning _____ prevents hotel guests from enjoying breakfast on the patio.

18. When _____ you expect the shipments to arrive?

19. The shipment from Hartfield Industries is _____ to arrive within the next three days.

20. You are _____ to have your annual company physical next month.

Die/Dye

21. Mark on the label the _____ lot number for each of these bolts of fabric.

22. If you do not water these young plants daily, they will _____.

23. Workers can easily _____ from the inhalation of these toxic fumes.

24. Do not allow the red _____ to bleed into any other colors in the fabric.

25. These washing machines may not be used to _____ clothing or any other articles.

Disapprove/Disprove

26. Did the zoning commission _____ our proposal?

27. The prosecuting attorney was unable to _____ the witness's testimony.

28. Although we can _____ his alibi, we cannot prove his presence at the scene of the crime.

29. If the insurance company _____ your claim, we will be forced to initiate legal proceedings.

30. The dean will automatically _____ any student petitions that request course waivers for state-mandated requirements.

Disburse/Disperse

31. The crowd began to _____ even before the football game ended.

32. Dividends for these bonds are _____ biannually on June 1 and December 1.

33. You may _____ these blank disks to those employees who use the computer stations.

34. When we entered the room, we found papers from the files _____ throughout the room.

35. We _____ all payroll checks through the Payroll Office.

Discreet/Discrete

36. You are to be commended for your _____ handling of these potentially embarrassing circumstances.

37. Mr. Jacob's administrative assistant is always _____ in discussing his availability and calendaring his appointments.

38. There must be a _____ reason why the committee did not approve our proposal.

39. Please be _____ in divulging any further information about our possible acquisition by AMCO Enterprises.

40. We have investigated several _____ possibilities for solving this problem.

Disinterested/Uninterested

41. Only _____ parties may serve as witnesses in cases involving traffic accidents.

42. If you are _____ in learning a software program, no amount of instruction will assist you with learning.

43. Most of the audience acted _____ in what the speaker had to say.

44. You will need two _____ persons to sign this affidavit in the presence of a notary.

45. If the client appears to be _____ in the property, do not attempt to convince him or her of its potential.

Done/Dun

46. In order to sell these _____-colored slacks, we will probably need to mark them down considerably.

47. You will need to _____ the people on this list to obtain at least a partial payment on their overdue accounts.

48. We have _____ everything we can to convince these customers to pay their accounts.

49. The white sandy beaches portrayed on the travel brochures turned out in reality to be dirty and _____ colored.

50. If you think we should no longer _____ these customers for payment, then I will turn their accounts over to an agency for collection.

E.g./I.e.

51. You may use our service to send shipments overnight within the United States, _____, the continental United States.

52. Observe E-mail "netiquette" in sending messages over the Internet; _____, compose messages off-line, confine the length of your message to a screenful of data, and be courteous.

53. To cite references in a research report, use a conventional style; _____, the Chicago manual style, the MLA style, or the APA style.

54. You may purchase from our catalog a variety of accessories to complement your business wardrobe; _____, shoes, purses, scarves, and jewelry.

55. None of these applicants appear to be qualified for the position we advertised; _____, all the applicants are lacking in the skills, abilities, and/or experience the position requires.

Elicit/Illicit

56. Were you able to _____ any further information from the witnesses?

57. The therapist has still not been able to _____ any verbal responses from the accident victim.

58. The FBI investigated the _____ activities of this company for over six months before making any arrests.

59. Reporters still have been unable to _____ a formal response from any company official.

60. You certainly cannot expect that such _____ maneuvers will be condoned by the Board of Directors.

Eligible/Illegible

61. How many of your students are _____ for graduation at the conclusion of the spring semester?

62. To be _____ for participation in the athletic program, students must maintain a "C" average.

63. Because of the severe water damage, this handwritten will is _____.

64. _____ signatures are easier to forge than those written clearly and distinctly.

65. You will become _____ for full benefits after six months' employment with the company.

Emigrate/Immigrate

66. Most of the new residents in our community have _____ from the Far East.

67. How many members of your family have _____ from South America?

68. Several members of our company plan to _____ to Australia to establish an import-export business there.

69. Although most of our employees were born in South Africa, their families originally _____ from England.

70. In what year did you _____ to Canada from Italy?

Eminent/Imminent

71. An _____ Miami physician has recently made major breakthroughs in rehabilitating patients with spinal cord injuries.

72. Were you able to engage an _____ speaker for the opening session of our convention?

73. If these trends continue, a substantial decline in stock market prices is

_____.

74. Foreclosure on these apartments is _____ unless the owner can raise sufficient capital elsewhere to make the loan payments.

75. The _____ success of this venture lies in the sales staff's ability to convince home owners that this device offers low-cost protection.

Envelop/Envelope

76. Please include a self-addressed _____ with your request.

77. An early morning fog often _____ this airport during the winter months and causes delays in scheduled arrivals and departures.

78. Mr. Ross is so _____ in this project that he has neglected his other duties.

79. A layer of pollution usually _____ the area and remains until wind or rain dissipates it.

80. All these _____ have been printed with an incorrect return address.

Every day/Everyday

81. _____ we receive at least one complaint about the new salesperson we hired last month.

82. _____ problems such as this one can be handled easily by one of my assistants.

83. _____ for the next week, we will receive at least three shipments from Richfield Industries.

84. For your _____ china pattern, you may wish to look at these less expensive selections.

85. Please be sure to sign out _____ after you finish your shift.

Every one/Everyone

86. _____ in our office will be attending the company holiday party.

87. _____ of the oak consoles was sold by the end of the first day of our sale.

88. Would you please ask _____ to check his or her book bag before entering the bookstore.

89. Almost _____ in the company has been notified of our plans to move the main plant to Springfield.

90. We have not yet been able to interview _____ of the qualified applicants.

Example/Sample

91. Offer our customers a _____-size vial of our new perfume when they purchase one of our other fragrances.

92. Before the customer confirms her purchase, she wishes to view a larger _____ of the fabric.

93. All members of our _____ population are from the Chicago area.

94. In our new training manual, be sure to provide ample _____ of screen displays.

95. As an _____ of an employment applicant tracking system, you may wish to describe the procedures used by AmCoast Financial Corporation.

Executioner/Executor

96. Whom has Mr. Benson named as _____ of his will?

97. The _____ was unable to locate several expensive paintings that were known to have been in the estate.

98. In many states the death penalty is carried out by a state _____.

99. The defendant is purported to be an _____ for an organized crime syndicate on the East Coast.

100. Please have the _____ prepare a list of the decedent's assets for the court.

Check your answers with those given on pages 336–337 before completing the following exercise.

Reinforcement Guide 6

Instructions: Select one of the words (or a form of the word) shown below to complete each of the following sentences.

Deprecate/Depreciate   Discreet/Discrete   Eminent/Imminent
Desert/Dessert   Disinterested/Uninterested   Envelop/Envelope
Device/Devise   Done/Dun   Every day/Everyday
Dew/Do/Due   E.g./I.e.   Every one/Everyone
Die/Dye   Elicit/Illicit   Example/Sample
Disapprove/Disprove   Eligible/Illegible   Executioner/Executor
Disburse/Disperse   Emigrate/Immigrate

1. Please give _____ at the meeting a copy of this report.

2. Several members of our staff have _____ from the Philippines.

3. If the hospital administrator _____ our budget request for an additional therapist, we will need to reduce our outpatient caseload.

4. Employees who continually _____ their supervisors are usually substandard workers who are unable to adjust to the work environment.

5. The court date for your official appointment as _____ of the estate has been set for August 21.

6. The _____ threat of further flood damage has caused the area to be evacuated.

7. Did you hire an agency to _____ these fliers throughout the neighborhood?

8. For the board meeting next week, we plan to serve coffee and _____.

9. Most of the _____ employees have enrolled in the stock-participation program.

10. All the employees stood in shock as they watched the flames _____ the warehouse.

11. The only distasteful part of this job is having to _____ slow-paying customers.

12. As soon as you _____ a new method for handling these payment coupons, please let me know.

13. This sales brochure is an excellent _____ of creative and aesthetically pleasing graphic design.

14. Our receptionist has been late to work _____ this week.

15. Were you able to _____ any further information about ITV's new operating system from any of our customers?

16. These payroll reports are _____ quarterly and must be submitted on time.

17. According to the decedent's will, his real estate holdings are to be sold and the proceeds _____ to the charities named.

18. When did you _____ to the United States?

19. _____ physicists from all over the world will gather for this convention.

20. Our editor in chief cannot allow the _____ problems of operating the division occupy the major part of her time.

21. All hair _____ on the market are now billed as "hair colorings."

22. During the negotiations both parties were _____ in releasing information to the press.

23. Most of the people who have viewed our video presentation of the Landmark Development have appeared _____ in investing in this project.

24. A truck will be in your neighborhood next week, and the Salvation Corps would appreciate receiving your donations; _____, used clothing, furniture, sports equipment, and appliances.

25. Our accountant informed us that we may _____ these computers over a three-year period.

*The answers to this exercise appear in the **Instructor's Manual and Key** for **HOW 8: A Handbook for Office Workers,** Eighth Edition.*

Practice Exercises for Words From *Expand/Expend* Through *Formally/Formerly*

Practice Guide 7

Instructions: Select the correct word or a form of the word from each set of word confusions to complete the following sentences. Write your choice in the blank provided.

Expand/Expend

1. Do not _____ any additional effort trying to convince Ms. Hall to remain with the company.

2. Within the next few months, we will _____ our operations to the Canadian provinces.

3. In revising this textbook, you may wish to _____ its information to include a chapter on international correspondence formats and standards.

4. As a result, we can _____ no additional funds for advertising during this quarter.

5. As soon as additional funds are available, we will _____ our offerings in computer applications courses.

Expansive/Expensive

6. _____ wastelands are dominant in this area of the country.

7. The cost of implementing your proposal is more _____ than we had anticipated.

8. Many _____ paintings were damaged by the fire.

9. Only _____ gourmet foods are stocked in this section of the store.

10. An _____ industrial center will be developed on this acreage.

Explicit/Implicit

11. The fact that you are qualified for the job is _____ in your being offered employment by three major corporations.

12. These instructions state _____, "Do not spray the saline solution directly into the eye."

13. _____ instructions for assembling these computers have been placed in each carton.

14. You are _____ consenting to these price increases by uttering no objections.

15. Your _____ directions were very easy to follow.

Extant/Extent

16. We have still been unable to determine the _____ of the damage caused by the warehouse fire.

17. All our _____ construction projects have been financed fully by various banks.

18. Some of the original buildings occupied by our company at the turn of the century are _____.

19. To what _____ do you foresee our involvement in this political campaign?

20. Most of the _____ earliest automobiles are owned by museums.

Facetious/Factious

21. Since the president lacks a sense of humor, please refrain from making any _____ remarks during his presentation.

22. Although seemingly _____, his statement bordered on sarcasm.

23. The new manager's _____ temperament can only result in continual dissension.

24. Our declining profit picture during the last year can be attributed directly to three board members' _____ personalities and their unwillingness to operate as a team.

25. Our manager is well-known for his _____ comments and dry sense of humor.

Factitious/Fictitious

26. Is this company still operating under a _____ business name?

27. The salesperson's _____ mannerisms and responses caused me to lose confidence in this potential real estate investment.

28. The hospital administrator's _____ concern for patient welfare has generated numerous complaints from the staff.

29. According to the author, all the characters in his new book, *The White House Controversy*, are _____.

30. The court has already established that the defendant has used at least three _____ names.

Fair/Fare

31. We can expect to see substantial _____ increases on all airlines for December.

32. The county _____ is held annually during the latter part of September.

33. Our firm has been engaged to ensure a _____ distribution of assets to all the creditors of record at the time of the bankruptcy.

34. We expect our employees to do more than just a _____ job.

WORDS OFTEN CONFUSED AND MISUSED

35. How well did you _____ in the forensics competition?

Farther/Further

36. If we can assist you any _____, please let us know.

37. Your office is _____ from the airport than mine.

38. Once I have had an opportunity to look into this matter _____, I will contact you again.

39. The _____ you live from campus, the better chance you will have of obtaining on-campus university housing.

40. Had you read _____, you would have seen the paragraph in the contract that grants the publisher full editing authority.

Feasible/Possible

41. Moving our offices from Woodland Hills to Westlake is certainly _____, but doing so at this time would involve a major expense for which we have not budgeted.

42. Is it _____ that you could have forgotten to mail the check?

43. Although on-line banking is _____, relatively few households are taking advantage of this service.

44. Connecting our local network to the campus network is _____, but the administration has been slow in implementing this proposal.

45. Increased budgets for this year have made _____ the purchase of three additional laser color printers.

Feat/Fete

46. The banquet to _____ our retiring football coach will be held on May 22.

47. The _____ accomplished by Rafer Johnson in the 1960 Olympics have yet to be exceeded—or even duplicated.

48. Such a _____ of daring and courage could have been accomplished by only a few.

49. How many people do you expect will attend this _____ to celebrate our company's one hundredth anniversary?

50. After the election the new mayor was _____ by his many supporters and friends.

Fever/Temperature

51. Be sure to record each patient's _____ in his or her chart directly after you read the thermometer.

52. The patient complained of having a _____ for the past three days.

53. Does the patient still have a _____?

54. If the child continues to have a _____, take him to the Emergency Department at West Hills Hospital.

55. This patient's _____ has been normal for the past 24 hours.

Fewer/Less

56. Because _____ than 15 people had registered for the class, the dean canceled it.

57. We received _____ responses to this advertisement than we had anticipated.

58. Please do not accept deposits that are _____ than half the total order.

59. Only orders containing ten or _____ items may be processed through our fast-service checkout line.

60. _____ than 30 percent of our investors have responded to the questionnaire.

Finally/Finely

61. We were _____ able to contact all the sweepstakes winners.

62. These walnut pieces are too coarse to be graded as "_____ chopped."

63. Our _____ trained athletes should perform well in the next Olympics.

64. When we _____ received the information from our central office, it arrived too late to assist us in making a decision.

65. We _____ raised enough capital to purchase the building site on Washington Boulevard.

Fiscal/Physical

66. Our company maintains a gym on the premises because the executive staff is interested in the _____ well-being of our employees.

67. The accompanying brochure outlines all the _____ benefits you can obtain from using the Schwer ExerBike.

68. Our school district's _____ period begins July 1 and ends June 30.

69. If you do not expend all the funds in your budget by the end of the _____ period, you will lose them.

70. Recent indiscreet investments by our company president have brought forth accusations of _____ irresponsibility from several board members.

Flagrant/Fragrant

71. The board of education could not even begin to defend the _____ actions of its newly appointed superintendent.

72. How could the governor have made such a _____ error?

73. Do not send highly _____ flowers to persons who suffer from allergies.

74. The newspapers were filled with stories of the _____ crimes committed by the hired assassins.

75. Our new line of _____ spices has achieved popularity as gift items for this holiday season.

Flair/Flare

76. Our new office manager has a _____ for color coordination and interior design.

77. Your _____ for calming irate customers will bring you much success in sales.

78. If Mr. Dodd allows his temper to _____ each time he encounters an adverse situation, he will certainly not be considered for promotion.

79. Be sure to get sufficient rest so that your laryngitis does not _____ up again.

80. _____ skirts are popular again this season.

Flaunt/Flout

81. People who _____ their wealth are usually not well liked by others.

82. American tourists should not _____ foreign customs when visiting other countries.

83. By _____ his attorney's advice, the defendant was sentenced to an even longer term.

84. Those construction workers who _____ the safety rules and procedures on this project will be dismissed immediately.

85. Bob distracts and embarrasses many members of the staff by continually _____ his vices.

Flew/Flu/Flue

86. Please call a service person to repair the chimney _____ in Suite 1420-22.

87. Most of our employees have had the _____ at least one time or another this winter.

88. Please instruct the hotel guests to open the _____ before using the fireplace.

89. The executive staff _____ first-class to New York, but all other company personnel were given coach class seating.

90. Do many of the elderly residents in this retirement home request _____ shots each season?

Foreword/Forward

91. Because Ryan Corporation appears to be a _____-looking company, its stock has risen steadily.

92. We are looking _____ to receiving your reply.

93. Have you read the _____ in Mark Lansing's new book?

94. The editor has requested David Baltimore, president of California Institute of Technology, to write the _____ for a book of readings on molecular biology and immunology.

95. In most cases the _____ of a book is written by a person other than the author or editor.

Formally/Formerly

96. The committee's selection will be announced _____ on July 14.

97. Ms. Greeley was _____ associated with Stanfield Industries.

98. Yes, we _____ were the primary distributors for this product line on the East Coast.

99. Our new product line will be _____ introduced at the International Computer Show in Chicago on March 25.

100. For this event all ladies and gentlemen must be _____ attired.

Check your answers with those given on pages 338–339 before completing the following exercise.

Reinforcement Guide 7

Instructions: Select one of the words (or a form of the word) shown below to complete each of the following sentences.

Expand/Expend
Expansive/Expensive
Explicit/Implicit
Extant/Extent
Facetious/Factious
Factitious/Fictitious
Fair/Fare

Farther/Further
Feasible/Possible
Feat/Fete
Fever/Temperature
Fewer/Less
Finally/Finely
Fiscal/Physical

Flagrant/Fragrant
Flair/Flare
Flaunt/Flout
Flew/Flu/Flue
Foreword/Forward
Formally/Formerly

1. Was your coughing and runny nose accompanied by a _____?

2. Any _____ memorabilia belonging to Elvis Presley has already been sold at public auction.

3. All funds raised by this telethon will be donated to _____ cancer research.

4. A large _____ is planned for the benefit of the proposed new hospital wing.

5. The hillside fires, which were thought to be under control yesterday evening, _____ out of control this morning.

6. Any child who continually _____ the school rules will be suspended.

7. An error in the advertising copy has caused a _____ demand for our 60-minute video cassettes.

8. By not objecting to the proposal, the national sales manager gave us her _____ consent to follow through with this new marketing plan.

9. Please telephone our travel agent and request information regarding _____ to Atlanta for the week of November 10.

10. Ms. Butler has a _____ for solving user problems with our word processing, spreadsheet, and database programs.

11. If _____ than ten people sign up for the seminar on August 10, we will need to reschedule it after the vacation period.

12. Our company was _____ a subsidiary of Walton Industries.

13. _____ deviations from company policy such as these will surely cost the manager his job.

14. To meet the deadline date on this project, our department worked together like a _____ tuned orchestra.

15. If you continue to foster _____ behavior among the office staff, we will be forced to hire a new office manager.

16. Because the _____ had inadvertently been closed, smoke from the fireplace filled the restaurant and set off the fire alarm.

17. Please supply us with _____ instructions for cleaning these tape decks.

18. Minors who present _____ identification are in violation of the law.

19. The speaker's presentation was filled with _____ remarks and humorous stories.

20. Although Don was elated that he had been chosen for the position, he should not have _____ his success in front of the others who had applied.

21. Do not _____ any additional time or effort attempting to locate these misplaced files.

22. To accommodate all the buildings in the architect's renderings, we will need a more _____ area than the site offered by your company.

23. Reaching the airport from the downtown area within 40 minutes is not _____ during traffic hours.

24. During the last _____ period, Hart Industries showed a profit increase of 7 percent.

25. Be sure to read the _____ before you begin reading *Business Etiquette Around the Globe*.

*The answers to this exercise appear in the **Instructor's Manual and Key** for **HOW 8: A Handbook for Office Workers,** Eighth Edition.*

Practice Exercises for Words From *Former/Latter* Through *Ideal/Idle/Idol*

Practice Guide 8

Instructions: Select the correct word or a form of the word from each set of word confusions to complete the following sentences. Write your choice in the blank provided.

Former/Latter

1. Please send a copy of this report to the _____ company president.

2. From among your present and _____ instructors, please list three references.

3. Our inventory must be completed during the _____ part of January.

4. Mr. Thompson's _____ proposal seems to be more practicable than this new one.

5. Both John Dixon, manager of our Toledo branch, and Brett Johnson, manager of our Louisville branch, applied for the position; but Brett, the _____, is more qualified.

Forth/Fourth

6. Amalgamated Enterprises represents the _____ contract we have received this month.

7. Please do not hesitate to set _____ any ideas you may have regarding this proposal.

8. Nearly one _____ of our sales staff has already reached its quota for the year.

9. You may need to reword for clarity the _____ question in this survey instrument.

10. Before we begin writing the grant proposal, we need to set _____ goals and objectives.

Fortunate/Fortuitous

11. Locating the long-lost heirs occurred only through a _____ incident.

12. Toys from this holiday toy drive will be distributed to less-_____ children.

13. Let us hope that we are _____ enough to outbid Lexigraph for this multimillion-dollar contract.

14. Their partner's embezzlement was discovered _____ by an accounting student who was working part-time for the company.

15. If I am _____ enough to obtain a position with your company, I would be willing to relocate.

Good/Well

16. The last group of candidates did very _____ on this promotional examination.

17. Since I did not feel _____ yesterday, I left the office early.

18. If employees do not feel _____ about themselves and their work, they will become disgruntled.

19. At the present time economic forecasts for our industry look _____.

20. Unfortunately, our basketball team did not do _____ enough in the preliminaries to qualify for the finals.

Grate/Great

21. I hope that the new mayor and his staff will meet the _____ expectations of our citizenry.

22. Please use a solid cover instead of a _____ for this open shaft.

23. You may wish to _____ all these smaller, unusable pieces into wood shavings.

24. Do his rude manners and loud voice _____ on your nerves too?

25. A number of _____ American leaders have stayed in this hotel during the last century.

Guarantee/Guaranty

26. Once your parents have signed the _____, we will begin processing the loan papers.

27. This one-year _____ includes parts and labor.

28. If you can _____ that the building will be ready for occupancy by October 15, we will sign the contract with your firm.

29. To lease this apartment for your mother, you must complete and sign this _____ for the rental payments.

30. For how long do you _____ your work?

Hail/Hale

31. Large pieces of _____ damaged windshields throughout the city during the storm.

32. Will I be able to _____ a taxi easily during the afternoon rush hour?

33. The falling _____ melted quickly once it hit the ground.

34. At eighty the chairman of the board is still _____ and hearty.

WORDS OFTEN CONFUSED AND MISUSED

35. All along the parade route, the crowd _____ the Rose Queen and her court.

He/Him/Himself

36. Although the choice is only between you and _____, the committee has still not made a decision.

37. We all suspected that the new president would be _____.

38. Since Bill agreed to write the report _____, the other committee members volunteered to assist him with editing and proofreading it.

39. The person selected for this top administrative post was not _____.

40. Please ask Marie, Chris, or _____ to assist you with compiling the sales figures for this month.

Healthful/Healthy

41. Daily running is considered by many to be a _____ activity.

42. Physical exercise contributes to a person's well-being and builds a _____ body.

43. Your condition can be improved only by following carefully a _____ diet.

44. Do not overwater your indoor plants if you wish to keep them green and _____.

45. Our manager always strives to keep a _____ spirit of cooperation among the members of her department.

Hear/Here

46. Return the form _____ when you have completed it.

47. Were you _____ when the manager requested us to join her for a brief meeting after the store closes?

48. None of us in the back row were able to _____ the general session speaker.

49. If you _____ of any job openings in this area, please let me know.

50. These tests are administered only _____ in the laboratory.

Her/Herself/She

51. Donna _____ was unsure whether or not she had set the alarm before leaving the office.

52. If Bob or _____ requests this confidential information, please give it to either one of them.

53. As soon as we receive the signed contracts, I will assign either my assistant or _____ to set up the account.

54. The most qualified person for this position is obviously _____.

55. If I were _____, I would request a leave of absence instead of resigning outright.

Hew/Hue

56. Most of the objects in our gallery are _____ from wood or stone.

57. This fabric contains most of the _____ of the rainbow.

58. Musicians and music fans of every _____ should be attracted to this exhibition.

59. We must _____ down this tree before its roots penetrate the retaining wall.

60. We have not yet been able to locate a silk with the particular pinkish _____ we need.

Hoard/Horde

61. _____ of locusts destroyed the crops in this region last season.

62. A _____ of fans gathered around the star as he attempted to leave the stadium.

63. Please request employees not to _____ quantities of blank floppy disks in their desks.

64. Rumors of shortages can cause consumers to _____ goods, which in turn can cause factitious demands for these products.

65. The officers seized the smugglers' _____ of contraband.

Hoarse/Horse

66. Because the caller had a _____ throat, my assistant had difficulty understanding his question.

67. Mr. Lyons' voice became _____ from lecturing over the continuous hum of the wall air-conditioners.

68. Your _____ throat will feel immediate relief once you try Baron's medicated throat lozenges.

69. All the properties in this canyon are zoned to permit _____.

70. Does Dr. Miller treat _____ as well as dogs and cats?

Hole/Whole

71. Our doughnut-_____ sales are almost one third of our doughnut sales.

72. Honey Baked Hams are sold only _____ or in halves.

73. We will not make any decisions until we have heard the _____ story.

74. If tenants drill _____ in the walls, they are responsible for the costs to patch and repaint the walls when they move.

75. The _____ conference will be devoted to research findings and methods.

Holy/Wholly

76. I am not _____ convinced that this proposal should be financed to its maximum.

77. A number of _____ relics were destroyed in the fire.

78. All members of the committee _____ support your idea.

79. The new stock issue was purchased _____ by small investors.

80. Although you may not _____ agree with them, I am sure you understand the reasons for our decision.

Human/Humane

81. This diagram illustrates the flow of blood through the _____ heart.

82. These new mannequins look almost _____.

83. _____ people are considerate of animals.

84. Our editor has requested us to submit more _____-interest stories for the Sunday edition.

85. The American prison system advocates the _____ treatment of inmates.

Hypercritical/Hypocritical

86. _____ and demanding supervisors generally experience a high degree of personnel turnover in their units.

87. Your inflexible and _____ view of office technologies will certainly cost you your job.

88. The press soon labeled this "would-be" council member _____ after citing several glaring inconsistencies in speeches to different community groups.

89. The Board of Directors was in my estimation _____ of the president's reorganization plan.

90. Too many politicians are _____; they tell the voters what they want to hear before the election but do as they please after the election.

I/Me/Myself

91. You may submit your reports to either Jan or _____.

92. It was _____ who conducted the in-service training program last month.

93. David, Lisa, and _____ are responsible for conducting this survey of consumer preferences.

94. Please ask the branch managers to fill out and return these questionnaires to Ms. Reynolds or _____.

95. The only person who has access to these files in our unit is _____.

Ideal/Idle/Idol

96. Our receptionist appears to have too much _____ time.

97. In just three years this pitcher has become a baseball _____ and made millions of dollars.

98. The site on the corner of Fourth Street and Jefferson Avenue is an _____ location for our proposed new branch office.

99. Our mainframe computer has already lain _____ for nearly seven hours.

100. Although none of these solutions is _____, we must select one.

Check your answers with those given on pages 339–340 before completing the following exercise.

Reinforcement Guide 8

Instructions: Select one of the words (or a form of the word) shown below to complete each of the following sentences.

Former/Latter
Forth/Fourth
Fortunate/Fortuitous
Good/Well
Grate/Great
Guarantee/Guaranty
Hail/Hale

He/Him/Himself
Healthful/Healthy
Hear/Here
Her/Herself/She
Hew/Hue
Hoard/Horde
Hoarse/Horse

Hole/Whole
Holy/Wholly
Human/Humane
Hypercritical/Hypocritical
I/Me/Myself
Ideal/Idle/Idol

1. Because she is consistently _____ of others' efforts, most members of the staff refuse to work closely with her.

2. Many people today still _____ large sums of cash instead of depositing them in savings accounts.

3. The winner of our monthly sales contest was _____, David Larson.

4. The prosecution's surprise witness seemed to come _____ from nowhere.

5. If you will return the completed application to either Ms. Davis or _____, we will process it without any further delays.

6. Once we receive the _____ shipment, we will send you full payment for Invoice 874659H.

7. Only through a _____ occurrence did we discover that one of our salespersons was selling competitive products while representing our line.

8. This student does not read _____ enough to work at grade level.

9. Your administrative assistant appears to have too much _____ time on his hands.

10. Based on the outcome of the vote, we can only assume that the board was not _____ convinced that our proposal is the solution to this problem.

11. Mary requested the respondents to return the questionnaire to _____ .

12. Mark down all our fireplace _____ 40 percent for this weekend sale.

13. As soon as we _____ from the lender, we will notify you.

14. Our society has dedicated itself to alleviating _____ suffering throughout the world.

15. Most of the stones used to build this home were _____ from giant rocks in the adjacent mountain area.

16. Once your parent company has signed the _____, we will issue a check for the amount of the loan.

17. Crowds _____ the athletes as they made their way to the center of the coliseum.

18. Politicians are often accused of being _____ when they do not fulfill their campaign promises.

19. Most of our students do _____ on college entrance examinations.

20. As I left the court, a _____ of reporters surrounded me.

21. The Northridge Chamber of Commerce will honor its _____ presidents at the next meeting.

22. After a two-week treatment at the Livingston Health Spa, you will leave feeling _____ and hearty.

23. Engage in _____ exercise daily to maintain your well-being.

24. Although my voice is still somewhat _____, I will do my best to deliver an interesting presentation at tomorrow's session.

25. All our products have a one-year _____ on parts and labor.

*The answers to this exercise appear in the **Instructor's Manual and Key** for **HOW 8: A Handbook for Office Workers,** Eighth Edition.*

Practice Exercises for Words From *Imply/Infer* Through *Liable/Libel/Likely*

Practice Guide 9

Instructions: Select the correct word or a form of the word from each set of word confusions to complete the following sentences. Write your choice in the blank provided.

Imply/Infer

1. To others, silence may _____ consent.

2. I did not mean to _____ that your statement was incorrect.

3. We _____ from the principal's statement that he knew who had broken the window.

4. The results of this survey _____ that our present computer installation is not paying for itself.

5. The newspaper article _____ that several computer software companies would be making significant announcements this month.

In behalf of/On behalf of

6. This plaque is being presented to the president of the Des Moines Chamber of Commerce _____ its members.

7. At the banquet Ms. Wells presented four scholarships _____ Midtown Industries.

8. Would you please speak to the dean of academic affairs _____ this student?

9. _____ Lismore Cosmetics, I am pleased to enclose a check to support your research program in skin abnormalities and disease.

10. The attorney requested to speak to the judge privately _____ his client.

Incidence/Incidents

11. Have you reported any of these _____ to the police?

12. We have yet to have any _____ requiring us to use this feature of your software program.

13. Because such an _____ in our company would be highly unlikely, your proposal does not suit our needs.

14. All the _____ you describe occurred without my knowledge or the knowledge of any other member of the administrative staff.

15. Too few _____ require our using teleconferencing for us to invest in our own facility.

Incite/Insight

16. Perhaps the new president will _____ more members to participate in our association's activities and projects.

17. A small group of agitators _____ the union members to strike.

18. The Board of Directors is looking for a chief executive officer with _____ and experience in human relations.

19. Without any _____ into the internal workings of the company, I cannot predict how successful it might become.

20. Do your political science courses _____ students to become more politically active?

Indigenous/Indigent/Indignant

21. Pineapples are not _____ to Hawaii; however, they are one of its major products.

22. Although his beginnings were _____, Mr. Simon has risen to become one of America's financial giants.

23. _____ accused of crimes in this state may secure the services of a public defender.

24. Your _____ attitude seems unjustified in this situation.

25. This kind of generosity and concern is _____ of her character and personality.

Ingenious/Ingenuous

26. _____ ideas such as this one come only once in a lifetime.

27. According to the news reports, the _____ boy was able to invade the computer files of many major corporations throughout the state.

28. Our _____ receptionist would never be suspicious of anything our clients tell her.

29. This makeshift car door opener formed from a wire coat hanger is an _____ device.

30. The defendant seemed to give an _____ account of his acts, concealing nothing.

Interstate/Intrastate

31. Since our food chain is _____, we are subject only to Colorado statutes.

32. Our _____ activities are primarily among Texas, Oklahoma, and New Mexico.

33. Commercial trucks traveling _____ must be licensed by all states in which their companies have offices.

34. The federal government regulates _____ commerce.

35. Our licensing program does not have reciprocity with any other state; therefore, you may practice _____ only.

Irregardless/Regardless

36. We must have these contracts prepared by tomorrow afternoon _____!

37. _____ of your company's current circumstances, would you reemploy this candidate if you had the opportunity to do so?

38. These outdoor sporting events will be held _____ of the weather forecasts projecting rain for the weekend.

39. Steve has permitted customers to purchase cars on credit _____ of their poor credit rating.

40. We will ship your order by Friday _____ of whether or not we have received payment.

Its/It's

41. If _____ too late for us to purchase tickets for the August 12 performance, please see if you can obtain tickets for August 19 or August 26.

42. We have been forced to close our Westchester branch temporarily because _____ new location is not yet ready for occupancy.

43. The building has been closed down by the fire department because _____ unsafe for occupancy.

44. The union has requested all _____ members to approve the new contract.

45. When will the chamber of commerce have _____ annual holiday party for needy children?

Later/Latter

46. All the electrical work in this housing tract must be completed by the _____ part of April.

47. Unfortunately, we are unable to schedule a _____ appointment for you.

48. Is this class offered at a _____ time also?

49. Her _____ design for the building facade is more creative and appealing.

50. Neither of his proposals was accepted by the committee, although the _____ one showed more promise.

Lay/Lie

51. Please request the patient to _____ down on the examination table.

52. Our computer system has _____ idle for nearly 24 hours.

53. The victim had _____ in his car for over two hours before the highway patrol discovered the wreckage in the gully beside the highway.

54. Why have these files been _____ on my desk for the last week?

55. The new shopping center _____ at the base of the Verdugo Foothills.

Lead/Led

56. Process Harman Manufacturing's order for 12 dozen No. 4384 _____ casings as soon as possible.

57. All crystal sold in the United States must be labeled clearly with the amount of _____ content.

58. Sandra has _____ in sales for the last three consecutive months.

59. The fire fighter _____ the three children to safety before the flames fully engulfed the house.

60. At yesterday's session Dr. Hansen _____ the discussion on downloading files from the Internet.

Lean/Lien

61. Our restaurant serves only _____ meats and fresh vegetables.

62. I believe the Board of Directors _____ toward divesting the company's interests in all oil stocks.

63. Several subcontractors have already placed _____ against the property.

64. Do not _____ the folding chairs against the newly painted walls.

65. After satisfying the _____ against the property, the owners will receive $10,085 upon the close of escrow.

Leased/Least

66. We have received at _____ 30 applications for this position.

67. The _____ we can do for our displaced employees is to offer them retraining for existing jobs or four weeks' severance pay.

68. Our company uses only _____ trucks and automobiles.

69. All our _____ properties are insured through Mutual Insurance Company of America.

70. We have _____ these offices for ten years.

Lend/Loan

71. We have sufficient collateral to obtain a _____ for $1 million.

72. If the bank will not _____ us these additional funds, we will be forced to curtail our expansion.

73. Would you be able to _____ me a few minutes of your time to go over yesterday's receipts?

74. The balloon payment on this _____ is due in six months.

75. None of the financial institutions we contacted would _____ us the funds for this housing development.

Lessee/Lesser/Lessor

76. Your monthly rental checks should be made payable to TRC Management Associates, the agent for the _____.

77. You, as the _____, are responsible for any damages to the property caused by you, your family members or friends, or any other person you willingly admit to the property.

78. Because the _____ wishes to convert these apartments to condominiums, he is not renewing any leases.

79. If you elect to receive the _____ amount, the annuity payments will continue for an additional five years.

80. Are we really qualified to decide which issue is of _____ importance?

Lessen/Lesson

81. Unless we _____ our efforts in this declining market, we will continue to suffer substantial losses.

82. The federal government has _____ its controls in this area and permitted state governments to assume jurisdiction.

83. Next week's _____ will cover importing spreadsheet and database files into a word processing file.

84. Perhaps we should _____ our commitment to those areas that produce long-term results and focus temporarily on achieving some necessary short-term goals.

85. We learned our _____ when we hired someone without first checking thoroughly her references.

Levee/Levy

86. There are _____ in many places along the lower Mississippi River.

87. This tax _____ will pay for local school improvements.

88. Every government must _____ taxes to pay its expenses.

89. During the summer season many tourists use this _____ to access our resorts by boat.

90. Unpaid tax _____ against these properties have resulted in foreclosure.

Liable/Libel/Likely

91. If you do not repair the cracks in the parking lot, you will be _____ for any damages resulting from this hazardous condition.

92. The U.S. Postal Service is not _____ for any parcel unless it is insured.

93. If your evidence is not conclusive, this statement about the mayor will be construed as _____.

94. Be sure to avoid making any _____ statements in your article.

95. If you do not purchase your airline ticket by the end of April, you are
_____ not to get a reservation.

Check your answers with those given on pages 341–342 before completing the following exercise.

Reinforcement Guide 9

Instructions: Select one of the words (or a form of the word) shown below to complete each of the following sentences.

Imply/Infer
In behalf of/On behalf of
Incidence/Incidents
Incite/Insight
Indigenous/Indigent
   Indignant
Ingenious/Ingenuous

Interstate/Intrastate
Irregardless/Regardless
Its/It's
Later/Latter
Lay/Lie
Lead/Led
Lean/Lien

Leased/Least
Lend/Loan
Lessee/Lesser/Lessor
Lessen/Lesson
Levee/Levy
Liable/Libel/Likely

1. Before occupying the premises, the _____ must sign the lease and give us a cashier's check to cover the first and last months' rent, a security deposit, and a nonrefundable cleaning fee.

2. If you need to _____ down, please use the cot in the employees' lounge.

3. Do not be deceived by his mild mannerisms and _____ smile.

4. Which financial institution has agreed to _____ us the money for this project?

5. I do not believe that our clients can be held _____ for these damages.

6. Although both her plans are sound, the accountant's _____ program for financing this project will probably be accepted by the board.

7. I did not intend to _____ that your products were inferior to those of your competitors.

8. This additional .01 percent _____ on real property will remain in effect for three years only.

9. We have already _____ all the office space in this building, even before it has been completed.

10. The council canceled _____ next meeting, which was scheduled for December 23.

11. These rallies are designed to _____ college students to take a more active role in politics and elections.

12. If we _____ our advertising efforts in this area, we are certain to lose sales to our major competitor.

13. To avoid having a _____ placed against your property, you must pay these subcontractors' charges.

14. If you plan to operate _____ only, you need not comply with these federal regulations.

15. In the future please file a written report for any _____ of this nature, regardless of whether or not a customer is injured.

16. Unless you can substantiate these allegations with concrete evidence, these statements can be construed as _____.

17. For this holiday season our bank is soliciting canned goods and toys for _____ families.

18. Our attorney believes that the company is _____ for the plaintiff's medical expenses and lost income for the past six years.

19. Our _____ research staff has made another breakthrough in miniaturizing the components for our portable video cameras.

20. If you travel _____ by truck or car, you may not transport fruit, vegetables, or plants across many state lines.

21. We have no other choice but to _____ from the number of complaint letters we have received that the service provided by your branch office needs to be improved.

22. Our attorney believes that the company is _____ for the plaintiff's medical expenses and lost income for the past six years.

23. At the closing session Ms. Harris will present the William S. Hartnell award _____ Western Publishing Company.

24. _____ of the stated guarantee, what has been your experience with A&A Computers' service center?

25. Drinking consistently from crystal with a high _____ content can prove hazardous to your health.

*The answers to this exercise appear in the **Instructor's Manual and Key** for **HOW 8: A Handbook for Office Workers,** Eighth Edition.*

WORDS OFTEN CONFUSED AND MISUSED

Practice Exercises for Words From *Lightening/Lightning* Through *Overdo/Overdue*

Practice Guide 10

Instructions: Select the correct word or a form of the word from each set of word confusions to complete the following sentences. Write your choice in the blank provided.

Lightening/Lightning

1. What _____ agent is used in these hair-coloring products?

2. By _____ our laptop computer, we were able to gain an additional 10 percent of the market share.

3. Remind the lifeguards to prohibit swimmers from entering the pools during the summer thunder and _____ storms.

4. Several plans for _____ airport congestion are presently under consideration by the city council.

5. Metal rods are often fixed on buildings to protect them from _____.

Local/Locale

6. _____ residents are protesting the construction of this youth detention camp in their community.

7. The _____ we had originally selected for our restaurant subsequently proved to be unsuitable.

8. Can you suggest a _____ for our West Coast distribution center?

9. Which television channel in our area provides the best _____ news coverage?

10. If you are interested in learning about our _____ government, you should attend a city council meeting.

Loose/Lose

11. When did you _____ your briefcase?

12. Please call our building maintenance service to have this _____ door handle repaired.

13. If we _____ this contract, our company will suffer a substantial loss in income.

14. If these _____ tiles are not repaired immediately, someone may fall and suffer a serious injury.

15. We cannot afford to _____ the confidence of our customers.

Magnate/Magnet

16. As you navigate your boat, be sure that no _____ is nearby to distort your compass readings.

17. A Texas oil _____ has purchased these lands.

18. Although his father was a railroad _____, he was unable to achieve any kind of success with the family fortune.

19. The carnival was like a _____, attracting children and their parents from miles around.

20. Many television stars have become famous because of their _____ personalities.

Main/Mane

21. Our _____ office is located in New York City.

22. One of our _____ concerns centers around the ability of this vendor to meet our delivery schedule.

23. The trainer grabbed the lion by its _____.

24. The _____ event is scheduled to begin at 9 p.m.

25. After the race the winning jockey stroked the horse's _____.

Manner/Manor

26. I am not sure whether or not we should proceed in this _____.

27. Many nineteenth-century European _____ have been converted into hotels or tourist sights.

28. The opening scene of this movie takes place in a French _____ in the outskirts of Paris around the turn of the century.

29. Perhaps we can find a more economical _____ for packaging our products.

30. His arrogant _____ has caused us to lose several valuable employees.

Marital/Marshal/Martial

31. May we request a prospective employee to indicate his or her _____ status on an employment application?

32. Each year the dean of the college acts as _____ of the graduation exercises.

33. High school bands in the Veterans Day parade commemorated the sacrifices of veterans throughout the country with _____ music.

34. A U.S. _____ is an officer of a federal court and has duties similar to those of a sheriff.

35. Do the current income tax laws permit a _____ deduction for a married couple filing jointly?

May be/Maybe

36. You _____ eligible for additional benefits upon retirement.

37. _____ you will be eligible for additional benefits upon retirement.

38. If you are unable to pick up this order by 5 p.m., _____ we can have it delivered to your store by a freight service.

39. As an investor in tax-free municipal bonds, you _____ interested in this new issue that has just become available.

40. This information _____ available through your local library.

Medal/Meddle

41. Do not _____ in the personal lives of your staff members.

42. How many gold _____ winners did the United States have in the last Olympics?

43. The _____ is silver and bears on the obverse an effigy of the Queen.

44. One country should not _____ in the internal affairs of another.

45. Please do not _____ with the books or papers on my desk.

Miner/Minor

46. Because the beneficiary is still a _____, the court must appoint a conservator.

47. We cannot deal with such _____ matters at this time.

48. He had been a coal _____ in Pennsylvania before he moved to Arizona.

49. In this state _____ may not enter into legal contracts.

50. Correct the important deficiencies in this report before you deal with the _____ errors.

Mode/Mood

51. Our supervisor always appears to be in a good _____.

52. The car is, comparatively speaking, a slow _____ of travel in the fast-paced business world.

53. What _____ will you use to pay for these purchases?

54. Natural hair styles became the _____ in the early 1980s.

55. When you are in the _____ to clean out the files, please let me know.

Moral/Morale

56. Under the direction of the new management, employee _____ has risen.

57. The team's _____ was low after its defeat.

58. Our company feels a _____ responsibility not to produce products that may be harmful to the health or well-being of society.

59. This speaker's topics all deal with _____ issues.

60. According to research, companies that sponsor profit-sharing plans have greater productivity and higher _____ than those that do not.

Morning/Mourning

61. All early _____ flights have been delayed because of the dense fog.

62. We serve complimentary coffee to our customers every _____ from 8 a.m. to 11 a.m.

63. The nation went into _____ upon the news of President Kennedy's assassination.

64. My most productive hours are those in the early _____.

65. Please do not disturb the family with business matters while they are in _____.

Naval/Navel

66. Two students from this year's graduating class have received appointments to the _____ academy.

67. This operation will leave you with a 3-inch scar directly below the _____.

68. We purchase all our _____ oranges from distributors in Florida.

69. The senator is a graduate of Harvard and a former _____ officer.

70. Our business depends entirely upon _____ contracts.

Ordinance/Ordnance

71. A local _____ prohibits excessive noise after 10 p.m.

72. Most large cities have _____ that control the use of smog-producing fuels.

73. The army has planned to move its _____ warehouse from Seal Beach to Oceanside.

74. Which officer is in charge of _____ procurement?

75. Fines for the violation of local traffic _____ range from $25 to $200.

Overdo/Overdue

76. This invoice is already 60 days _____.

77. If you _____ the comedy scenes, you will lose your audience.

78. Two of our cooks seem to _____ the meats and vegetables.

79. His plane is already three hours _____.

80. You cannot continue to ignore your _____ bills.

Check your answers with those given on pages 342–343 before completing the following exercise.

Reinforcement Guide 10

Instructions: Select one of the words (or a form of the word) shown below to complete each of the following sentences.

Lightening/Lightning
Local/Locale
Loose/Lose
Magnate/Magnet
Main/Mane
Manner/Manor

Marital/Marshal/Martial
May be/Maybe
Medal/Meddle
Miner/Minor
Mode/Mood
Moral/Morale

Morning/Mourning
Naval/Navel
Ordinance/Ordnance
Overdo/Overdue

1. News of our new employee profit-sharing program has certainly boosted employee _____.

2. Because of rebel attacks on the capital, the president of the country declared a state of _____ law.

3. This _____ was selected for our next convention because of its central location.

4. The family has closed the business for three days during this _____ period.

5. We _____ interested in computerizing our billing system, so please call me for a demonstration of your software.

6. If you _____ any items while on campus, please check with the Campus Police Department.

7. The fire on the _____ base destroyed nearly $2 million in supplies and equipment.

8. Enclosed is a list of the police officers in our precinct who have received a _____ for bravery beyond the call of duty.

9. Hilton was a hotel _____ of an earlier era.

10. Because the sale and use of fireworks without a license are prohibited by a city _____, individuals may not purchase them for private Independence Day celebrations.

11. Although a seemingly _____ consideration, our all-day complimentary cookie-and-coffee service attracts many customers.

12. The lion's _____ had become tangled in the bars of the cage.

13. Your _____ invoices must be paid before we can ship any additional merchandise.

14. Our primary _____ of shipment is via surface carriers.

15. This expansive _____ has been in the Winchester family for nearly two centuries.

16. _____ and thunder storms are forecast for this evening.

17. You cannot expect Johnson Industries to pay $23 million for a company and then not _____ in its internal operations.

18. Please have a _____ deliver the summons to the defendant.

19. These specialized high-quality _____ schools are designed to draw children from all parts of Los Angeles.

20. Hydro-Clor bleach may be used safely for _____ all dull, gray-looking white fabrics.

21. Although daily exercise is healthful, be careful not to _____ an exercise program.

22. When assisting customers with their purchases, you should always project a cheerful _____.

23. Our counseling staff specializes in assisting couples with _____ problems.

24. The applicant's _____ source of income is from a trust fund left to him by his parents.

25. All our new procedures manuals are being assembled in _____-leaf binders.

*The answers to this exercise appear in the **Instructor's Manual and Key** for **HOW 8: A Handbook for Office Workers,** Eighth Edition.*

WORDS OFTEN CONFUSED AND MISUSED

Practice Exercises for Words From *Pair/Pare/Pear* Through *Practicable/Practical*

Practice Guide 11

Instructions: Select the correct word or a form of the word from each set of word confusions to complete the following sentences. Write your choice in the blank provided.

Pair/Pare/Pear

1. Did the chef _____ the apples before putting them in the salad?

2. The landscape design includes several Oriental _____ trees.

3. During the sale one customer purchased 17 _____ of shoes.

4. We have been directed to _____ all expenses by 10 percent during the next quarter.

5. Pictures of the bridal _____ appeared in yesterday's newspaper.

Partition/Petition

6. How many registered voters signed the _____?

7. In our new offices a _____ separates each work station.

8. The remainder of the estate will be _____ among various relatives and friends.

9. We plan to renovate the second floor and _____ it into four medical suites.

10. Please have the client file a naturalization _____ as the first step toward obtaining United States citizenship.

Passed/Past

11. Based on this company's _____ performance, we cannot rely on it to complete a job according to schedule.

12. He has continually been _____ up for promotion.

13. In the _____ we have always closed our offices the Friday after Thanksgiving.

14. Has this information been _____ on to all our employees?

15. As a _____ award winner, you are invited to attend each annual banquet as a guest of the foundation.

Patience/Patients

16. Be sure to notify all our _____ of our new address and telephone number.

17. You will need to exhibit more _____ in dealing with clients and potential investors.

18. During this flu season the waiting room has been filled with _____ from early morning until late afternoon.

19. All new _____ must complete this information form before seeing the doctor.

20. An effective supervisor must show _____ and understanding in dealing with employees.

Peace/Piece

21. If you are interested in becoming a _____ officer, our counseling office can provide you with information about this career.

22. These offices have been leased by a new world _____ organization.

23. The _____ of land upon which ATV Industries bid contains 77 acres.

24. Most of the properties in this area are second homes owned by city dwellers who enjoy the _____ and quiet of the countryside.

25. This manufacturer's china sets all contain 144 _____.

Peak/Peek

26. What has been the _____ price of this stock?

27. This talented, ambitious young lawyer has yet to reach the _____ of her career.

28. The unemployment rate reached its _____ for the year in July.

29. Children often stop to _____ in the window of our candy store.

30. Place this answer sheet out of sight so that students cannot inadvertently _____ at it.

Peal/Peel

31. At the first _____ of thunder, be sure to stop the construction crew and begin transporting the workers and equipment back to the service facility.

32. The backers knew their play was a success as _____ of laughter resounded throughout the theater.

33. Ask the chef to _____ the tomatoes before cutting them into any salads.

34. The bells _____ forth their message of Christmas joy.

35. Please inform the landlord that the paint on the outside of our office building is _____.

Peer/Pier

36. If you must _____ closely to read newspapers and magazines, you should have an optometrist check your eyes.

37. At this university, advancement in academic rank is determined solely by a committee of one's _____ .

38. Our new restaurant will be located at the end of the _____, overlooking the harbor.

39. Many of the younger children _____ at Santa Claus awhile before mustering up enough courage to approach him.

40. No night fishing is permitted on the _____.

Persecute/Prosecute

41. You must prohibit the other employees from continuing to _____ Ms. Smith.

42. During August this region is _____ by small stinging insects.

43. Has the state decided whether or not it will _____ your client?

44. Because they do not take the time to read, students _____ our clerical staff with silly questions.

45. Drunken drivers will be _____ to the fullest extent of the law.

Personal/Personnel

46. Most of our _____ have been employed by the company for over five years.

47. These benefits are for full-time _____ only.

48. Employees' _____ phone calls during working hours should be limited to emergencies only.

49. If you wish to view your _____ file, please contact the director of employee relations.

50. The former tenant still needs to remove his _____ possessions from this furnished apartment.

Perspective/Prospective

51. To increase sales, we must broaden our market _____.

52. Please have a member of our sales staff visit each of these _____ clients personally.

53. All _____ employees must submit a letter of application and a résumé.

54. To be a successful leader, one must be able to view issues in their proper _____.

55. His lack of _____ has caused us substantial losses in the foreign market.

Peruse/Pursue

56. If the company does not _____ a different course, it will certainly end up in bankruptcy.

57. Much of the E-mail I receive may be left unread or just _____.

58. You may wish to _____ the final draft of this report before it is distributed to the staff.

59. She _____ a wise course by investing in this shopping center project.

60. Alan _____ the study of music for four years before his interests turned to computer applications and technology.

Plaintiff/Plaintive

61. Who is the _____ in this case?

62. The _____ were unable to provide sufficient evidence to substantiate their case.

63. The _____ testimony of the witness seemingly stirred the jury.

64. The _____ has accused the defendant of fraud.

65. This particular songwriter is best known for his _____ lyrics.

Pole/Poll

66. A car has evidently crashed into and damaged this light _____.

67. A _____ of the day students has indicated that they prefer morning classes instead of afternoon classes.

68. Underground utilities free areas from unsightly telephone and electric _____.

69. For local elections there is usually a light _____.

70. In 1968 the _____ declared the election too close to call.

Populace/Populous

71. So far we have polled the _____ of three Midwestern cities.

72. Less _____ areas such as Greenview and Bellhaven have been slow in obtaining cable television.

73. Is California the most _____ state in the United States?

74. In your opinion, which of these two candidates will have greater appeal to the general _____?

75. The _____ in these regions is increasing at the rate of 4.5 percent annually.

Pore/Pour

76. Our new cleansing formula removes excess oil buildup from your _____ while keeping your skin soft and moist.

77. We will just have to _____ over this problem until we solve it.

78. The company cannot continue to _____ money into subsidiaries that fail to show reasonable earnings.

79. As the three-day weekend began, holiday travelers by the thousands _____ out of the city.

80. We spent nearly three hours _____ over past invoices to locate the cause of the discrepancy.

Practicable/Practical

81. Although your plan is _____, we do not have sufficient budget this year to finance it.

82. His three years in law school were no longer _____ when he decided to become a chemist.

83. The _____ choice would be to limit all our product warranties to six months

84. With advancing technology and lower costs, the "robot in every broom closet" may soon become _____.

85. If the majority of consumers are indeed _____, they will not spend their time and money foolishly on this product line.

Check your answers with those given on pages 343–344 before completing the following exercise.

Reinforcement Guide 11

Instructions: Select one of the words (or a form of the word) shown below to complete each of the following sentences.

Pair/Pare/Pear   Peal/Peel   Plaintiff/Plaintive
Partition/Petition   Peer/Pier   Pole/Poll
Passed/Past   Persecute/Prosecute   Populace/Populous
Patience/Patients   Personal/Personnel   Pore/Pour
Peace/Piece   Perspective/Prospective Practicable/Practical
Peak/Peek   Peruse/Pursue

1. A _____ of our employees revealed that almost 30 percent would be willing to work overtime during the inventory period.

2. If he continues to _____ the smaller children in the class, Tom will be suspended from school.

3. To function successfully as a manager, you will need to develop more _____ in dealing with difficult situations.

4. On the surface this plan appears to be the best one, but in reality it is too costly to be _____.

5. This applicant's _____ voice and mannerisms are unsuitable for the receptionist position we have open.

6. Do not allow anyone to _____ over your shoulder as you tally the daily receipts.

7. We have been audited by the Internal Revenue Service for the _____ three years.

8. If you continue to _____ over these books in such poor lighting, you will certainly damage your eyesight.

9. You must evaluate all these sudden sales increases in their proper _____.

10. The hourly _____ of our grandfather clocks often turns away potential purchasers.

11. Residents on our street signed a _____ requesting the city council to approve funds for repaving our street.

12. Franchises are available only in the less _____ cities; the other franchises have already been sold.

13. Most of our _____ are highly trained chemists or engineers.

14. Until we receive this _____ of information, the entire project remains at a standstill.

15. Please _____ at least $3,000 from this budget.

16. Our firm represents the _____ in this case.

17. We cannot afford to _____ resources into a project that has so little promise of a substantial return.

18. During the remodeling of our offices, the _____ between the two conference rooms will be removed.

19. Two _____ clients wish to discuss their investment portfolios with you.

20. The _____ of this city has remained stable since 1980.

21. You should take an alternate route to the airport during _____ traffic hours.

22. This federal grant will permit him to _____ further his study of spinal cord regeneration.

23. Our company has just _____ through a difficult transition resulting from decreased government defense contracts.

24. Many of the _____ admitted to our hospital are insured by health maintenance organizations (HMOs).

25. Applications for employment are not permitted to solicit _____ information such as age, gender, marital status, religious preference, or ethnicity.

*The answers to this exercise appear in the **Instructor's Manual and Key** for **HOW 8: A Handbook for Office Workers,** Eighth Edition.*

Practice Exercises for Words From *Pray/Prey* Through *Scene/Seen*

Practice Guide 12

Instructions: Select the correct word or a form of the word from each set of word confusions to complete the following sentences. Write your choice in the blank provided.

Pray/Prey

1. Inexperienced investors often fall _____ to land investment schemes.

2. After each service the minister asks the congregation to _____ in silence for 30 seconds before leaving the church.

3. I _____ your forgiveness for losing these valuable papers.

4. Each year more and more people are _____ to this dreaded disease.

5. Small struggling companies are often _____ to large powerful conglomerates.

Precede/Proceed

6. The committee has decided to _____ in the usual manner with this case.

7. Please note that in each letter the reference initials should _____ the enclosure notation.

8. You may wish to _____ the demonstration with a brief overview of the capabilities of the laser printer.

9. Bill Harris _____ Jill Newcomb as president of the local chamber of commerce.

10. We will be unable to _____ with this project until early spring.

Precedence/Precedents

11. We have agreed to give _____ to all requests from the governor's office.

12. This project takes _____ over all other projects handled by our office.

13. There were no _____ for our firm's venturing into sales and production outside the United States.

14. Last year's fund-raising banquet set a _____ for sponsoring this event annually.

15. In the military a general takes _____ over a captain.

Presence/Presents

16. All these _____ must be wrapped for the holiday party.

17. This subpoena requires your _____ in court on October 23.

18. Everyone in the courtroom was amazed at the calm _____ of the witness as the district attorney continued to fire questions at him.

19. Did you purchase _____ for each of the administrative assistants in our office?

20. The _____ of the internal auditors disrupted our office routine for nearly a week.

Principal/Principle

21. Our _____ branch in your city is located on the corner of Fifth and Main Streets.

22. How much of the _____ still remains unpaid after this year's payments?

23. If you wish to discuss this problem with the high school _____, please call her office for an appointment.

24. Not only was it a matter of _____ to bring the issue out into the open but also it was good politics.

25. Many people make it a _____ to save a regular amount from each paycheck.

Propose/Purpose

26. How do you _____ we rectify this deficit?

27. The _____ of our survey is to assess the effectiveness of our newspaper advertising.

28. After sitting and listening for over an hour, I still could not determine the _____ for the meeting.

29. Residents in the area have already begun to oppose the _____ freeway extension.

30. May I _____ that we investigate further the suitability of this site for a new branch before we make an offer on the property.

Quiet/Quite

31. These clients wish to purchase a home in a _____ residential neighborhood.

32. We were _____ disappointed when the contract was awarded to another company.

33. I am _____ sure you recognize the importance of turning in these reports on time.

34. Many executives contend that they are able to get more work done in the _____ of their homes than they are in their busy offices.

35. These charges are so serious that you should be _____ sure they are valid before you proceed.

Raise/Raze/Rise

36. How much did interest rates _____ this week?

37. The city council had approved the petition to _____ this old building until a committee proved it was a historical site.

38. Last week the legislature voted to _____ the state sales tax 1/2 percent.

39. This stock _____ 16 points before it suffered any decline.

40. The old church was _____, and a new one was built in its place.

Real/Really

41. We are _____ pleased that you will be joining our firm as a financial analyst.

42. All the consultant's suggestions have been _____ helpful in setting up our training center.

43. Working with you on this proposal has been a _____ pleasure for me.

44. Does Carnation use imitation or _____ chocolate chips in its ice cream?

45. If you are _____ concerned about the integrity of this company, perhaps you should take your business to another vendor.

Reality/Realty

46. Have you dealt with this _____ company in the past?

47. The _____ of the situation was that the company's bankruptcy left over a thousand workers unemployed.

48. After your _____ agent contacted us, we notified the buyers that you had accepted their offer.

49. From the beginning I doubted the _____ of what he had reportedly seen.

50. The company owns over $190 million worth of _____ in the Chicago downtown area.

Receipt/Recipe

51. Please consider your canceled check to be your _____.

52. Many people claim to have the _____ for See's famous fudge.

53. Is there a book that publishes _____ from famous restaurants throughout the world?

54. Save this _____ for income tax purposes.

55. Be sure to obtain a _____ for all your purchases so that you may be adequately reimbursed for your expenses.

Residence/Residents

56. _____ from the community have signed a petition to halt the airport expansion.

57. If you are interested in selling your _____, please contact me for an appraisal.

58. Please list the address of your current _____ on this form; do not list a post office box address.

59. How many _____ live in this retirement community?

60. As the hurricane approached the coastal region, all _____ were requested to evacuate the area.

Respectably/Respectfully/Respectively

61. If your client does not address the court _____, he will be fined for contempt.

62. John, Lisa, and Karen are our senior employees; they have been with the company eight, seven, and five years, _____.

63. We insist that the nursing staff in our convalescent facility treat the patients _____.

64. Although she was a poor, struggling widow, Mrs. Smith raised her five children _____.

65. This month's first- and second-prize winners were Ann Freeman and Carl Irwin, _____.

Ring/Wring

66. Do not _____ this sweater while it is wet.

67. If the doorbell does not _____, just knock on the door.

68. Whenever I am on-line and this telephone _____, it is answered by the telephone message center in my computer.

69. If you _____ out this bathing suit after swimming, it will lose its shape.

70. This fraudulent banker could _____ money from almost anyone with his smooth line and promise of greater return.

Role/Roll

71. Congratulations upon your making the Dean's Honor _____ this semester.

72. Our senator played a major _____ in getting this piece of legislation through Congress.

73. Please have someone _____ down the sun screens each day by two o'clock to protect diners from the ocean glare.

74. Who played the _____ of Dolly in the senior class's production of *Hello, Dolly?*

75. Every instructor should have his or her _____ sheet for the opening class session.

Rote/Wrote

76. Who _____ this report for the Board of Directors?

77. Most children know the alphabet by _____ before entering school.

78. The author of this play _____ the script while serving in the army.

79. Administrative assistants should know by _____ the two-letter postal designations for all states and territories within the United States.

80. How much _____ script learning is required of television actors and personalities?

Rout/Route

81. What _____ should we take from the office to reach your home?

82. The police were summoned when the concert turned into a _____.

83. The flight _____ from Los Angeles to Indianapolis requires a stopover or a change of plane in Chicago.

84. The home football team _____ its opponent by a score of 40 to 7.

85. Most mail _____ in this section of the city permit mail carriers to use electric carts.

Scene/Seen

86. We have not yet _____ any results from this advertising campaign.

87. The opening _____ of the play is in 1929 on Wall Street.

88. If a customer begins to create a _____, politely invite him or her into your office.

89. How many times has the patient _____ Dr. Moyer?

90. I have not yet _____ the final draft of the contract.

Check your answers with those given on pages 344–345 before completing the following exercise.

Reinforcement Guide 12

Instructions: Select one of the words (or a form of the word) shown below to complete each of the following sentences.

Pray/Prey	Quiet/Quite	Respectably/Respectfully/Respectively
Precede/Proceed	Raise/Raze/Rise	Ring/Wring
Precedence/Precedents	Real/Really	Role/Roll
Presence/Presents	Reality/Realty	Rote/Wrote
Principal/Principle	Receipt/Recipe	Rout/Route
Propose/Purpose	Residence/Residents	Scene/Seen

1. The bridesmaids—Sue Smith, Beverly Brown, and Mary Moore—require dress sizes 6, 10, and 8, _____.

2. We were _____ disappointed to learn that our company president has accepted a position with another firm.

3. Many people still follow the _____ of never doing business with friends or relatives.

4. Do not allow yourself to fall _____ to any of his investment schemes.

5. What _____ will our company play in the development and construction of the proposed new shopping center?

6. The listing _____ company has served this area for nearly twenty years.

7. When should we _____ this project to the city council?

8. We cannot _____ with this project until we obtain final approval from the federal government.

9. Most of these third-grade children already know the multiplication tables *one* through *ten* by _____.

10. You must show your _____ to exchange or return this merchandise.

11. We have received _____ a number of complaints regarding the paint quality on our bicycles.

12. Mailing this contract by 5 p.m. today takes _____ over any of our other responsibilities.

13. Unfortunately, the character part for which you have been cast appears only in the opening _____.

14. All the _____ were requested to evacuate the hotel during the emergency.

15. The builder plans to _____ the present house and construct a multimillion-dollar home in its place.

16. The only way you can ensure the _____ of this witness is to issue him a subpoena.

17. Your monthly statement shows your payment breakdown in terms of
    _____ and interest.

18. Our company has no written policy or _____ regarding a married couple
    working in the same department.

19. The home team's defeat soon became a _____.

20. Whenever interest rates _____ considerably, the construction industry
    suffers.

21. Warn purchasers not to _____ out this garment after washing.

22. Before you begin to write a letter, be sure you have clearly in mind its
    _____.

23. The Chart House restaurant shares its famous blue cheese dressing
    _____ with those customers who request it.

24. Did you _____ John Corbin as president of the chamber of commerce?

25. In public schools teachers may not require children to _____.

*The answers to this exercise appear in the **Instructor's Manual and Key** for **HOW 8: A
Handbook for Office Workers,** Eighth Edition.*

Practice Exercises for Words From *Set/Sit* Through *Sure/Surely*

Practice Guide 13

Instructions: Select the correct word or a form of the word from each set of word confusions to complete the following sentences. Write your choice in the blank provided.

Set/Sit

1. Please _____ these boxes on the counter in my office.

2. Do not allow patients to _____ any longer than five minutes in the waiting room before recognizing their presence.

3. We _____ in the waiting room for nearly two hours before the doctor would see us.

4. Who has been _____ these dirty coffee cups on the sink instead of placing them in the dishwasher?

5. The customer has been _____ here for nearly an hour.

Sew/So/Sow

6. How often do you _____ these fields?

7. Our manager was _____ pleased with her work that he offered her a permanent position.

8. Most of the farms in this area are _____ with wheat.

9. Someone in our Alterations Department will be able to _____ the emblems on these shirts by Friday afternoon.

10. Who supplies the thread for our _____ classes?

Shall/Will

11. The corporation _____ not assume any liabilities over $1,000 not authorized specifically by the Board of Directors.

12. I _____ contact you as soon as the merchandise arrives.

13. If you are interested in viewing this property personally, we _____ be pleased to schedule an appointment.

14. Our agency _____ be responsible for screening prospective employees and furnishing information about their qualifications.

15. I _____ send you this information by the end of the week.

Shear/Sheer

16. This fabric is too _____ for the draperies in the outer office.

17. The purchase of this electric collator was a _____ waste of money.

18. The fabric has been _____ too close to the seams on all these garments.

19. From the top of the wall, there was a _____ drop of 100 feet to the sidewalk below.

20. Extreme force on the scissor handles can _____ the rivet holding the blades together.

Shone/Shown

21. The sun has not _____ for the past week in this resort area.

22. Have you _____ these plans to our new architect?

23. All these new fashions are scheduled to be _____ next month.

24. The outside lights have _____ continuously for the past week.

25. Your headlights _____ only briefly before flickering out.

Should/Would

26. If the owner is still interested in selling the property, we _____ like to make an offer.

27. I _____ have this information available within the next week.

28. When _____ I file these papers with the court?

29. If you _____ like additional information, please call my office.

30. If we _____ be able to obtain additional shipments of these silks, we will contact you immediately.

Soar/Sore

31. Prices of raw materials in our industry have continued to _____.

32. Our new medication relieves pain from _____ and aching muscles.

33. Our hopes _____ when we heard that the contract had not yet been awarded.

34. A _____ skyscraper will replace the building on the corner of Broadway and Seventh Street.

35. You should consult a doctor about your _____ leg.

Sole/Soul

36. Our trademark is embossed on the _____ of every shoe we manufacture.

37. The _____ deterrent to our accepting this offer is the short time allowed for fulfilling the contract.

38. This artist puts her whole _____ into her work.

39. Please do not breathe a word about this merger to a _____.

40. At present my _____ responsibility is to prepare a grant proposal for our college.

Some/Somewhat

41. Although we were _____ disappointed with your last construction job, we have decided to accept your bid for the current project.

42. We will need to make _____ modifications in these plans.

43. If you wish _____ legal advice, please contact our attorney.

44. These wood carvings are _____ more expensive than we had expected.

45. A mystery novel loses _____ of its suspense when read a second time.

Some time/Sometime/Sometimes

46. Please call our office _____ next week for an appointment.

47. Our new building should be completed _____ next month.

48. We sent you this information _____ ago.

49. _____ we receive requests for information about our competitor's products.

50. We have been working on this project for _____.

Staid/Stayed

51. During the holiday season most of the stores _____ open until 10 p.m.

52. Successful salespeople do not usually have _____ personalities.

53. Have you ever _____ at the Regency Hotel?

54. In the opening scene of the play, Grant portrays a _____, boring university professor.

55. If you had _____ a while longer, you would have met the new company president.

Stationary/Stationery

56. Our new _____ will be printed on beige-colored paper.

57. The _____ supplies are stored in the closet next to Ms. Dillon's desk.

58. Both the wall units are _____ fixtures in these offices.

59. Please order an additional supply of letterhead _____.

60. Interest rates have remained relatively _____ during the last month.

Statue/Stature/Statute

61. Our store specializes in clothing for men with above-average _____.

62. The architect designed a _____ to be placed in the middle of the fountain.

63. _____ in this state prohibit gambling.

64. Nearly every city has a _____ of a famous personality.

65. Bob Hope is regarded as a man of _____ by millions of Americans.

Straight/Strait

66. If you have a complaint, please take it _____ to the manager.

67. The ship caught fire at the entrance to the _____.

68. To qualify for this job, you must be able to sew a _____ seam.

69. The _____ of Gibraltar connects the Mediterranean Sea and the Atlantic Ocean.

70. The sheet feeder on our new printer does not feed in the paper _____.

Suit/Suite

71. Please reserve a _____ of rooms at the Hotel Grande for the medical convention.

72. Your _____ will be returned from our Alterations Department by Thursday afternoon.

73. Will you be able to deliver this customer's bedroom _____ by November 15?

74. This living room _____ will be placed on sale next week.

75. A _____ against your company was filed by our attorneys yesterday.

Sure/Surely

76. We are _____ pleased with the outcome of the negotiations.

77. If you need additional information, please be _____ to call me.

78. We can _____ use some additional help.

79. Our manager _____ does not understand the situation, or he would have given us additional assistance.

80. Are you _____ the door was locked when you left the office?

Check your answers with those given on pages 346–347 before completing the following exercise.

Reinforcement Guide 13

Instructions: Select one of the words (or a form of the word) shown below to complete each of the following sentences.

Set/Sit	Soar/Sore	Statue/Stature/Statute
Sew/So/Sow	Sole/Soul	Straight/Strait
Shall/Will	Some/Somewhat	Suit/Suite
Shear/Sheer	Some time/Sometime/Sometimes	Sure/Surely
Shone/Shown	Staid/Stayed	
Should/Would	Stationary/Stationery	

1. The state legislature has enacted a _____ regulating the sale of firearms within the state.

2. I believe the owner's assessment of the value of this property is _____ exaggerated.

3. The lighthouse beacon _____ through the heavy New England fog.

4. Please _____ these figurines in the display case.

5. The Panama Canal is a _____ that connects the Atlantic and Pacific Oceans.

6. Our company plans _____ in the future to erect a branch office on this site.

7. I _____ appreciate your filling out and returning the enclosed forms as soon as possible.

8. Our factory _____ garments for well-known clothing designers on a contract basis.

9. Our offices will be relocated to a _____ on the third floor.

10. This applicant's personality is too _____ for him to be successful in the position of national sales manager.

11. Real estate prices continue to _____ as we enter a new year.

12. As soon as we receive your completed loan application, we _____ begin processing your loan.

13. You are _____ correct in assuming that this book will be available for classes next fall.

14. Please send your requests for all _____ and supplies to me.

15. There was hardly a _____ in the store at what is normally a prime shopping time.

16. In _____ desperation, the company executives decided to recall our Model 50 automatic garage door opener.

17. These _____ cabinets need to be refinished in light oak to match the remainder of the office decor.

18. We were fortunate to obtain a person of Judge Hill's _____ to deliver the graduation address.

19. My _____ concern regarding this loan centers around the applicant's ability to meet the monthly payments based upon the income shown in the application.

20. In which court will you file _____?

21. This new computer chip will be ready for shipment to computer manufacturers _____ next month.

22. Since the security guard has lost the key, we will need to _____ the lock off this gate.

23. AloRub will soothe your _____ and aching muscles with only a single application.

24. Which artist did the city council commission for the _____ to be placed at the entrance of the municipal court building?

25. Our tailor will complete the alterations on your _____ by the end of next week, Friday, April 3.

*The answers to this exercise appear in the **Instructor's Manual and Key** for **HOW 8: A Handbook for Office Workers,** Eighth Edition.*

Practice Exercises for Words From *Tare/Tear/Tier* Through *Your/You're*

Practice Guide 14

Instructions: Select the correct word or a form of the word from each set of word confusions to complete the following sentences. Write your choice in the blank provided.

Tare/Tear/Tier

1. The _____ of this shipment is 1,380 pounds.

2. Only one _____ of the wedding cake was eaten.

3. You may repair this _____ in the envelope with transparent tape.

4. Please record the _____ on each bill of lading.

5. We have seats available only on the third _____ of the stadium.

Than/Then

6. You have higher seniority _____ anyone else in the department.

7. This conference is being held sooner _____ I expected.

8. You will _____ be reimbursed for your expenses.

9. As soon as escrow closes, you may _____ begin moving your possessions onto the property.

10. Certificates of deposit earn interest at a higher rate _____ money market accounts.

That/Which

11. The textbook _____ you requested is no longer in print.

12. Milton Industries, _____ is located in Albany, is our sole source for these metal bolts.

13. Your July payment, _____ we received yesterday, was $20 less than the amount stipulated in the contract.

14. One of the dining room sets _____ you shipped us arrived in damaged condition.

15. Any garments _____ are left over 30 days are subject to being sold to recover cleaning costs.

Their/There/They're

16. If _____ unable to make further payments, we must repossess the car.

17. Will you be able to meet me _____ at 2 p.m.?

18. We will provide you with samples as soon as _____ available.

19. None of _____ invoices since October have been paid.

20. Do you have _____ current address and telephone number?

Theirs/There's

21. _____ still ample opportunity for young men and women to be successful in our industry.

22. If _____ no advantage to upgrading our software immediately, let us wait until we find it necessary to do so.

23. All these clip art images on compact disks are _____.

24. As long as _____ a 10 percent profit margin on these disks, we will continue to manufacture them.

25. Since these reference books are _____, please treat them carefully.

Them/They

26. Was it _____ who requested this information?

27. Either we or _____ will represent the company at this conference.

28. The last two people to leave the room were _____.

29. If I were either one of _____, I would consult an attorney before taking any further action.

30. As soon as _____ arrive, I will begin the meeting.

Threw/Through

31. My assistant _____ out all these outdated files last week.

32. Only _____ your efforts and hard work were we able to obtain this contract.

33. This sale runs _____ Friday, November 21.

34. Who _____ all these papers on the floor?

35. To drive _____ the city took us nearly two hours.

To/Too/Two

36. This office is entirely _____ cold during the morning hours.

37. Please enclose the top part of your statement in the envelope _____.

38. Your clients did not seem _____ interested in purchasing the property.

39. If you wish _____ bid on the contract, please submit your formal offer by June 30.

40. _____ many of our clients have complained about the poor service in this branch office.

Tortuous/Torturous

41. Grading these lengthy, complicated accounting examinations is always a
_____ experience for most of our staff.

42. This _____ mountain road is too treacherous for us to drive during the
snow season.

43. Movie watching should be an enjoyable, not a _____, experience.

44. The patient's _____ reasoning prompted the doctor to order a series of
psychological examinations.

45. Executives responsible for downsizing their companies have found this process to be a
_____ task.

Toward/Towards

46. Every day we move closer _____ our goal as the donations continue to
arrive from all parts of the country.

47. About 50 percent of the rooms in our hotel have large patios or windows facing
_____ the ocean.

48. The main entrance to our new office building faces _____ Grand Avenue.

49. To reach our office, continue driving north _____ the mountains.

50. We are working _____ achieving an Internet connection for all
workstations in our company.

Us/We

51. The property was divided equally among the Johnsons, the Coxes, and
_____.

52. If you were _____, would you purchase this property?

53. The managers and _____ assistants should rotate this responsibility
among ourselves.

54. The manager took the visiting dignitaries and _____ on a tour of the
plant.

55. The persons in charge of the project are _____, Don and I.

Vain/Van/Vane/Vein

56. Because she appears to be so _____, other employees have difficulty
working with her.

57. The weather _____ on the old cottage had blown off during the storm.

58. Our new line of Ford _____ will be on display next week.

59. I tried in _____ for a week to reach him by telephone.

60. The customer complained about a large _____ of gristle in his meat.

Vary/Very

61. We were _____ pleased with the results of the survey.

62. If the writer would learn to _____ his sentence structure, his writing style would be more interesting.

63. Each month the sales in this district _____ considerably.

64. None of us are _____ interested in taking this tour.

65. Our office routine does not _____ much from day to day.

Vice/Vise

66. The handle on this _____ is stuck.

67. Unfortunately, lying is one of this inmate's many _____.

68. Gossiping about the _____ of your fellow workers can only lead to dissension.

69. Every time I see Detective Burns, he has a cigar _____ between his teeth.

70. Child abuse is a _____ that must be eradicated among parents in our civilized society.

Waive/Wave

71. Be sure to _____ at the crowds along the parade route.

72. If you sign this form, you will _____ your rights to sue for malpractice.

73. Too many people think they can buy anything just by _____ money in front of other people.

74. The lawyer _____ the privilege of cross-examining the witness.

75. The announcement caused a _____ of enthusiasm.

Waiver/Waver

76. Please ask the department chair to sign this course _____.

77. If you _____ from this position, you are sure to receive criticism from your supporters.

78. Our choice _____ between Springfield and Peoria for the location of our next branch office.

79. If your client will sign this _____, we will settle this case for $15,000.

80. As the child hit the showcase, the expensive figurine _____ and then toppled and broke on the shelf.

Weather/Whether

81. Please place the daily _____ reports on my desk as soon as you receive them.

WORDS OFTEN CONFUSED AND MISUSED

82. We have not yet decided _____ or not we will invest in this shopping mall.

83. Have you decided _____ to reinvest these funds or withdraw them?

84. We cannot resume work on the outside of the hotel until the _____ becomes warmer.

85. I do not believe our company will be able to _____ another financial crisis such as the last one.

Who/Whom

86. Our manager is a person _____ deals fairly with each employee.

87. I do not know to _____ this letter should be addressed.

88. _____ should I contact for an interview?

89. _____ is in charge of customer relations?

90. The only applicant _____ we have not yet interviewed is Sharon Blake.

Who's/Whose

91. Do you know _____ scheduled to work in my place tomorrow?

92. When you learn _____ briefcase was left here, please let me know.

93. Please let me know _____ rent has not yet been paid this month.

94. If you know of anyone _____ interested in renting this apartment, please let me know.

95. The person _____ last on the promotion list has little chance of being placed.

Your/You're

96. If _____ interested in applying for this position, please let us know.

97. As soon as we receive _____ verification of employment, we will approve the loan.

98. Please print _____ name legibly under the signature line.

99. Because _____ one of our best customers, we are inviting you to attend a special showing of Avant Fashions on Friday, April 3.

100. _____ certainly welcome to visit our showroom anytime to see personally the beauty and luxury of the new Sarona.

Check your answers with those given on pages 347–348 before completing the following exercise.

Name _____ Date _____

Reinforcement Guide 14

Instructions: Select one of the words (or a form of the word) shown below to complete each of the following sentences.

Tare/Tear/Tier
Than/Then
That/Which
Their/There/They're
Them/They
Threw/Through
To/Too/Two

Tortuous/Torturous
Toward/Towards
Us/We
Vain/Van/Vane/Vein
Vary/Very
Vice/Vise
Waive/Wave

Waiver/Waver
Weather/Whether
Who/Whom
Who's/Whose
Your/You're

1. We do not yet know _____ we will be able to obtain the necessary financing to construct an additional wing to the hospital.

2. Most of our beauty consultants are quite _____, but clients still seek their advice and services.

3. If we were _____, we would not have entered into a contract with this particular construction firm.

4. Does the bill of lading show the _____ of the shipment?

5. Do you know _____ we can employ to reorganize our filing system?

6. Although the fire fighters' time schedules _____ from month to month, they are made available to each employee three months before taking effect.

7. We will be in these temporary offices from December 1 _____ the end of March.

8. The flight delay in Chicago held us up longer _____ we had originally expected.

9. Do you know _____ responsible for approving these budget requests?

10. If you wish, you may _____ your rights to a trial by jury.

11. Because the bank is usually _____ crowded at the noon hour, I delay making our deposits until early afternoon.

12. Our closest branch office, _____ is located at 15150 Camelback Road, would be pleased to open an account for you.

13. When _____ ready to refurnish your home, please visit our showroom.

14. The witness did not _____ once in his testimony as he was cross-examined by the defendant's attorney.

15. The manager never consults _____ employees for information or advice on customer preferences.

16. Unless you hear from me to the contrary, we will meet with the other college presidents and _____ administrative staffs on September 1.

17. The orders for those customers _____ merchandise has not yet been shipped are arranged by date in the Orders Pending file.

18. Please have the claimant sign this _____ before you disburse the settlement check.

19. The crews drilled through several _____ of hard rock before they were able to sink a well.

20. The patient is complaining that the large _____ in her legs are causing pain.

21. _____ been too little time for us to work on this project.

22. Some of the tourists have complained that the course of the river is too _____, and they have had difficulty maneuvering our houseboats.

23. What is the president's attitude _____ increased medical benefits for our employees?

24. When visiting the Florida Everglades, beware of alligators and their _____-like jaws.

25. Dawn Perry is the candidate _____ I believe will be appointed to head the Traffic Enforcement Department.

*The answers to this exercise appear in the **Instructor's Manual and Key** for **HOW 8: A Handbook for Office Workers,** Eighth Edition.*

WORDS OFTEN CONFUSED AND MISUSED

Additional Practice Exercises for *Affect/Effect*

Practice Guide 15, Part A

Instructions: Use a form of *affect* or *effect* to complete the following sentences.

1. What _____ do you believe this unstable stock market will have on the economy?

2. This price increase is too small to _____ our sales substantially.

3. Continued rainy weather will surely _____ adversely the completion of our new housing tract.

4. The new management has been slow in _____ any major policy changes.

5. Yesterday's announcement about our company's new PZAZZ computer had a startling _____ on the price of our stock.

6. The president's decision to reduce staff at our Burbank plant will _____ approximately 200 workers.

7. Pressure groups have been lobbying to _____ legislation that will prohibit smoking in public buildings.

8. We are yet unable to determine the _____ these new tax laws will have on our firm.

9. How can you possibly _____ additional savings when the price of raw materials continues to rise?

10. Has the laboratory been able to determine if this new medication has any side _____?

11. Unfortunately, Mr. Dunn's personal problems are beginning to _____ his job performance.

12. Overexposure to sunlight can _____ the quality of your photographs.

13. You can achieve this _____ only by following these step-by-step instructions.

14. This month *The Journal of Psychology* will feature several articles on _____ behavioral changes in emotionally disturbed children.

15. We have yet to determine the full _____ this merger will have on our employees.

Check your answers with those given on page 348 before completing the following exercise.

Practice Guide 15, Part B

Instructions: Use a form of *affect* or *effect* to complete the following sentences.

1. Do the research findings reveal that this medication will have an adverse _____ on adults over thirty?

2. Excessive rains this winter will surely _____ the completion date of our new office building.

3. What _____ will the president's speech have on stock prices?

4. The rise in the number of insurance claims in this area will _____ an increase in premium rates.

5. How were your insurance rates _____ by the recent accident?

6. Home videotape recorders have had a stimulating _____ in the revival of old movies.

7. Our new supervisor has already _____ several startling changes in the department.

8. Over 30 percent of our employees will be _____ by the impending strike.

9. How can we possibly _____ reductions in our manufacturing costs when material and labor costs continue to rise?

10. The major _____ of this new economic proposal will not be felt until the early 2000s.

11. Please determine what _____ the addition of three new microcomputers will have on our office operations.

12. None of our clients have been _____ by the recent strike in the automobile industry.

13. Long-term _____ such as these are not easily predicted.

14. Consumer furniture purchases continue to be _____ by new home construction and full employment.

15. Vigorous protests by citizens' groups may _____ legislation to prohibit the sale of identification cards by mail.

16. Have you been able to determine what _____, if any, this advertising campaign has had on sales?

17. The number of air-conditioning ducts installed with each system _____ the efficiency of the motor and the costs of operation.

18. Further investments in this company could have a substantial _____ in minimizing our losses for the current tax year.

19. Recent federal legislation will _____ several important changes in our accounting procedures.

20. Significant temperature changes in the work environment _____ the efficiency of office personnel.

*The answers to this exercise appear in the **Instructor's Manual and Key** for **HOW 8: A Handbook for Office Workers**, Eighth Edition.*

WORDS OFTEN CONFUSED AND MISUSED

Reinforcement Guide 15

Instructions: Use a form of *affect* or *effect* to complete the following paragraphs.

We have not yet been able to determine what _____ our new pricing policy will have on sales. With the present sales volume, we can only predict that unless our manager, Mr. Jones, can _____ significant cost reductions, this pricing policy will result in declining profits. If, on the other hand, the _____ of our present sales campaign escalates our sales volume, then we can expect the new pricing policy to be successful. In summary, sales volume and costs will _____ directly the new pricing structure initiated by Mr. Jones.

During the next quarter we will be able to analyze the overall _____ of the new policy and how it has _____ our profit picture. Before Mr. Jones is permitted to _____ any additional changes, though, the Board of Directors must review carefully how any new recommendations will _____ our entire operation in light of the potential problems that may exist with our new pricing policy. Too many unprecedented policy decisions could _____ adversely the price of our stock, and we might encounter difficulty in _____ changes to restore the price to its normal high level.

*The answers to this exercise appear in the **Instructor's Manual and Key** for **HOW 8: A Handbook for Office Workers,** Eighth Edition.*

Cumulative Practice Guide 1

Part A

Instructions: Select the correct alternative from the words shown in parentheses. Write your answer in the blank provided to the right of each sentence.

1. Did you know that Mr. Sooyun is (a/an) authority on rare coins? _____

2. We are not permitted to (accept/except) second-party checks. _____

3. Will you be able to (adapt/adept/adopt) this recorder to operate on 110-volt electricity? _____

4. I recommend that you follow the (advice/advise) of our tax consultant. _____

5. The strike should not (affect/effect) our sales volume immediately. _____

6. All the homes in this development have (all ready/already) been sold. _____

7. The research team was (all together/altogether) disappointed in the results of the survey. _____

8. No matter how hard he tried, Mr. Abrams was unable to (allude/elude) the persistent sales representative. _____

9. (Almost/Most) everyone in our office has contributed to the social fund. _____

10. Please divide the remaining supplies (among/between) the three offices on the second floor. _____

11. You may offer this film on a free one-week loan basis to (any one/anyone) who requests it. _____

12. May we have your check for $100, (as/like) you promised. _____

13. Can the seller (assure/ensure/insure) that the present tenants will vacate the building by May 1? _____

14. He has been treated very (bad/badly) by some of his colleagues. _____

15. Dividends are paid (biannually/biennially) on this stock—once in March and again in September. _____

16. Ex-Senator Rifkin must vacate his office in the (capital/capitol) by the first of next week. _____

17. Who will be in charge of selecting the (cite/sight/site) for our new warehouse? _____

18. The new painting in the reception area (complements/compliments) the carpeting, draperies, and furnishings. _____

19. His (continual/continuous) complaining makes him a difficult person with whom to deal. _____

20. Only one person was absent from the (council/counsel) meeting. _____

21. All the board members were concerned about the apparent (decent/descent/dissent) among the executive officers. _____

22. The speaker continued to (deprecate/depreciate) the young candidate in the eyes of the public. _____

23. Did Ms. McKearin (device/devise) this new method for crating eggs? _____

24. Your contract is (dew/do/due) for review on the 15th. _____

25. Our South Bend factory has been known to (disburse/disperse) pollutants in the surrounding area. _____

Check your answers with those given on page 348 before completing the following exercise.

Part B

Instructions: Select the correct alternative from the words shown in parentheses. Write your answer in the blank provided to the right of each sentence.

1. How many responses was this ad able to (elicit/illicit)? _____

2. Do you know why the Valerios (emigrated/immigrated) from the United States? _____

3. Several of our investors feel that the collapse of savings and loan institutions is (eminent/imminent). _____

4. At least ten people have called (every day/everyday) since the ad appeared last Thursday. _____

5. Please ask (every one/everyone) to sign his or her time card each Friday. _____

6. We have asked the district attorney to investigate these charges (farther/further). _____

7. Our express lines will accommodate customers with 12 or (fewer/less) items. _____

8. Did you know that our sales manager was (formally/formerly) with the Atlas Corporation? _____

9. You did very (good/well) on the last examination. _____

10. The recent publicity has caused people to (hoard/horde) aluminum foil. _____

11. Please send copies of this report to Paul and (I/me/myself). _____

12. I did not mean to (imply/infer) that you were not doing your job properly.

_____

13. Mrs. Melhorn, our company president, reminds us frequently of her (indigenous/indigent/indignant) beginnings.

_____

14. Once we expand our operations to Virginia and Delaware, we will be subject to all laws governing (interstate/intrastate) commerce.

_____

15. The company must expand (its/it's) sales force by January 1.

_____

16. Please ask Ms. Feldman to (lay/lie) down.

_____

17. Unfortunately, Ron is (liable/libel) for the debts incurred by his partner.

_____

18. The belt on this wheelchair motor appears to be too (loose/lose).

_____

19. Many of our customers find Mr. Brown's (marital/marshal/martial) manner offensive.

_____

20. (May be/Maybe) one of our consultants can help you solve this problem.

_____

21. There has definitely been a decline in employee (moral/morale) since the new executive group took over the operations.

_____

22. Caution our readers not to (overdo/overdue) this exercise program.

_____

23. Three years have (passed/past) since I was transferred to the East Coast.

_____

24. I admire your (patience/patients) in dealing with all these production problems.

_____

25. This is not the first time the manager has been charged with (persecuting/prosecuting) one of his employees.

_____

Check your answers with those given on page 349 before completing the following exercise.

Part C

Instructions: Select the correct alternative from the words shown in parentheses. Write your answer in the blank provided to the right of each sentence.

1. On this application you are not required to disclose any (personal/personnel) information.

_____

2. Be sure to send copies of this brochure to all (perspective/prospective) clients.

_____

3. You must obtain Ms. Goto's approval before you (proceed/precede) any further with this research.

_____

4. All accounts marked with a star must be given (precedence/precedents).

_____

5. If I felt he were a person of (principal/principle), I would gladly enter into this agreement. _____

6. This office needs peace and (quiet/quite) for a few days. _____

7. Do you expect the price of gold to (raise/rise) within the next few weeks? _____

8. Our personnel manager is (real/really) impressed with the qualifications of these applicants. _____

9. Contact at least three (reality/realty) firms for an appraisal of this property. _____

10. Did you obtain a (receipt/recipe) for your October payment? _____

11. Mr. Webb (respectfully/respectively) requested the governor to review his petition. _____

12. What (route/rout) will the truck take from El Paso to Chicago? _____

13. Please (set/sit) the heavy packages on the counter. _____

14. Whom have you employed to (sew/so/sow) the costumes for our grand opening? _____

15. I have never before seen a customer with such (shear/sheer) gall. _____

16. If we could have your order (some time/sometime/sometimes) before November 1, we can guarantee delivery before Christmas. _____

17. None of the walls on this floor are (stationary/stationery). _____

18. The (statue/stature/statute) of this art object is too great for the museum patio. _____

19. Your travel agent is (sure/surely) pleased with the arrangements he was able to make for you. _____

20. At present we have more orders for this electronic game (than/then) we have inventory in our warehouse. _____

21. Before we can make any recommendations, we must study (their/there/they're) operations more fully. _____

22. Dr. Mendoza takes (to/too/two) personally the problems of her patients. _____

23. Many of us believe the zoning commission will (waiver/waver) once it is confronted with the citizens' demands. _____

24. All employees have been instructed not to disclose (weather/whether) our stock will go public. _____

25. (Your/You're) one of the leading contenders for this position. _____

Check your answers with those given on page 349 before completing the following exercise.

Name _____   Date _____

Cumulative Practice Guide 2

Instructions: Select the correct words from the word confusions shown in parentheses in the following letter. Write your answers in the numbered blanks that appear at the right.

Dear Mr. Newsome:

(Your, You're) request to refinance your plumbing and

1. _____

hardware supply business has been tentatively approved. When

we receive your (explicit, implicit) written statement that you

2. _____

will (accede, exceed) to our request to place as additional

3. _____

collateral your newly acquired plant (cite, sight, site), we will

4. _____

be able to initiate the formal paperwork.

Please excuse our delay in answering your request; we

were under the (allusion, delusion, illusion) that you were also

5. _____

seeking financing elsewhere to (ensure, insure) sufficient (capital,

6. _____

capitol) for your expansion program. As you know, we are

7. _____

(principal, principle) lenders only and do not provide secondary

8. _____

financing.

The opinions of (every one, everyone) on our loan committee

9. _____

were (all together, altogether) favorable, and the members

10. _____

agreed to approve the loan tentatively. (Their, There, They're)

11. _____

only concern was that the amount requested is in (access,

12. _____

excess) of the present (appraised, apprised) value of your

13. _____

business. Consequently, we are requesting the additional

collateral before we (precede, proceed) with this loan any

14. _____

(farther, further).

15. _____

Speaking for the entire loan committee, I can (assure,

16. _____

ensure, insure) you that we will (dew, do, due) everything

17. _____

possible to assist you with your financing needs. We (to,

too, two) are interested in the growth and development of

18. _____

this community and wish to encourage (perspective,

prospective) investors.

19. _____

Please contact me as soon as possible to arrange a

meeting to tie up the (loose, lose) ends. We should not

20. _____

(defer, differ) getting the paperwork under way any longer.

Any afternoon next week will be (all right, alright) with me;

the sooner we have this meeting, the sooner we will be able

to (disburse, disperse) your funds.

    I look forward to hearing from you and appreciate

that you (choose, chose) our bank to obtain your (capital,

capitol) funding.

                Sincerely yours,

21. _____

22. _____

23. _____

24. _____

25. _____

The answers to this exercise appear in the **Instructor's Manual and Key** *for* **HOW 8: A Handbook for Office Workers,** *Eighth Edition.*

WORDS OFTEN CONFUSED AND MISUSED

Name _____ Date _____

Cumulative Practice Guide 3

Instructions: Select the correct words from the word confusions shown in parentheses in the following memorandum. Write your answers in the numbered blanks that appear at the right.

TO: Karen Williams, Director of (Personal, Personnel)   1. _____

FROM: Gary Morgan, Executive Vice President

SUBJECT: THE (AFFECT, EFFECT) OF RECRUITMENT,   2. _____
          SELECTION, AND IN-SERVICE TRAINING ON
          OVERALL PLANT OPERATIONS

I wish to (complement, compliment) you on the excellent job   3. _____

you did in recruiting and hiring (personal, personnel) for our new   4. _____

plant that opened last year. You are to be (commanded,

commended) for adding such a large number of new employees   5. _____

during such a short time period.

Our production and sales this year will (accede, exceed) last   6. _____

year's by 30 percent. Much of this increase is (dew, due, do) to   7. _____

your (continual, continuous) efforts to hire and train well-   8. _____

qualified people.

Last year when we set a (precedence, precedent) in the   9. _____

Industry by staffing an entire plant with predominantly new

employees, I was concerned (weather, whether) or not this   10. _____

action would adversely (affect, effect) our production. However,   11. _____

my concern was (shear, sheer) nonsense. The people you have   12. _____

hired are more qualified, efficient, and dependable (than, then)   13. _____

I had expected. I wish to (formally, formerly) congratulate you   14. _____

on your progressive personnel practices.

May I also indicate that I agree in (principal, principle) with   15. _____

the extensive in-service training program you have initiated.

We have (all ready, already) promoted a number of people   16. _____

from within the company, and this policy of internal promotion   17. _____

has certainly helped the (moral, morale) of all (who, whom) work   18. _____

here. Although the cost of this in-service program is relatively

(expansive, expensive), it appears to be worth the investment.　　19. _____

Other members of the executive staff (appraise, apprise) this　　20. _____

program in the same manner.

　　Your contributions and innovative ideas have (allowed,　　21. _____

aloud) us to plan for the future with a (confidant, confident)　　22. _____

outlook. We will keep you informed of our (coarse, course)　　23. _____

of action so that we may continue to rely on your (assistance,　　24. _____

assistants) to (assure, ensure, insure) our continued success.　　25. _____

*The answers to this exercise appear in the **Instructor's Manual and Key** for **HOW 8: A Handbook for Office Workers,** Eighth Edition.*

Name _____ Score _____

Testing Your Understanding, Part 1 (2 points each)

Instructions: Read the following sentences carefully for meaning. If a word has been used incorrectly, UNDERLINE it. Then write the correct word in the blank at the end of the sentence. If a sentence is correct, write *OK* in the blank.

1. At the present time I am adverse to accepting any additional responsibilities. _____

2. Our clients' annual income exceeds the minimum requirement for this home by $8,450. _____

3. Upon the advise of our attorney, we have decided not to invest in this property. _____

4. Large increases in materials costs have affected price increases in nearly all our products. _____

5. A large amount of stockholders have protested our proposal to merge with ICA Corporation. _____

6. Although we cannot ensure that these condominiums will be ready for occupancy on October 1, we are promising purchasers this date. _____

7. Our company has born financial burdens since the early 1990s. _____

8. The state game licensing bureau is located in Room 480 of the California State Capital. _____

9. This manual explains how to sight sources and prepare footnotes for term papers and reports. _____

10. To receive your complementary copy, just fill out and return the enclosed postcard. _____

11. A number of credible financial institutions are endorsing the new issue of our stock. _____

12. You may wish to seek counsel from your attorney before making a decision on this issue. _____

13. Companies that continue to disburse pollutants in the environment will be fined heavily. _____

14. Not everyone is familiar with the works of the imminent English playwright Shakespeare. _____

15. Most of the employees in our organization have immigrated from Mexico. _____

16. Almost everyday we receive a complaint about the service in our Denver office. _____

17. What effect has this advertising campaign had on sales? _____

WORDS OFTEN CONFUSED AND MISUSED

271

18. The police in this area are attempting to stop the elicit sale of drugs.
   _____

19. Every one in the company should receive this information on employee medical and retirement benefits.
   _____

20. Do you foresee any substantial decent in interest rates within the next three months?
   _____

21. At yesterday's meeting the board disproved the purchase of these desert properties.
   _____

22. Although many people depreciate the commercialism associated with Christmas, they still join the millions of holiday shoppers.
   _____

23. Personalized sales letters tend to elicit a greater response than nonpersonalized ones.
   _____

24. The stories being sent by these foreign correspondents seem hardly creditable.
   _____

25. Our new file clerk is continuously misplacing or misfiling important documents.
   _____

26. Buckingham Palace is a frequently visited tourist site in London.
   _____

27. These two textbooks compliment each other; what one touches upon lightly, the other delves into heavily.
   _____

28. His employer censored him for neglecting his work.
   _____

29. All these Italian chains are 18-carat gold.
   _____

30. How many people have you hired to canvas neighborhoods in the vicinities of our three offices?
   _____

31. You may obtain this information from any one of my assistants.
   _____

32. If you wish to invest any additional capitol in this project, please let me know.
   _____

33. Who beside you in the office has been able to get tickets to the opening game of the World Series?
   _____

34. I feel badly that we are unable to offer you a position at the present time.
   _____

35. I have learned to pack only the bare necessities for my business trips.
   _____

36. Anytime you are interested in learning more about real estate investments, just give me a call at 555-7439.
   _____

37. Have you appraised anyone on the staff of the change in your plans?
   _____

38. Like I stated in my July 16 memo, we will continue to honor the 25 percent discount on all our products in the FS-200 series line through July 31. _____

39. The rapid assent of interest rates during the last three weeks has curtailed the home-buying market considerably. _____

40. Between all of us, we should be able to devise a plan to solve this problem. _____

41. Most everyone on our staff has attended at least one of your computer seminars. _____

42. We have not all together determined the projected final cost of this construction project. _____

43. The cause of cancer continues to allude all medical researchers. _____

44. Effective television advertising creates an allusion of reality in the minds of viewers _____

45. Fluctuations in oil prices effect consumer automobile purchasing patterns. _____

46. Unless you adopt readily to change, you will have difficulty working for such a progressive, forward-looking company like Amgen. _____

47. We are unable to except these expired coupons. _____

48. You will need a court order to obtain excess to the files. _____

49. You may wish to seek advice from your accountant before selling these properties. _____

50. What kind of affect, if any, will the retail clerks' strike have on our industry? _____

*The answers to this exercise appear in the **Instructor's Manual and Key** for **HOW 8: A Handbook for Office Workers,** Eighth Edition.*

Name _____ Score _____

Testing Your Understanding, Part 2 (2 points each)

Instructions: Read the following sentences carefully for meaning. If a word has been used incorrectly, UNDERLINE it. Then write the correct word in the blank at the right of the sentence. If a sentence is correct, write *OK* in the blank.

1. Unless you give implicit instructions to our administrative assistant, the job will not be done correctly. _____

2. Most of our extant projects have been financed by Washington Federal Bank. _____

3. Less people than we had expected responded to our newspaper advertisements. _____

4. If you were me, would you accept this position? _____

5. Trees from which we obtain this kind of lumber are indigent to the Northwest. _____

6. These books have lain on the shelves for years without anyone even opening them. _____

7. We are not libel for any damage caused by the trucking company. _____

8. If you are interested in purchasing additional computers, we maybe able to obtain them for you at discount prices. _____

9. A local ordnance prohibits gambling within the city limits. _____

10. If the manager continues to prosecute individual members in his department, they will file a formal grievance against him. _____

11. How many hours did our assistants pore over books in the law library before finding these legal precedents? _____

12. Our principle stockholder has expressed opposition to our acquiring additional properties in this area. _____

13. Before constructing any type of building on this property, we will need to raise the existing structures. _____

14. The founder of our company played a major roll in the development of our city. _____

15. We may sometime in the future be able to do business with you. _____

16. When did the state legislature enact this stature? _____

17. As a result of there inquiry, the grand jury has begun an investigation. _____

18. Only the department chair can waive this requirement. _____

19. Within the last decade persons involved in realty sales have been forced to whether periods of high interest rates. _____

20. Since you are located further from the airport than I, I will pick up the shipment. _____

21. As long as you continue to flaunt authority and proper work ethics, you will have difficulty holding a job. _____

22. You did good on this examination. _____

23. A hoard of reporters surrounded the rock star as he stepped from his limousine. _____

24. Did the vice president infer that our manager had been replaced because our office has shown a declining sales record? _____

25. During the last two years, the company has reached it's sales quotas six of the eight quarters. _____

26. If the bank will loan us the money, we will be able to enlarge our restaurant. _____

27. Please have the marshal subpoena this witness. _____

28. We would appreciate your sending us a check to settle your overdo account. _____

29. Please refer any perspective clients to me personally. _____

30. A pole of our employees revealed that the majority preferred receiving stock options and benefit programs over salary increases. _____

31. Which of these requests should receive precedence? _____

32. We are real enthusiastic about the possibility of Thornton Industries acquiring our company. _____

33. Rote learning does not come easily to most people. _____

34. Hurricane-like winds sheered the roofs off three houses in this Florida neighborhood. _____

35. Our new stationary has been ordered and should arrive within the next week. _____

36. At the present time we have more employees in this branch office then we need. _____

37. There are to many students enrolled in this class. _____

38. No matter how intimidating the opposition may be, do not waiver if you feel your position is correct. _____

39. We called a consultant who we had met in Atlanta. _____

40. If your interested in these kinds of investment opportunities, please give me a call. _____

WORDS OFTEN CONFUSED AND MISUSED

41. Only if someone in your family is willing to sign a guaranty can we approve this loan.

          _____

42. Because this sales territory includes California, Oregon, Washington, Nevada, and Arizona, my job involves considerable intrastate travel.

          _____

43. Our goal is to establish branch offices in the most populace areas of the state.

          _____

44. Most of the residence in this convalescent home are in need of constant care and supervision.

          _____

45. Since all our floor models will be placed on sale this weekend, you may wish to select a bedroom suit at that time.

          _____

46. If home prices continue to sore, fewer and fewer people will be able to purchase single-family dwellings in our city.

          _____

47. Our personnel manager could not overlook such a fragrant violation of company policy.

          _____

48. Students from almost every cultural hew attend our university.

          _____

49. Such an ingenious plan should surely give us a competitive advantage in marketing our new video cameras.

          _____

50. Please have someone from our maintenance crew repair this lose door plate before one of our students trips and falls.

          _____

*The answers to this exercise appear in the **Instructor's Manual and Key** for **HOW 8: A Handbook for Office Workers**, Eighth Edition.*

Section 8 Spelling, Proofreading, and Editing

Proofreading (8-4 and 8-5)

Practice Guide 1

Instructions: Proofread the sentences in Column B by checking them against the ones in Column A. Use proofreader's marks to make the necessary corrections in Column B.

Column A	*Column B*
1. We are in the process of planning fund-raising activities for the college's proposed building program.	1. We are in the process of planning fund raising activitys for the colleges proposed building program.
2. Since the exterminators must tent the building, all tenants will be required to vacate their offices from August 3 through August 5.	2. Since the exterminaters must tent the building all tenants will be required to vacate there offices from August 3 thru August 6.
3. Perhaps we should engage a freelance photographer to obtain professional pictures for the sales brochure of our new Willow Brook Development.	3. Perhaps, we should engage a free lance photographer to obtain proffesional pictures for the sales brochure of our new Willowbrook Development.
4. During this three-day Memorial Day sale, you can save up to 50 percent on regular items that have been reduced only temporarily for this sale.	4. During this 3-day Memorial day sale, you can save up to 50% on regular items that have been reduced temporarly for this sale.
5. In your job search visit the Web site of MedSearch America <http://www.medsearch.com>; this on-line career center posts résumés and lists job opportunities in a wide range of health-related occupations throughout the United States.	5. In your job search, visit the web sight of MedSearch America <http://www.medsearch.com>, this on line career center posts résumés and lists job opportunities in a wide range of health related occupations throughout the U.S.

6. New keys will be issued for the parking gate entrances to all employee parking lots.

7. Before entering the premises, all visitors must stop at the kiosk to obtain a permit from the security guard.

8. Plan to register early for this conference; after November 2 registration fees will be $150.

9. You are among our preferred customers, and we are pleased to invite you to this special by-invitation-only sale.

10. We cannot accept any out-of-state or third-party checks; therefore, you will need to find another means for making this payment.

11. If you will fax me your E-mail address, I will let you know the dates of the convention as soon as the executive board determines them.

12. Will you be able to attend the luncheon that has been scheduled for Thursday, September 20, at 12 noon?

13. CliniShare has been able to serve most of our patients' needs for medical equipment, medical supplies, and nursing care.

6. New keys will be issued for all parking gates at entrances to the employee's parking lots.

7. Before entering the premises all visitors must stop at the keosk to obtain a permit from the security guard

8. Plan to register early for this conferance, after November 2nd, registration fees for this conference will be $150.00.

9. You are amoung our prefered customers and we are pleased to invite you to this special by invitation only sale.

10. We can not except out-of-state or third party checks, therefore, you will need to find another means of making payment.

11. If you will fax me your E-Mail address I will let you know the date of the convention as soon the executive board determines it.

12. Will you be able to attend the luncheon which has been scheduled for Thursday, September 20th, at 12 Noon.

13. Clini Share have been able to serve most of our patient's needs for medical equipment, medical supplies and nursing care.

14. Ms. Deborah Marton has been appointed manager of the Accounting Department; she will assume this position on July 1.

14. Ms. Deborah Martin has been appointed Manager of the Accounting department: she will assume this position July 1.

15. According to the posted sign, "Vehicles not displaying a valid parking permit will be towed away at owner's expense."

15. According to the sign posted, "Vehicals not displaying a valid parking permit will be towed away at owners' expense".

16. Stocks, corporate bonds, mutual funds, unit trusts, government bonds, tax-free municipal bonds, and precious metals—all these investment opportunities are available through T. R. Noble.

16. Stocks, corporate bonds, mutual funds, unit trusts, goverment bonds, tax free municiple bonds and precious metals-all of these investment opportunities are available through T.R. Noble.

17. For reservations for the nights of April 19 and 20 at the Park Regency Hotel in Atlanta, your confirmation number is JRK1892.

17. For reservations for the nights April 19 and 20 at the Park Regency hotel in Atlanta your confirmation number is JRk1892.

18. Copies of the agenda, last year's minutes, a list of advisory committee members, a campus map, and a parking permit are enclosed.

18. Copys of the agenda, last years minutes, a list of advisory committee members, a campus map and a parking permit is enclosed.

19. Do you foresee that these changes will affect our ability to market this high-end software to home computer users?

19. Do you forsee that these changes will effect our ability to market this high end software to home-computer users.

20. All these grant proposals must be submitted to the appropriate offices in Washington, D.C., by March 31, or they will not be funded.

20. All of these grant proposals must be submitted to the apropriate office in Washington D. C. by March 31, or they will not be be funded.

Check your answers with those given on pages 349–350 before completing the following exercise.

Editing (8-6 and 8-7)

Practice Guide 2

Instructions: Edit the following letter for errors in grammar, punctuation, and spelling. Use proofreader's marks to show your corrections.

Dear Mr. Elliott:

Let me take this opportunity to thank you for doing business with M.T. Stein & Co. Inc. Your confidence and patronage is truly appreciated.

You are the most important ingredient to our success. We are commited to doing everything we can to give you the best service in the fields of tax free municipal bonds, mutual funds, unit trusts, United States government obligations, corporate bonds, and precious metals.

Often I avoid showing particular products to a client because I assume that they may not be interested. On the other hand, however, they may very well be. In an effort to provide more prompt and comprehensive service to my valued clients like you, Mr. Elliot, I am conducting a survay to obtain a better understanding of your investment needs. Therefore, would you please fill out the enclosed questionaire and return it in the enclosed envelope.

Your response would be greatly appreciated in my continuing efforts to better serve you.

Sincerely yours,

*The answers to this exercise appear in the **Instructor's Manual and Key** for **HOW 8: A Handbook for Office Workers,** Eighth Edition.*

Practice Guide 3

Instructions: Edit the following letter for errors in grammar, punctuation, and spelling. Use proofreader's marks to show your corrections.

Dear Ms. Nye:

I think you will agree that the potential for saving hundreds of dollars a year on your auto insurance is an opportunity you can not afford to miss. That is why I am urging you to take advantage of this excellant offer.

As part of this program you will receive the following

- Real savings

- Convenience

- First rate service and dependability

Saving however, is not the whole story. With Nationwide Insurances superior reputation, you will feel confident that you selected a company with stability and integrity. Nationwide Insurance has been in business since 1926, and is the fourth largest auto insurer in the United states. They are rated A+ (Superior) by A.M. Best, the leading independant analyst of insurance companies.

Call now for your free no obligation rate quote. To find out how much you can save with Nationwide Insurance, just call toll-free (800) 555-3465, extension 827. Be assured there are no high pressure sales tactics. You are under no obligation whatsoever but if you like the quote you can arrange to apply for your coverage right away.

Sincerely,

*The answers to this exercise appear in the **Instructor's Manual and Key** for **HOW 8: A Handbook for Office Workers,** Eighth Edition.*

Part 3

Section 1 Address Format and Forms of Address

Address Format (9-1 Through 9-8)

Practice Guide 1

Instructions: For each of the following exercises, format the inside address and furnish an appropriate salutation.

Ex. *Man within a company*

John R. Dillon, Manager, Production Department, Ellis Decor and Designs, 13500 E. Base Line Rd., Columbus, IN 47203-9652

Inside address

Mr. John R. Dillon, Manager
Production Department
Ellis Decor and Designs
13500 East Base Line Road
Columbus, IN 47203-9652

Salutation
Dear Mr. Dillon:

1. Individual woman

Lisa Williams, 2853 Elliott Ave., Apt. 17, Medford, OR 97501-1258

Inside address

Salutation

2. Individual man

Allen Mercer, 2823 Manzano St. NE, Albuquerque, NM 87110

Inside address

Salutation

3. Woman within a company

Alecia Robertson, Sales Manager, Young America Designs, Inc., 580 Freeman Ave., Suite 300, Kansas City, KS 66101-2204

Inside address

Salutation

4. Company

AmerGeneral Insurance Company,
Claims Department, Nations Trust Bank
Building, Suite 450, 700 Curtiss St.,
Hartford, CT 06106-1354

Inside address

Salutation

5. Company

Atlantic Wrought Iron Works, 800 N.
Lincoln Ave., P.O. Box 447, Pittsburgh,
PA 15233-3768

Inside address

Salutation

6. Individual, gender unknown

Terry Thompson, 1 Nash St. E., Wilson,
NC 27893-2741

Inside address

Salutation

7. Individual married woman

Andrea Matthewson, 1230 W. 14 Ave.,
Anchorage, AK 99501-1064

Inside address

Salutation

8. Individual (gender unknown) within a
company

Tran Nguyen, Manager, Hawaiian
Imports, Inc., 1778 Ala Moana Blvd.,
Honolulu, HI 96815-4922

Inside address

Salutation

9. Man within a company (foreign address)

Rafael Marqués, Subdirector, Hotel
Zoraida Garden, Avenida de Venezuela,
04740 Roquetas de Mar, España (Spain)

Inside address

Salutation

10. Man within a company

Sid Leavitt, Plant Manager, GDC Manufacturing Corp., 8100 Thom Blvd., Las Vegas, NV 89131-3612

Inside address

Salutation

11. Individual woman

Marlene Begosian, 13233 4th Ave. SW, Seattle, WA 98146-1165

Inside address

Salutation

12. Married woman within a company

Carolyn Yeager, Management Consultant, Brooks, Kline & Stewart, Barnhardt Financial Center, Suite 200, 400 Columbus Ave., Boston, MA 02116-3868

Inside address

Salutation

13. Individual man

Kenneth Killian, 4751 NW 24 St., Unit 105, Oklahoma City, OK 73127-6213

Inside address

Salutation

14. Woman within a company (foreign address)

Maureen L. Parry, Managing Director, Eaton Bankers & Trust Ltd., 55 Hornby Ave., Whetstone, London N22, England

Inside address

Salutation

15. Department within a company

Department of Human Resources, Advanced Powder Coating, 1487 S. 1100th E., Salt Lake City, UT 84105-2423

Inside address

Salutation

*The answers to this exercise appear in the **Instructor's Manual and Key** for **HOW 8: A Handbook for Office Workers,** Eighth Edition.*

Forms of Address (9-9, 9-11 Through 9-14)

Practice Guide 2

Instructions: For each of the following exercises, format the inside address and furnish an appropriate salutation.

Ex. *Married couple*

Michelle and David Allen, 2775 N. 38 St., Boise, ID 83703-4815

Inside address

Mr. and Mrs. David Allen
2775 North 38th Street
Boise, Idaho 83703-4815

Salutation

Dear Mr. and Mrs. Allen:

1. Physician

   Shari Thomas, Facey Medical Clinic, 2113 E. Martin Luther King Jr. Blvd., Austin, TX 78702-1357

   Inside address

   Salutation

2. Lawyer

   William Armstrong, Doyle, Menning & Gemmingen, Rochester Towers, Suites 800-850, 1050 Fairfax Ave., Birmingham, AL 35214-5488

   Inside address

Salutation

3. Professor (with doctor's degree)

   Patricia Atkinson, Department of Business and Economics, Livingston Technical University, 2400 University Ave., Griffin, GA 30223-1000

   Inside Address

   Salutation

4. Service person, lieutenant, United States Navy

   Jack Clemens, USS Dwight D. Eisenhower, CV 69 FPO AE, Norfolk, VA 09532-2830

   Inside address

   Salutation

5. Dean of a college

   Lonnie S. Beacon, Academic Affairs, Whitmore College, 220 St. John St., Portland, ME 04102

   Inside address

   Salutation

6. Two or more men

   John Buenzli and Robert Carroll, Buenzli & Carroll Auto Imports, 6950 Raymond Ave., Charleston, SC 29406-2103

   Inside address

   Salutation

7. Two or more women

   Dorothy Colbert and Eleanor Griffith, Inspection Coordinators, Burlington Woolen Mills, 100 Booth St., Burlington, VT 05401-2210

   Inside address

   Salutation

8. United States representative for Colorado or your state (names available on the Internet at <http://www.house.com> or <http://clerkweb.house.gov/members/house.htm>)

   Diana DeGette

   Inside address

   Salutation

9. President of the United States

   William Clinton

   Inside address

   Salutation

10. United States senator for Illinois or your state (names available on the Internet at <http://www.senate.gov/senator/state.html>)

    Richard J. Durbin

    Inside address

    Salutation

11. Governor of Oklahoma or your state (addresses available on Internet at <http://www.trytel.com/~aberdeen/ub.html#UB1>)

    Frank Keating, State Capitol, Rm. 212, Oklahoma City, OK 73105

    Inside address

    Salutation

12. Mayor of Salt Lake City, Utah, or mayor of your city (local telephone and fax numbers are available on the Internet at <http://www.usmayors.org/meet_mayors/>)

    Deedee Corradini, 451 S. State St., Room 306, Salt Lake City, UT 84111-3104.

    Inside address

    Salutation

13. Catholic bishop

    Vernon E. Meehan, St. John Baptist de la Salle, 7001 Fair Oaks Ave., Dallas, TX 75231-6032

Inside address

Salutation

14. Protestant minister

    Christopher Flanagan, Hillcrest Presbyterian Church, 1151 Thornton Rd., Bangor, ME 04401-3866.

    Inside address

    Salutation

15. Undetermined individual or group

    No name

    Inside address

    Salutation

*The answers to this exercise appear in the **Instructor's Manual and Key** for **HOW 8: A Handbook for Office Workers,** Eighth Edition.*

Section 2 Business Letters and Memorandums

Formatting Business Letters and Memorandums (10-5 Through 10-23 and 10-36)

Practice Guide 1

Instructions: Each of the exercise instructions provided below corresponds with a letter or memorandum exercise in Part 2, Section 1 (pp. 15–56) of this workbook. These letters and memorandums reinforce the principles of punctuation in *HOW 8.* Using your word processor, prepare the documents according to the instructions provided for each exercise and supply the proper punctuation. Use correct formats for each letter or memorandum, and remember to balance letters vertically.

1. **Comma Placement, Series, Reinforcement Letter 1 (p. 18)**
   Memorandum format
   Addressed to John Cole, Manager, Research Department
   Written by Rory Silva, Senior Partner
   Subject: Research Procedures for New Cases

2. **Comma Placement, Parenthetical, Reinforcement Letter 2 (p. 20)**
   Memorandum format
   Addressed to David Post, Vice President, Sales
   Written by Anne Kelly, President
   Subject: Opening of New Branch Offices

3. **Comma Placement, Direct Address, Reinforcement Letter 3 (p. 22)**
   Modified block format, blocked paragraphs, mixed punctuation
   Delivery notation—express mail
   Addressed to Mrs. June Smith, 3624 West 59th Place, Los Angeles, California 90043-1753
   Written by Valley Department Store, Joyce Arntson, Manager

4. **Comma Placement, Appositives, Reinforcement Letter 4 (p. 24)**
   Full block format, open punctuation
   Addressed to Mr. Eric L. Ray, Sales Manager, Fairmont Publishing Company, Inc., 4900 Avenue of the Americas, New York, New York 10026-3020
   Subject: New Title, *Writing Résumés That Get Jobs*
   Written by Donald R. Hirschell, Editor in Chief, Business and Economics
   Copies to be sent to Edward Sharp, Advertising Department, and Lisa Tsutsui, Editorial Department

12. **Comma Placement, Contrasting/Contingent Expressions and Omitted Words, Reinforcement Letter 12 (p. 40)**

Full block format, open punctuation

Addressee notation—fax confirmation

Addressed to Ms. Alice Stadthaus, Buyer, Broude's Department Store, 1900 Russell Cave Road, Lexington, Kentucky 40511-3012

Subject: Your Order No. 87392T

Written by Jean Chung, Manager, Sales Department

13. **Comma Placement, Clarity, Reinforcement Letter 13 (p. 42)**

Memorandum format

Addressed to John Allen, National Sales Manager

Written by Roberta Alvarez, Southern Regional Sales Manager

Subject: January Sales Conference

14. **Comma Placement, Short Quotations, Reinforcement Letter 14 (p. 44)**

Modified block format, blocked paragraphs, mixed punctuation

Delivery notation—certified mail

Addressed to Mr. Conrad B. Ryan, Owner, Ryan's Stationers, Inc., 735 Punahou Street, Honolulu, Hawaii 96826-1430

Written by Janet Horne, Manager, Credit Department

15. **Semicolon Placement, No Conjunction, Reinforcement Letter 15 (p. 46)**

Memorandum format

Addressed to Carol Smith, President

Written by George Borg, Vice President, Marketing

Subject: Incentive Commission Plan

16. **Semicolon Placement, With Conjunction, Reinforcement Letter 16 (p. 48)**

Modified block format, indented paragraphs, mixed punctuation

Delivery notation, certified mail—return receipt requested

Addressed to Mr. Curtis L. Mason, House of Fabrics, 4556 Detroit Road, Cleveland, Ohio 44102-7343

Written by Crest Button and Sash, Helen Sellman, Credit Manager

Copy to the Corrigan Collection Agency

Postscript: We hope you choose to protect your credit rating!

17. **Semicolon Placement, With Transitional Expressions, Reinforcement Letter 17 (p. 50)**

Memorandum format

Addressed to Kristin Harris, Regional Sales Manager

Written by Ross Byrd, National Sales Manager

Subject: Sales Decline in the Boston Area

Copy to be sent to Lynn Reed, Sales Supervisor

18. **Semicolon Placement, Series and Enumerations, Reinforcement Letter 18 (p. 52)**

Full block format, mixed punctuation

Addressed to Mr. Jason Williams, President, National Association of Plant Managers, Ludlow Manufacturing Company, Inc., 1550 West Liberty Avenue, Pittsburgh, Pennsylvania 15226-3448

Written by Keri L. Clark, Executive Director

19. **Colon Placement, Formally Enumerated or Listed Items and Explanatory Sentences, Reinforcement Letter 19 (p. 54)**

Modified block format, blocked paragraphs, mixed punctuation

Addressed to Mrs. Dianne Farmer, Manager, Mid-Valley Office Equipment Company, 3412 South Mountain Avenue, Tucson, Arizona 85713-3398

Subject: Your Order 873962 dated January 5, 1999

Written by Kevin Mulcahy, Sales Manager

20. **Dash Placement—Parenthetical Elements, Appositives, and Summaries, Reinforcement Letter 20 (p. 56)**

Memorandum format

Addressed to Susan Brady, Vice President, Real Estate and Development

Written by Cory Armon, Executive Vice President

Subject: Closing of Branch Offices

Copies to be sent to Gail Davis, Chris Ellis, and Tony Garcia

*The answers to this exercise appear in the **Instructor's Manual and Key** for **HOW 8: A Handbook for Office Workers,** Eighth Edition.*

Practice Guide 2

Instructions: Each of the exercise instructions provided below corresponds with a letter or memorandum exercise in Part 2, Section 3 (pp. 69–94) of this workbook. These letters and memorandums reinforce the principles of capitalization in *HOW 8.* Using your word processor, prepare the documents according to the instructions provided for each exercise and make any needed corrections in capitalization. Use correct formats for each letter or memorandum, and remember to balance letters vertically.

1. **Capitalization, Proper Nouns and Adjectives, Reinforcement Letter 1 (p. 72)**

Modified block format, indented paragraphs, mixed punctuation

Addressed to Ms. Janice Harris, 6923 Hughes Terrace, Apt. 1B, Detroit, Michigan 48208-5639

Written by Travelwell Luggage, Leroy S. Speidel, Adjustment Department

2. **Capitalization, Abbreviations and Numbered or Lettered Items, Reinforcement Letter 2 (p. 74)**

Full block format, open punctuation

Personal notation

Addressed to Mrs. Denise R. Rice, Vice President, Leland Cole Cosmetics, 10400 Lafayette Street, Denver, Colorado 80233-4351

Written by Arthur J. Anderson, Travel Agent

Blind copy to be sent to Ms. Jane Hughes, Norris Travel Agency, New York City branch

3. **Capitalization, Personal and Professional Titles, Reinforcement Letter 3 (p. 76)**

   Modified block format, indented paragraphs, mixed punctuation

   Delivery notation—fax confirmation

   Addressed to Mr. Vernon C. Ross, Chairperson, Committee for the Reelection of Councilman John Rogers, 630 South Figueroa Street, Suite 830, Los Angeles, California 90017-2073

   Written by Doris Chamberlain

4. **Capitalization, Literary or Artistic Works/Academic Subjects, Courses, and Degrees, Reinforcement Letter 4 (p. 78)**

   Full block format, open punctuation

   Addressed to Dr. Maxine Carnes, Professor, School of Business and Economics, Jackson State University, 1325 Lynch Street, Jackson, Mississippi 39203-1023

   Written by Anthony T. Beller; signature line is Patricia R. Lowman, Editor in Chief

5. **Capitalization, Organizations, Reinforcement Letter 5 (p. 80)**

   Simplified letter format

   Addressed to Mr. Mark Smith, Manager, Accounting Department, Watson Corporation, 10420 Ninth Street, N.W., Oklahoma City, Oklahoma 73127-1397

   Subject: Conclusion of Yearly Audit

   Written by J. T. Rheingold, Chief Auditor, Gleason, Stone & Hale

   Blind copy to be sent to John Jones, Vice President, Ryan Corporation

*The answers to this exercise appear in the **Instructor's Manual and Key** for **HOW 8: A Handbook for Office Workers,** Eighth Edition.*

Practice Guide 3

Instructions: Each of the exercise instructions provided below corresponds with a letter or memorandum exercise in Part 2, Section 4 (pp. 95–111) of this workbook. These letters and memorandums reinforce the principles of number format in *HOW 8.* Using your word processor, prepare the documents according to the instructions provided for each exercise and make any needed corrections in number format. Use correct formats for each letter or memorandum, and remember to balance letters vertically.

1. **Numbers, General Rules, Reinforcement Letter 1 (p. 98)**

   Full block format, mixed punctuation

   Delivery notation—fax confirmation

   Attention: Ms. Sally Fields, Order Desk

   Addressed to Johnson Furniture Manufacturing, Inc., 2400 North Elm Street, Greensboro, North Carolina 27408-3124

   Written by Mayo Department Stores, David Seigel, Manager, Furniture Department

2. **Numbers, Related Numbers, Reinforcement Letter 2 (p. 100)**

   Social business format

   Addressed to Mr. Robert Bradley, Arrangements Chairman, New Jersey Information Processing Association, 260 Ridgewood Avenue, Newark, New Jersey 07108-9214

   Written by Gloria McKimmey, President

3. Numbers, Money and Percentages/With Nouns and Abbreviations, Reinforcement Letter 3 (p. 102)

Simplified Letter Format

Addressed to Wards and Company, Plumbing and Heating Supplies, 1105 East Madison Street, Springfield, Illinois 62702-3242

Attention: Mr. George Black, Manager

Subject: Damaged Electric Motors

Written by Gino P. Scopesi, Manager, Adjustment and Claims Department

Blind copy to be sent to Phil Hernandez, Chicago Branch Office

4. Numbers, Weights and Measures/Dates and Periods of Time, Reinforcement Letter 4 (p. 104)

Modified block format, blocked paragraphs, mixed punctuation

Addressed to Mr. and Mrs. Anthony Reed, 438 Penny Lane, Unit 2, Austin, Texas 78758-6921

Written by Sunset West, Inc., James Bennett, Vice President, Sales

*The answers to this exercise appear in the **Instructor's Manual and Key** for **HOW 8: A Handbook for Office Workers,** Eighth Edition.*

Section 3 Indexing for Filing

Indexing and Alphabetizing (14-3 Through 14-5)

Practice Guide 1

Instructions: In Column B write in indexing order the names of the individuals listed in Column A. In the space below the listing, write the numbers appearing before each name as they should appear in alphabetical sequence.

Column A	Column B
1. Mrs. Jo Lee R. McElvey	_____ _____ _____ _____ _____
2. John G. Martin, Jr., M.D.	_____ _____ _____ _____ _____
3. Wm. J. MacIntyre	_____ _____ _____ _____ _____
4. Mary Lou Morton-Duben	_____ _____ _____ _____ _____
5. Marly Louise Mason	_____ _____ _____ _____ _____
6. John G. Martin, Sr., M.D.	_____ _____ _____ _____ _____
7. Mrs. McKimmey	_____ _____ _____ _____ _____
8. William J. MacIntyre	_____ _____ _____ _____ _____
9. Mrs. Mary Morton	_____ _____ _____ _____ _____
10. John G. Martin, III, M.D.	_____ _____ _____ _____ _____

Alphabetized Listing

___ ___ ___ ___ ___ ___ ___ ___ ___ ___
 1   2   3   4   5   6   7   8   9   10

Practice Guide 2

Instructions: In Column B write in indexing order the names of the individuals listed in Column A. In the space below the listing, write the numbers appearing before each name as they should appear in alphabetical sequence.

Column A	Column B
1. Jas. David Del Monico	_____ _____ _____ _____ _____
2. Mrs. Jo Anne C. DeSantis	_____ _____ _____ _____ _____
3. Joan M. DeSantis	_____ _____ _____ _____ _____
4. James D. Del Monico, Jr.	_____ _____ _____ _____ _____
5. Professor J. T. Dell, Ph.D.	_____ _____ _____ _____ _____
6. Johanna S. Delmar-Larson	_____ _____ _____ _____ _____

7. John Philip Del Mario   _____ _____ _____ _____ _____

8. James R. D'Amato, D.D.S.   _____ _____ _____ _____ _____

9. Mrs. Del Monte   _____ _____ _____ _____ _____

10. James D. Delmonico   _____ _____ _____ _____ _____

Alphabetized Listing

_____ _____ _____ _____ _____ _____ _____ _____ _____ _____
  1   2   3   4   5   6   7   8   9   10

Practice Guide 3

Instructions: In Column B write in indexing order the organizational names listed in Column A. In the space below the listing, write the numbers appearing before each name as they should appear in alphabetical sequence.

         Column A   *Column B*

1. The Fortune Cookie Café   _____ _____ _____ _____ _____

2. Dr. Forkner's Pet Clinic   _____ _____ _____ _____ _____

3. Ford & Young's Showcase   _____ _____ _____ _____ _____

4. *F R T* Worldwide Delivery   _____ _____ _____ _____ _____

5. Fast-and-Clean Linen
Service   _____ _____ _____ _____ _____

6. Formann, Drake, Greco &
Richards   _____ _____ _____ _____ _____

7. FBLA   _____ _____ _____ _____ _____

8. Fort Wayne Auto Leasing,
Inc.   _____ _____ _____ _____ _____

9. D & D Pet Hospital   _____ _____ _____ _____ _____

10. Francois Fornier's French
Cuisine   _____ _____ _____ _____ _____

Alphabetized Listing

_____ _____ _____ _____ _____ _____ _____ _____ _____ _____
  1   2   3   4   5   6   7   8   9   10

Practice Guide 4

Instructions: In Column B write in indexing order the organizational names listed in Column A. In the space below the listing, write the numbers appearing before each name as they should appear in alphabetical sequence.

Column A   Column B

1. 7th Avenue Deli   _____ _____ _____ _____ _____

2. A1 Financial Corporation   _____ _____ _____ _____ _____

3. San Diego Cultural Center   _____ _____ _____ _____ _____

4. Santiago Export & Import
   Co.   _____ _____ _____ _____ _____

5. Sandy Beach Golf & Tennis
   Club   _____ _____ _____ _____ _____

6. 7-11 Minimart   _____ _____ _____ _____ _____

7. The San Marcos Inn   _____ _____ _____ _____ _____

8. SDSU   _____ _____ _____ _____ _____

9. Seventh Street
   Wholesalers, Inc.   _____ _____ _____ _____ _____

10. Sandy Beech's Nail
    Boutique   _____ _____ _____ _____ _____

Alphabetized Listing

_____ _____ _____ _____ _____ _____ _____ _____ _____ _____
   1   2   3   4   5   6   7   8   9   10

Practice Guide 5

Instructions: In Column B write in indexing order the names of government entities listed in Column A. In the space below the listing, write the numbers appearing before each name as they should appear in alphabetical sequence.

Column A   Column B

1. Arizona Department of
   Justice (state)   _____ _____ _____ _____ _____

2. Phoenix Police
   Department (city)   _____ _____ _____ _____ _____

3. Federal Bureau of
   Investigation (national)   _____ _____ _____ _____ _____

4. San Bernardino Board of
   Supervisors (county)   _____ _____ _____ _____ _____

5. Department of Justice,
   Immigration and
   Naturalization Service
   (national)   _____ _____ _____ _____ _____

6. Arizona Department of
   Highways (state)
   _____ _____ _____ _____ _____

7. Phoenix Department of
   Sanitation (city)
   _____ _____ _____ _____ _____

8. Glendale Department of
   Health and Safety (county)
   _____ _____ _____ _____ _____

9. Navy Department
   (national)
   _____ _____ _____ _____ _____

10. Glendale Commission on
    Disabilities (county)
    _____ _____ _____ _____ _____

Alphabetized Listing

_____ _____ _____ _____ _____ _____ _____ _____ _____ _____
  1   2   3   4   5   6   7   8   9   10

*The answers to this exercise appear in the **Instructor's Manual and Key** for **HOW 8: A Handbook for Office Workers,** Eighth Edition.*

Section 4 Information Sources

Accessing Internet Web Sites (15-12 and 15-13)

Practice Guide 1

Instructions: Access the Internet. Follow the specific instructions given for each exercise.

1. Visit the U.S. Postal Service's ZIP + 4 Code Lookup site <http://www.usps.gov/ncsc/lookups/lookup_zip+4.html> to locate nine-digit zip codes for the following addresses:

   - 1000 Harbor Boulevard, Suite 3, Weehawken, NJ   _____

   - One Active Aid Road, Redwood Falls, MN   _____

   - P.O. Box 5270, Denver, CO   _____

   - 6368 Lake Avenue, S.W., Tacoma, WA   _____

   - 418 North 64th Street, Kansas City, KS   _____

2. Access the U.S. Senate site <http://www.senate.gov/senator/state.html> that lists the states and the names of their current United States senators. This site also provides a link to each senator's home page.

   - List the names of the two senators from Montana.   _____

        _____

   - Visit the home page of one of the senators from Montana. List the name of the senator. Describe the contents of the home page, noting briefly any links to other sites.

        Senator _____

   _____

   _____

   _____

   _____

3. Visit a site of the U.S. Census Bureau (<http://www.census.gov/statab/ccdb/ccdb301.txt> or <http://www.census.gov/> using appropriate links) to answer the following questions about the population and geographical area of United States cities:

   - How many United States cities have populations of more than 1 million?   _____

   - What city in the United States has the fourth largest population?   _____

   - How many United States cities have populations ranging between 500,000 and 999,000?   _____

- How many United States cities have populations numbering 200,000 or more? _____

- Among those cities with populations of 200,000 or more, which one has the largest land area? _____

- Among those cities with populations of 200,000 or more, which one has the second largest land area? _____

Practice Guide 2

1. Access *Merriam-Webster Online* <http://www.m-w.com>. Locate the definitions for *millennium.* Briefly summarize the contemporary meanings.

   _____

   _____

   _____

   _____

2. Access *Merriam-Webster Online* <http://www.m-w.com>. Select the *Word of the Day* link. Provide the date of access, the word defined, and a brief definition.

   Date _____

   Word _____

   Definition _____

   _____

   _____

3. Access an on-line version of *Roget's Thesaurus of English Words and Phrases* <http://home.thesaurus.com/thesaurus/search.html>. Search for the noun *job* as it relates to *business.* List ten words that could be used as substitutes.

   _____ _____ _____ _____ _____

   _____ _____ _____ _____ _____

4. Access *The WorldWideWeb Acronym and Abbreviation Server* <http://www.ucc.ie/info/net/acronyms/index.html>. Search for the acronym D.A.R.E.; ***do not*** include periods or spaces in your search. List two meanings for this acronym.

   _____

   _____

Practice Guide 3

Instructions: Access *USA TODAY* on-line <http://www.usatoday.com>. Select an article from the links provided. Provide the date of access, the title of the article, and a summary of its contents.

Date _____

Title _____

Summary _____

_____

_____

_____

_____

_____

_____

_____

_____

_____

_____

_____

_____

_____

*The answers to these practice guides appear in the **Instructor's Manual and Key** for **HOW 8: A Handbook for Office Workers,** Eighth Edition.*

Part 4

Key to Familiarization Exercise for *HOW* (pages 3–11)

Answer	Section
1. c	Preface, page viii
2. d	Preface, page viii
3. b	Preface, page viii
4. b	Preface, page viii, and inside front cover
5. c	Preface, page viii
6. c	9-12
7. b	15-11, 15-12, 15-13
8. c	11-19
9. a	4-26
10. d	pages 201–202
11. b	1-33, 1-41e
12. c, d	3-15e
13. b	4-2a, b, c
14. b, c, d	4-1d
15. a, c, d	6-7b
16. b, d	6-21
17. a, c, d	3-16a, c
18. d, e	3-6
19. c	1-15a, d or 1-47, 1-54
20. b	1-2
21. b	9-2b or 10-12c
22. b, c	6-4b
23. c, d	page 204
24. a	5-12 or inside back cover
25. c, d	6-18f

Answer	Section
26. c, d	10-37
27. d	4-9
28. d	10-8
29. b, c	2-5g, h; 2-6c
30. b, d	3-5a, c, d
31. b	page 231
32. b, c	3-4
33. d	1-5a
34. b, c	2-2a, b, f, h
35. b, d	10-11
36. b, c	14-3a
37. b	10-26b
38. a	9-9, 13-4e
39. d	9-12
40. a, d, e	10-9b, c
41. a, e	6-12c
42. a, d	3-13, 3-14
43. d	10-21, 10-36d
44. c	4-4a, b, c
45. a, c	8-3b, c, d
46. b, d	3-6
47. a, d	4-1
48. d	1-19
49. b, d	1-55a, c, d, e or 6-5a, c, d, h
50. b, c	page 226

Key to Practice Exercises

Section 1 Punctuation

Practice Sentences 1 (page 17)

1. ...rain, sleet, and ice ....
2. ...uses a word processor, prepares spreadsheets, and answers ....
3. ...Arizona, Nevada, Utah, and Montana.
4. ...changed all the locks, barred the outside windows, and installed ....
5. Trees, shrubs, and ground cover ....
6. Call Henry Smith, offer him the job, and ask ....
7. Many doctors, dentists, and lawyers ....
8. ...obtained a permit, purchased the building materials, and hired ....
9. Proofread the report, make three copies, and mail ....
10. ...stationery store, post office, and grocery store ....

Practice Paragraph 1 (page 17)

We must correspond with Mr. Jones regarding our inventory, sales, and profit picture. Ask him to let us know how our high inventory, low sales volume, and declining profits during the last quarter will affect our status for the entire year. Write the letter, sign it, and mail it.

Practice Sentences 2 (page 19)

1. In fact, ...
2. ..., nevertheless, ...
3. ..., fortunately, ...
4. Yes, ...
5. No commas. (*Perhaps* flows smoothly into the rest of the sentence.)
6. ..., in other words, ...
7. Between you and me, ...
8. No commas preferred. (Optional commas around *therefore*).
9. ..., without a doubt, ...
10. No commas preferred. (Optional commas around *indeed*.)

Practice Paragraph 2 (page 19)

We, as a rule, do not employ inexperienced workers. However, Mr. Williams has so many excellent recommendations that we could not afford to turn down his application. Perhaps you will wish to meet him personally before assigning him to a supervisor. I can, of course, have him stop by your office tomorrow.

Practice Sentences 3 (page 21)

1. Brett, ...
2. ..., class, ...
3. ..., Mrs. Davis.
4. ..., ladies and gentlemen, ...
5. ..., Gary, ...
6. Yes, fellow citizens of Spokane, ...
7. No commas.
8. ..., Dr. Bush.
9. No commas.
10. ..., friends and neighbors, ...

Practice Paragraph 3 (page 21)

Would you, Ms. White, please review the financial report. I would appreciate your doing so too, Ms. Smith. Gentlemen, please check with both Ms. White and Ms. Smith for their advice before making any further financial commitments.

Practice Sentences 4 (page 23)

1. ..., Stan Hughes, ...
2. ..., the author of a best-seller, ...
3. ..., a member of the finance committee, ...
4. No commas.
5. ..., "Skiing in California," ...?
6. No commas.
7. ..., our new assistant, ...
8. ..., two prominent authorities on the subject of consumer finance.
9. ..., Bill Thompson.
10. ..., Crutchfield Industries, ...

Practice Paragraph 4 (page 23)

We have just learned that our president, Mr. Black, will retire next June. He has been president of Data Products, Inc., for the past ten years. My assistant received the news yesterday and believes that Stephen Gold, Ph.D., will be asked to fill the position. We will keep our employees informed of further developments through our monthly newsletter, *Data Jottings*.

Practice Sentences 5 (page 25)

1. ... February 28, 1998.
2. No commas.
3. ... 8 p.m., EST?
4. No commas.
5. ... Thursday, June 12, 1999.
6. No commas.
7. ... November 4, 1997, ...
8. No commas.
9. ... 8:40 a.m., CST.
10. On Wednesday, December 6, 2001, ...

Practice Paragraph 5 (page 25)

We will meet on April 1 to plan the scheduled opening of two new branch offices on Tuesday, May 3, and Thursday, May 19. These offices are the first ones we have opened since August 22, 1997. We will need to plan these openings carefully because we will be directly responsible for two additional openings in September 2000 and April 2001.

Practice Sentences 6 (page 27)

1. ... College, 6201 Winnetka Avenue, Woodland Hills, California 91371.
2. ... Lane, Los Angeles, California 90041-2027.
3. ... London, England, and Paris, France, ...
4. ... Honolulu, Hawaii.
5. ... Albuquerque, New Mexico, ...
6. ... Avenue, Knoxville, Tennessee 37912-5821.

7. ...Stocker, Office Manager, Smythe & Ryan Investment Counselors, 3370 Ravenwood Avenue, Suite 120, Baltimore, Maryland 21213-1648.
8. ...Box 360, Rural Route 2, Bangor, Maine 04401-9802.
9. Dallas, Texas, ...
10. ...Madrid, Spain.

Practice Paragraph 6 (page 27)

We sent the information to Mr. David Hope, Manager, Larry's Clothing Store, 2001 Adams Street, S.W., Atlanta, Georgia 30315-5901. The information should have been sent to Mr. Hope's new address in Columbus, Ohio. It is 2970 Olive Avenue, Columbus, Ohio 43204-2535.

Practice Sentences 7 (page 29)

1. ...January, and ....
2. ...3 p.m., but ....
3. ...office, or....
4. ...well, nor ....
5. No comma. (Second clause incomplete.)
6. ...publication, and ....
7. No comma. (The words *and that* result in a dependent clause.)
8. ...himself, or ....
9. ...Akron, nor ....
10. No comma. (Second clause incomplete.)

Practice Paragraph 7 (page 29)

We have checked our records and find that you are correct. Our deposit was mailed to your branch office, but no record of this deposit was entered into our check record. Our records have been corrected, and we appreciate your help in solving this problem. We hope that we have not caused you any inconvenience and that we may rely upon your help in the future.

Practice Sentences 8 (page 31)

1. ...pleasant, patient ....
2. No commas.
3. No commas.
4. ...elegant, secluded ....
5. No commas.
6. ...ambitious, greedy ....
7. No commas.
8. Your outgoing, cheerful ....
9. ...wealthy, well-known ....
10. No commas.

Practice Paragraph 8 (page 31)

Your informative, well-written report was submitted to the board of education yesterday. You will certainly be permitted to purchase some inexpensive modern equipment on the basis of the facts presented. I am sure the board will agree that the present facilities do not reflect a realistic, practical learning environment for business students.

Practice Sentences 9 (page 33)

1. When you see John, ...
2. While you were in New York, ...

3. Before you leave for Denver, . . . ?
4. As stated previously, ...
5. Because Mr. Logan wishes to move to Indianapolis, ...
6. If so, . . . ?
7. While Ms. Smith was conferring with her attorney, ...
8. Provided we have an adequate budget, ...
9. If you cannot make an appointment at this time, ...
10. As explained above, ...

Practice Paragraph 9 (page 33)

When you receive the material, please review it carefully and return it to our office within two weeks. If possible, note all changes in red. As soon as we receive your corrections, we will be able to submit the manuscript to the printer. We expect that if the current production schedule is maintained, the book will be released early in March.

Practice Sentences 10 (page 35)

1. To continue with this project, ...
2. Seeing that John had made a mistake, ...
3. After viewing the offices in the Hudson Building, ...
4. Near the top of the new listings, ...
5. Tired of her usual routine, ...
6. No comma.
7. No comma.
8. To be interviewed for this position, ...
9. Until the end of the month, ...
10. Encouraged by recent sales increases, ...

Practice Paragraph 10 (page 35)

For the past one hundred years, our bank has served the needs of the people of Hartford. At the present time we wish to attract more depositors to our institution. To attract new customers to the Bank of Connecticut, we have established a premium plan. Hoping that such an incentive will draw a large group of new depositors, we have provided a number of gift items to be given away with the opening of new accounts for $1,000 or more.

Practice Sentences 11 (page 37)

1. Mr. Sims, who has responsibility for reviewing all appeals, will . . . .
2. No commas.
3. . . . article, which appeared in last Sunday's local paper, discussed . . . .
4. No commas.
5. . . . shipped, even though I tried to cancel it.
6. No commas.
7. Mr. Davis, who has attended many of our seminars, is . . . .
8. . . . report, which was distributed at the last meeting of department heads.
9. . . . Inn, regardless of its expensive meals and remote location.
10. . . . president, planning to make major organizational changes, first . . . .

Practice Paragraph 11 (page 37)

The new community library, which is located on South Main Street, is presently recruiting employees to serve the public during the evening hours. Mr. Davis is looking for staff members who would be willing to work from 5 to 9 p.m. on weekday evenings. He would be pleased to receive your recommendations if you know of any qualified individuals who would be interested in such a position. We would appreciate receiving your recommendations within the next few days since Mr. Davis must hire the evening staff by May 10, before the library opens on May 13.

Practice Sentences 12 (page 39)

1. The format, not the content, of . . . .
2. . . . forms, the sooner we can . . . .
3. . . . July 1, but only to . . . .
4. . . . Internet sites, the more adept . . . .
5. . . . report, not just a short memo, outlining . . . .
6. . . . June 9; Mary, June 15; Ted, June 22; and Rosa, June 30.
7. . . . suites; yesterday, three; and the day before, two.
8. . . . report; the Personnel Department, 12; and the other departments, 8.
9. . . . supplies; this month, only one.
10. . . . in 2000; three, in 2001; two, in 2002.

Practice Paragraph 12 (page 39)

Last week our agent sold six homes; this week, just four. Mr. Stevens maintains that our construction site is not appealing to home buyers. His argument is plausible, yet weak. Other builders in the area have been more successful in their marketing efforts. The more competition Mr. Stevens encounters, the more his sales efforts seem to decline.

Practice Sentences 13 (page 41)

1. . . . many, many years.
2. A long time before, she had spoken . . . .
3. Whoever wins, wins a . . . .
4. Ever since, Mr. Salazar . . . .
5. We were very, very . . . .
6. Students who cheat, cheat . . . .
7. Three months before, our sales manager . . . .
8. Whoever begins, begins . . . .
9. Even before, he had . . . .
10. After this, time will . . . .

Practice Paragraph 13 (page 41)

All the meeting was, was a discussion of Mr. Green's plan to move the plant. Mr. Green has presented this same plan many, many times. A few weeks before, another committee totally rejected his proposal. Ever since, he has looked for another group to endorse his ideas.

Practice Sentences 14 (page 43)

1. . . . sign," said Mr. Grey.
2. "How long," asked Ms. Foster, "will it . . . monitor?"
3. No commas.
4. Mr. Hughes said, "Everyone . . . ."
5. No commas.
6. "Are you finished," asked Scott, "with . . . ?"
7. The witness reaffirmed, "That . . . ."
8. "Please . . . Friday, May 5," said . . . .
9. No commas.
10. "Mr. David Brown," said Ms. Burns, the Department of Human Resources head, "has . . . ."

Practice Paragraph 14 (page 43)

Mr. Dallas answered the reporter's question with a simple "yes." His philosophy appeared to be "A bird in hand is worth two in the bush." The reporter then asked, "Do you believe this labor problem will be settled within the next week?" Mr. Dallas answered confidently, "I believe the terms of the contract will be accepted by a clear majority." "I am sure," added Ms. Hill, "that the employees will be especially pleased with the additional insurance benefits offered."

Practice Sentences 15 (page 45)

1. ...products; we feel....
2. ...reports; she wishes....
3. Andrea collated, Kim stapled.
4. ...table; I will....
5. ...project; he will....
6. I dusted furniture, John cleaned the showcase, Mary vacuumed—all just....
7. ...meeting; he will....
8. ...today; the committee....
9. The thief entered, he grabbed the jewels, he exited swiftly.
10. ...low; they increased somewhat during September; November....

Practice Paragraph 15 (page 45)

We need someone to meet with the Atlas Corporation representatives. Please call Mr. Green; ask him to be in my office by 10 a.m. tomorrow morning. He knows Piedmont, he knows commercial real estate, he knows prices. Mr. Green would be my first choice for the job; Ms. Jones would be my second choice; my final choice would be Mr. Bruce.

Practice Sentences 16 (page 47)

1. James Hogan, who is originally from Nevada, has written a book about tourist sights in Las Vegas; and....
2. Cliff Lightfoot, our supervisor, has been ill for several weeks; but he plans to return to the office next Wednesday, November 19, in time....
3. ...offices, and we....
4. We cannot, Ms. Baron, repair the radio under the terms of the warranty; nor.... (*or* ...of the warranty, nor....)
5. Nevertheless, the committee must meet again next Friday, but....
6. ...nearby, and....
7. Unfortunately, ...engine problems; but according to the latest information we have received, they....
8. I believe, Ms. Edwards, that....
9. You may, of course, wish to keep your original appointment, or....
10. ...return; but we cannot guarantee that our next program, or any other programs planned for the future, will do as well.

Practice Paragraph 16 (page 48)

We were pleased to learn, Mr. Bell, that you have opened a new store on West Main Street, (*or* Street;) and you may be sure that we look forward to establishing a mutually profitable business relationship. Our new line of stationery, greeting cards, and other paper products should be of interest to you; and we will have our sales representative in your area, Jack Dale, phone you for an appointment to view them. He can leave a catalog with you, (*or* you;) or he can take you personally to our showroom, which is located only three miles from your store.

Practice Sentences 17 (page 49)

1. ...year; therefore,....
2. ...schedule; however,....
3. ...remodeling; on the contrary,....
4. ...wing; consequently,....
5. ...textbooks; moreover,....
6. ...novel; then we....
7. ...sharpeners; however,....
8. Mr. Cooper, vice president of Western Bank, will not be able to attend our meeting; consequently,....
9. ...hours; thus all....
10. ...area; therefore,....

Practice Paragraph 17 (page 50)

Our order for 24 sets of china arrived yesterday; however, more than half the sets have broken pieces. These china sets are a featured item for our May sale; thus we would appreciate your sending an additional 14 sets to replace the broken ones. Please ship these replacements immediately so that they will arrive in time for our sale.

Practice Sentences 18 (page 51)

1. ...Miami, Florida; Houston, Texas; and Portland, Oregon.
2. ...David Stevens, president, North Hills Academy; Agnes Moore, assistant principal, Rhodes School; and Vera Caruso, director, Flintridge Preparatory School.
3. ...campaign; for example,.....
4. ...problem; namely, labor shortages, wage increases, and frequent strikes.
5. Esther has done all the fact-finding for this case; Jim has verified her findings; and Paul will....
6. ...San Fernando, California; Phoenix, Arizona; and Reno, Nevada, plan to....
7. ...July 4, 1776; October 24, 1929; and November 22, 1963.
8. ...procedures; for example, we....
9. ...year; namely, Charles Brubaker, Dana Walters, Phillip Gordon, and Lisa Stanzell.
10. ...Dayton, Ohio; sales territories will be expanded from eight to ten; and the position....

Practice Paragraph 18 (pages 51–52)

Our next student travel tour will include visits to London, England; Madrid, Spain; and Frankfurt, Germany. Two years ago we received 200 applications for our European tour; last year we received nearly 400; and this year we expect over 700 students to apply for this tour. This tour is one of the most popular ones we offer because the Smith Foundation underwrites many of the costs; namely, hotel accommodations, meals, and surface transportation.

Practice Sentences 19 (page 53)

1. ...supplies: bond paper, pencils, pens, and writing pads.
2. ...out: Marguerite Rodriguez from Atlas Corporation, Robert Wong from the Accounting Department, Lynne Hale from Thompson Industries, and....
3. ...viewpoint: she has....
4. ...bills for January 4, January 8, February 1, and February 7.
5. ...catalogs: Spring 1999 or Summer 1999.
6. ...February were Naomi Chahinian, Bertha Granados, and Kelly Crockett.
7. ...line: shirts, shoes, belts, skirts, and hats.

8. . . . year: Belmont . . . .
9. . . . discontinued: we have . . . .
10. . . . sale; namely, 3 cashiers, 5 salespersons, and 6 inventory clerks.

Practice Paragraph 19 (page 54)

New offices were opened in the following cities last year: Albany, Billings, Dayton, and
Fresno. We had planned to add additional offices in Portland and San Antonio: the high cost
of financing has delayed the openings of these offices until next year. Both the planning and
the development of the new offices have been handled by five persons in our home office:
Bill Collins, Brad Morgan, Susan Smith, Carol White, and David Williams.

Practice Sentences 20 (page 55)

1. Former employers and teachers—these are the only names . . . .
2. A number of urgent E-mail messages—one from Mary Thompson, two from Laura Woo,
   and two from Michael Benton—still need to be answered.
3. Several major factors—increased interest rates, higher property values, and a general
   business slowdown—have caused a real estate decline in this area.
4. The administrative staff—hoping to boost employee morale, increase sales, and raise
   profit levels—instituted a bonus-commission program.
5. Sunburst, Apollo, Courtyard, and Terrace Blossom—these four china patterns . . . .
6. Any number of private delivery services—Airborne Express, Federal Express, United
   Parcel Service, etc.—can provide you with overnight service to Cincinnati.
7. All our staff members—with possibly only one or two exceptions—are Certified Public
   Accountants. (or . . . , with possibly only one or two exceptions, ...)
8. You may choose from a variety of colors—black, navy, gray, white, bone, red, pink,
   yellow, brown, taupe, emerald, and sky blue.
9. Three commercial on-line service providers—America Online, CompuServe, and
   Prodigy—are being evaluated by our manager.
10. Word processing, spreadsheet, and database—any applicant we interview must have
    recent training or experience in all three areas.

Practice Paragraph 20 (pages 55–56)

Crestview Wood Finishing—manufacturers of French doors and windows, main entrance
doors, and window boxes—has been serving our community for more than twenty-five years.
Our quality workmanship—which can be seen in the lustrous wood finish, elegant hardware,
and precision fit of our doors and windows—is guaranteed for five years. Stop by our
showroom to view our new display of French doors and windows. Single pane, double
panes, beveled, or frosted—you may choose any of these glass types for your French doors
or windows.

Section 2 Hyphenating and Dividing Words

Practice Guide 1 (pages 57–58)

1. five-minute
2. OK
3. word processing
4. OK
5. alarmingly toxic
6. OK
7. three- and four-bedroom
8. Oklahoma University
9. newly acquired
10. kindhearted
11. thirty-year
12. charge account
13. snow-white
14. OK
15. part-time
16. OK
17. interest-free
18. government sponsored
19. OK
20. air-conditioning
21. high and low selling prices
22. Main Street
23. OK
24. hit-and-miss
25. large- and small-scale
26. redeemable store coupons
27. Little League
28. OK
29. basic accounting
30. home-study

Practice Guide 4 (pages 65–66)

1. nov/elty
2. unde/sir/able
3. ND
4. 4397 Halstead / Street
5. ND
6. ND
7. Mary N. / Gomez
8. ND
9. 25 per/cent
10. Columbus, / Ohio / 43210
11. read/ers
12. criti/cal
13. tech/niques
14. San / Fran/cisco
15. Agri/cul/ture
16. Ms. Darlene / Jackson
17. 3942 East / 21st / Street
18. December 17, / 1999
19. pos/si/ble
20. con/nec/tion
21. brother-/in-/law
22. thor/oughly
23. Mas/sa/chu/setts
24. self-/reliance
25. ND

Section 3 Capitalization

Practice Sentences 1 (page 71)

1. Dr. Chu's, Medical Arts Building
2. Promenade Shopping Mall, Franciscan china
3. Caribbean, Viking Queen
4. Green Tree Bridge, Suwannee River
5. Sharp calculators, Dorsey Memocalcs
6. Caesar salad, beef Stroganoff
7. Montclair Hotel, City of Angels
8. venetian blinds
9. Dakota County Fair, Norfolk
10. John Sreveski, india ink

Practice Paragraph 1 (page 71)

In April we will meet in the Islands to discuss the reorganization of territories in Alaska, California, Hawaii, Oregon, and Washington. Reservations have been made for April 7 on a United Airlines flight to Honolulu. Either American Motors or Ford Motor Company cars may be rented from Budget Car Rental for those agents attending the meeting.

Practice Sentences 2 (page 73)

1. c.o.d., 2 p.m.
2. CPA, USC
3. TWA Flight 82
4. Invoice 578391
5. page 28, Model 1738 VCR
6. No. 347
7. Figure 3, page 23
8. paragraph 4
9. Policy No. 6429518-C
10. Model No. 17 desk

Practice Paragraph 2 (page 73)

The cost of damages resulting from your accident is covered by your policy, No. 846821. However, as stated in Section B, paragraph 3, the company will cover medical costs only after the $100 deductible stipulation has been satisfied. If your medical expenses since January 1 have exceeded the deductible amount, please have your doctor fill out Form 6B and return it in the enclosed envelope. If you have any questions, call me at 759-6382 any weekday between 9 a.m. and 4 p.m.

Practice Sentences 3 (page 75)

1. governor
2. Professor Carlos Rodriguez
3. Mark Swenson, president of Georgetown Steel
4. vice president, Joshua Wooldridge
5. Professor
6. Mayor-elect Ann Brown
7. Byron Teague, assistant dean of instruction
8. personnel director
9. Lieutenant Colonel Bruno Furtado
10. Bill Clinton, the president

Practice Paragraph 3 (page 75)

The purchasing agents' convention in Miami was well attended this year. After a welcoming speech by Mayor Frank Barnes, John Lang, the president of Williams Manufacturing Company, spoke on how inflation is affecting the inventories of many companies throughout the country. Also speaking on the same subject was Professor Roberta Holt.

Practice Sentences 4 (page 77)

1. *A History of the Americas* or <u>A History of the Americas</u> . . . History 12
2. *Music World of Wonder* or <u>Music World of Wonder</u>
3. Theresa Flores, Ph.D., . . . conversational Spanish
4. Walt Disney's movie *The Lion King* or <u>The Lion King</u>
5. Lisa Gartlan, M.D.
6. "A Look at Teenage Life in These United States" . . . *Outlook Magazine* or <u>Outlook Magazine</u>
7. master of science degree in engineering
8. "Singing in the Rain"
9. *The New York Times* or <u>The New York Times</u>   *The Wall Street Journal* or The Wall Street Journal
10. Theater Arts 23 . . . *Fiddler on the Roof* or <u>Fiddler on the Roof</u>

Practice Paragraph 4 (page 77)

I plan to interview Fred Case, Ph.D., the author of the book *It's Easy to Make A Million Dollars* (or <u>It's Easy to Make a Million Dollars</u>). This interview will be the basis for a feature article that will appear in the "People Today" section of the Sunday *Chronicle* (or <u>Chronicle</u>). I am interested to learn whether the ideas outlined in his book came from actual experience, research, or both. I understand, too, that the newly released movie, *How to Make a Million Without Really Trying* (or <u>How to Make A Million Without Really Trying</u>), is based on Dr. Case's book.

Practice Sentences 5 (page 79)

1. National Fund for the Protection of American Wildlife
2. Senate
3. company
4. Accounting Department, Payroll Department
5. Advertising Department
6. county
7. Department of Human Resources
8. government
9. Board of Directors
10. National Council of Teachers of English

Practice Paragraph 5 (page 79)

Bill Hughes has recently been promoted to head our Public Relations Department. As a former president of both the Chamber of Commerce and the Rotary Club, he is well acquainted with many members of the business community. One of his main responsibilities in his new position at Fairchild Enterprises will be to promote the company among his business contacts.

Section 4 Numbers

Practice Sentences 1 (page 97)

1. 27
2. six
3. Thirty-six
4. ten
5. five
6. 38
7. Eighty-six
8. 3 million
9. 25
10. 12

Practice Paragraph 1 (page 97)

Mr. Wells requested that we send him 75 copies of our latest catalog. He is conducting three separate workshops at Eastern Business College and believes that over 20 (*or* twenty) business teachers will sign up for each course. So that the business teachers can become acquainted with the materials we have available, Mr. Wells would like to give each teacher a copy of our catalog.

Practice Sentences 2 (page 99)

1. 3
2. 1,000,000
3. 10
4. 11, four
5. 7
6. 382, 9
7. two
8. 8
9. 1 million, 1.5 million
10. four

Practice Paragraph 2 (page 100)

We appreciate your order for 8 pocket radios, 22 cassette tape recorders, and 6 portable television sets. At the present time we have only 9 cassette tape recorders in our Dallas warehouse. We will check with our three branch offices and our two retail stores to determine whether they have available the remaining 13. In the meantime, we are shipping you 8 pocket radios, 9 cassette tape recorders, and 6 portable television sets.

Practice Sentences 3 (page 101)

1. page 7
2. Policy 83478
3. No. 3
4. Number 1886
5. paragraph 8
6. $4
7. 6 percent
8. $.20
9. 8 percent
10. 85 cents
11. $1,000,000
12. $4 million
13. 22 percent
14. 20 cents
15. 0.4

Practice Paragraph 3 (pages 101–102)

A copy of your homeowner's policy, Policy 7832146, is enclosed. As you will note on page 1, line 6, the total company liability under this policy cannot exceed $47,000. Please submit this year's premium of $168. Because increasing costs have forced us to raise our premium rates, this premium reflects an increase of 8 percent over last year's premium.

Practice Sentences 4 (page 103)

1. 9 pounds 12 ounces
2. 3
3. June 3
4. 6 p.m.
5. 8 inches
6. 4 pounds 2 ounces
7. October 25
8. 9 o'clock in the morning
9. 1st of January
10. eighteen
11. 30
12. 18
13. thirty-three
14. 125th
15. 63

Practice Paragraph 4 (page 104)

When we were in Phoenix from August 13 until August 24, the average high temperature reading was 116 degrees. On the 25th of August, the temperature reading dropped to 110 degrees. We did enjoy our twelve-day vacation but wished our stay had been a cooler one.

Section 5   Abbreviated Forms

Practice Guide 1 (pages 113–114)

1. CST
2. 900 B.C.
3. CLU
4. OK
5. NBC
6. Dr.
7. OK
8. OK
9. Model No. 1417
10. c.o.d.
11. OK
12. Ext. 327
13. U.K.
14. N.E.
15. Brig. Gen. Ret. Foster L. Klein
16. etc.
17. OK
18. M.D.
19. Ralph T. Drengson Sr.
20. IBM Aptiva
21. Esq.
22. 5 p.m.
23. OK
24. Ph.D.
25. CD-ROM

Practice Guide 3 (page 117)

1. OK
2. I'm not
3. isn't
4. OK
5. You're
6. hasn't
7. OK
8. its
9. they're
10. OK

Section 6   Grammar and Usage

Noun Plurals

Practice Guide 1 (page 119)

1. policies
2. churches
3. radios
4. lives
5. Montgomerys
6. tomatoes
7. curricula
8. statistics
9. mumps
10. brigadier generals
11. yeses and noes
12. cupfuls
13. bookshelves
14. brothers-in-law
15. bases
16. pants
17. 9s
18. roofs
19. attorneys
20. waltzes
21. altos
22. cargoes
23. thises and thats
24. monkeys
25. analyses
26. alumni
27. per diems
28. counties
29. boxes
30. Koltzes
31. A's
32. bronchi
33. lessees
34. father figures
35. fathers-in-law
36. valleys
37. R.N.s
38. Mses. Ross *or* Ms. Rosses
39. data
40. Mickey Mouses
41. goings-over
42. t's
43. jockeys
44. Japanese
45. Messrs. Ramirez *or* Mr. Ramirezes
46. embargoes
47. yourselves
48. chassis
49. halves
50. Germans

Practice Guide 2 (page 120)

1. valleys
2. cargoes
3. halves
4. mice
5. bills of lading
6. OK
7. 2s
8. crises
9. OK
10. parentheses
11. freshmen
12. W-4s
13. companies
14. IDs
15. OK
16. mosquitoes
17. zeros
18. themselves
19. alumni
20. economics

Noun Possessives

Practice Guide 4 (page 123)

1. son-in-law's
2. children's
3. Everyone else's
4. week's
5. personnel managers'
6. Rosses and Lopezes'
7. girls'
8. Mr. Beaty's
9. Bob's and Phil's
10. company's
11. ladies'
12. months'
13. Mary's
14. Mrs. Joneses'
15. chief of police's
16. Alumni's
17. ITT's
18. expiration date of the lease
19. men's, boys'
20. Martha and Don's

Practice Guide 5 (page 124)

1. women's
2. floppy disk drive of this computer
3. Julie and Brad's
4. company's
5. OK
6. stone's
7. Bob's
8. students'
9. brother-in-law's
10. Ms. Joneses'
11. Adam's and Barbara's
12. moment's
13. attorney's
14. Mr. Steven's
15. company's, company's
16. OK
17. editor in chief's
18. week's
19. managers
20. truck engines

Pronouns

Practice Guide 7 (pages 127–128)

Part 1

1. We
2. me
3. he
4. I
5. she
8. us
9. he
10. me
11. her
12. I

Part 2

1. Between you and *me,* . . . .
2. . . . was *she?*
3. . . . to be *she* . . . .
4. . . . have been *he.*
5. . . . Paul and *me.*
6. . . . Teri and *me* . . . .
7. OK
8. . . . Bob, Arlene, and *I* . . . .
9. If you were *I,* . . . ?
10. OK

Part 3

1. who
2. whom
3. who
4. who
5. Whoever
6. who
7. Whom
8. whoever
9. who
10. whom
11. Whoever
12. who
13. whom
14. whom
15. who

Practice Guide 8 (page 129)

1. she
2. us
3. OK
4. she
5. whoever
6. person *who*
7. I
8. me
9. its
10. OK
11. I
12. us
13. him
14. Ms. Lloyd herself
15. who
16. us
17. their
18. whom
19. I
20. company *that*

Practice Guide 9 (pages 131–132)

1. *their* assignments
2. submit *his or her*
3. OK
4. clear *his or her*
5. *their* free time
6. to *her.*
7. refer *him or her*
8. of *its*
9. guarantee *its*
10. solve *their*
11. introduce *its*
12. OK
13. at *their* high
14. list *it*
15. praising *their*
16. guaranteed *its*
17. return *his or her*
18. completed *his or her*
19. provide *them*
20. read *her*

Verbs

Practice Guide 11 (pages 135–136)

1. client *paid*
2. Susan *called* all
3. we *will ship* your
4. also *teaches*
5. after we *had* already
6. OK
7. region *have* increased
8. has *lain* idle
9. are *using*
10. OK
11. have *grown*
12. will *choose*
13. sale *began* on
14. have *laid*
15. workers *hung*
16. credit union *lends*
17. to *lose*
18. have *spoken*
19. *lying* around
20. anyone *verified*

Practice Guide 12 (pages 137–138)

1. Pork and beans *is*
2. supply . . . *is* rapidly
3. OK
4. *are* planning
5. Someone . . . *needs* to
6. *is* all you need
7. *have* been
8. OK
9. There *are*
10. OK
11. The number . . . *is*
12. If I *were* you,
13. college *need*
14. company *approves*
15. Everything . . . *needs*
16. OK
17. Each . . . *has* been
18. *is* included
19. Neither . . . *has*
20. *have* requested

Practice Guide 13 (pages 139–140)

1. Have you <u>written</u> letters to the two agencies?
2. The tract of new homes <u>was</u> laid out to attract buyers with growing families.
3. Our client has already <u>spoken</u> to several agents in your firm.
4. The patient asked if he could <u>lie</u> down on the cot.
5. <u>Have</u> the criteria been ranked in the order of their importance?
6. There <u>are</u> several alternatives you may wish to consider.
7. Neither of them <u>wishes</u> to postpone his vacation.
8. OK
9. Dr. Saunders is one of those doctors who <u>know</u> a great deal about law.
10. Our stock of felt-tip pens <u>has</u> disappeared from the supply cabinet.
11. He had <u>forgotten</u> about this appointment until his secretary reminded him.
12. Until last Wednesday the book had <u>lain</u> on top of the counter.
13. All the juice in these bottles <u>has</u> been drunk.
14. OK
15. Neither you nor the other accountant <u>has</u> been absent this year.
16. OK
17. The staff <u>were</u> arguing loudly about their duties. (*or* The staff members <u>were</u> . . . .)
18. One of the mothers <u>has</u> consented to bring donuts for the class.
19. All our bills for this month have been <u>paid</u>.
20. OK
21. <u>Has</u> the Board of Directors approved this purchase?
22. There <u>are</u> still a number of options we need to explore before we can institute a new loan-tracking system.
23. Michael has <u>driven</u> nearly 15,000 miles this month visiting all the doctors in his territory.
24. OK
25. The stock market has <u>sunk</u> 107 points within the last two days.
26. I sent you this information after the 1998 financial information <u>had been</u> compiled.
27. Bob <u>has worked</u> in our Research Department since 1991.
28. <u>Has</u> the committee submitted <u>its</u> report?
29. None of the antiques <u>were</u> damaged during the earthquake.
30. OK

Adjectives

Practice Guide 15 (pages 143–144)

1. *a* one-bedroom
2. *a lighter oak finish*
3. any *other* programmer
4. more *nearly* impossible
5. feel *well*
6. *an* hour.
7. OK
8. felt *worse*
9. feel *bad*
10. anyone *else*
11. *a* historical
12. The *promptest* response
13. *a better way*
14. *out-of-state* cars
15. *12-foot* fence
16. *an* eight-unit
17. most *nearly* sturdy
18. *create unique*
19. *more noticeable* every
20. any *other* unit

Adverbs

Practice Guide 16 (pages 145–146)

1. less *carefully*
2. netted *nearly*
3. OK
4. looked *good*
5. company *the longest*—
6. with *anybody*
7. to *receive shortly*
8. OK
9. delivered *regularly*
10. do *well*
11. more *slowly*
12. have *barely* scratched
13. We *can* hardly
14. feel *bad*
15. working *well?*
16. *most* widely
17. *really* disappointed
18. *any* information
19. run *more smoothly*
20. to *evaluate carefully*

Prepositions

Practice Guide 17 (pages 147–148)

1. *Among* the three
2. OK
3. different *from*
4. discrepancy *between*
5. identical *with*
6. plan *to expand* its
7. retroactive *to*
8. *All the* computers
9. *opposite* Westlake
10. *inside* the main
11. *off* this counter?
12. hardly *help* hearing
13. OK
14. convenient *for* you?
15. *Both these* recommendations
16. compliance *with*
17. angry *with*
18. *Among* themselves
19. OK
20. buy *from* Midtown

Conjunctions

Practice Guide 18 (pages 149–150)

1. by *either* fax or E-mail.
2. but *becoming* one
3. OK
4. company *not only* manufactures
5. Neither Dana *nor*
6. and *a signed lease.*
7. look *as*
8. and *preparing the agenda.*
9. become *as* popular
10. *and return it*
11. assistance *not only* to
12. OK
13. on *not only* the written
14. *as* we had hoped.
15. *nor the understanding*
16. by *either* Standard Mail (B) or
17. affairs, you may
18. and *assisting* visitors
19. *week because*
20. just *as* the diagram illustrates

Section 7   Words Often Confused and Misused

Practice Exercises for Words From *A/An* Through *Aisle/Isle*

Practice Guide 1 (pages 151–155)

A/An

1. an
2. a
3. a
4. an
5. a

A lot/allot/alot

6. a lot
7. allot
8. allot
9. a lot
10. allotted

A while/Awhile

11. a while
12. awhile
13. A while
14. a while
15. awhile

Accede/Exceed

16. exceed
17. accede
18. exceed
19. accede
20. exceed

Accelerate/Exhilarate

21. accelerate
22. accelerate
23. exhilarate
24. accelerate
25. exhilarated

Accept/Except

26. accept
27. except
28. except
29. accept
30. accepted

Access/Excess

31. access
32. excess
33. excess
34. access
35. access

Ad/Add

36. add
37. add
38. ad
39. add
40. ad

Adapt/Adept/Adopt

41. adopt
42. adapt
43. adept
44. adapt
45. adopt

Addict/Edict

46. addicts
47. edict
48. edict
49. addicts
50. edict

Addition/Edition

51. edition
52. additions
53. addition
54. editions
55. edition

Adherence/Adherents

56. Adherence
57. adherence
58. adherents
59. adherents
60. adherence

Adverse/Averse

61. averse
62. adverse
63. averse
64. Adverse
65. averse

Advice/Advise

66. advise
67. advice
68. advice
69. advice
70. advise

Affect/Effect

71. effect
72. affect
73. effect
74. affect
75. effect

Aid/Aide

76. aid
77. aid
78. aide
79. aid
80. aides

Aisle/Isle

81. aisle
82. aisles
83. isle
84. isle
85. aisle

Practice Exercises for Words From *All ready/Already* Through *Any Way/Anyway*

Practice Guide 2 (pages 159–163)

All ready/Already

1. all ready
2. already
3. already
4. already
5. all ready

All right/Alright

6. all right
7. all right
8. all right
9. all right
10. all right

All together/altogether

11. altogether
12. all together
13. all together
14. altogether
15. altogether

All ways/Always

16. always
17. always
18. all ways
19. always
20. all ways

Allowed/Aloud

21. allowed
22. allowed
23. aloud
24. allowed
25. aloud

Allude/Elude

26. allude
27. elude
28. allude
29. elude
30. allude

Allusion/Delusion/Illusion

31. illusion
32. illusion
33. delusion
34. allusion
35. illusion

Almost/Most

36. Almost
37. Most
38. almost
39. almost
40. almost

Altar/Alter

41. alter
42. altars
43. altar
44. alter
45. alter

Alternate/Alternative

46. alternate
47. alternative
48. alternate
49. alternate
50. alternatives

Among/Between

51. among
52. between
53. between
54. between
55. among

Amount/Number

56. number
57. number
58. number
59. amount
60. number

Anecdote/Antidote

61. anecdote
62. anecdote
63. antidote
64. antidotes
65. anecdotes

Annual/Annul

66. annul
67. annual
68. annual
69. annual
70. annul

Anxious/Eager

71. anxious
72. eager
73. eager
74. anxious
75. eager

Any one/Anyone

76. anyone
77. Any one
78. any one
79. Anyone
80. anyone

Any time/Anytime

81. Any time
82. anytime
83. anytime
84. any time
85. any time

Any way/Anyway

86. anyway
87. Any way
88. any way
89. any way
90. Anyway

Practice Exercises for Words From *Appraise/Apprise* Through *Bolder/Boulder*

Practice Guide 3 (pages 167–172)

Appraise/Apprise

1. apprise
2. apprised
3. appraised
4. appraise
5. apprised

As/Like

6. as
7. like
8. as
9. like
10. As

Ascent/Assent

11. ascent
12. assent
13. ascent
14. ascent
15. assent

Assistance/Assistants

16. assistance
17. assistance
18. assistance
19. assistants
20. assistants

Assume/Presume

21. assume
22. assumed
23. presume
24. assume
25. presume

Assure/Ensure/Insure

26. ensure
27. insure
28. ensure
29. assure
30. assure

Attendance/Attendants

31. attendance
32. attendance
33. attendants
34. attendance
35. attendants

Bad/Badly

36. bad
37. badly
38. badly
39. bad
40. bad

Bail/Bale

41. bales
42. bail
43. bail
44. bales
45. bales

Bare/Bear

46. bare
47. bear
48. bare
49. bare
50. bare

Base/Bass

51. bass
52. base
53. base
54. base
55. bass

Bazaar/Bizarre

56. bizarre
57. bazaars
58. bazaar
59. bizarre
60. bizarre

Berth/Birth

61. berth
62. birth
63. birth
64. berths
65. berths

Beside/Besides

66. besides
67. beside
68. beside
69. besides
70. besides

Bi-/Semi-

71. semi-
72. semi
73. Bi-
74. bi-
75. semi-

Biannual/Biennial

76. biannual
77. biannual
78. Biennial
79. biannual
80. biennially

Bibliography/Biography

81. bibliography
82. bibliography
83. biography
84. bibliography
85. biography

Billed/Build

86. billed
87. build
88. build
89. build
90. billed

Boarder/Border

91. border
92. boarder
93. boarders
94. border
95. border

Bolder/Boulder

96. bolder
97. boulder
98. bolder
99. bolder
100. boulders

Practice Exercises for Words From *Born/Borne* Through *Coarse/Course*

Practice Guide 4 (pages 175–180)

Born/Borne

1. borne
2. borne
3. born
4. borne
5. born

Bouillon/Bullion

6. bouillon
7. bullion
8. bullion
9. bouillon
10. bouillon

Breach/Breech

11. breach
12. breached
13. breech
14. breach
15. breach

Bring/Take

16. bring
17. take
18. bring
19. bring
20. take

Calendar/Colander

21. colanders
22. calendars
23. calendar
24. calendar
25. colander

Callous/Callus

26. callous
27. callous
28. callus
29. callous
30. callus

Can/May

31. may
32. may
33. can
34. Can
35. may

Canvas/Canvass

36. canvas
37. canvass
38. canvas
39. canvass
40. canvass

Capital/Capitol

41. capital
42. capitol
43. capital
44. capital
45. Capitol

Carat/Caret/Carrot/Karat

46. carat
47. karat
48. caret
49. carrot
50. karat

Cease/Seize

51. cease
52. cease
53. seize
54. seize
55. cease

Ceiling/Sealing

56. sealing
57. ceilings
58. Sealing
59. ceiling
60. ceilings

Censor/Censure

61. censor
62. censure
63. censured
64. censors
65. censored

Census/Senses

66. senses
67. census
68. census
69. census
70. senses

Cent/Scent/Sent

71. cent
72. sent
73. scents
74. scent
75. cent

Cereal/Serial

76. serial
77. cereal
78. cereal
79. serial
80. serial

Choose/Chose

81. chose
82. choose
83. choose
84. chose
85. choose

Cite/Sight/Site

86. site
87. cite
88. sight
89. cited
90. sites

Close/Clothes/Cloths

91. close
92. clothes
93. cloths
94. close
95. clothes

Coarse/Course

96. course
97. course
98. coarse
00. course
100. course

Practice Exercises for Words From *Collision/Collusion* Through *Deference/Difference*

Practice Guide 5 (pages 183–187)

Collision/Collusion

1. collusion
2. collision
3. collusion
4. collision
5. collusion

Command/Commend

6. commend
7. commended
8. commands
9. command
10. commend

Complement/Compliment

11. complement
12. complement
13. complement
14. compliments
15. compliment

Complementary/Complimentary

16. complimentary
17. complementary
18. complementary
19. complimentary
20. complimentary

Confidant/Confident

21. confidant
22. confident
23. confident
24. confidant
25. confident

Conscience/Conscious

26. conscience
27. conscious
28. conscience
29. conscious
30. conscious

Console/Consul

31. console
32. consoles
33. consul
34. console
35. consul

Continual/Continuous

36. continual
37. continually
38. continuous
39. continuously
40. continually

Convince/Persuade

41. persuade
42. persuade
43. convince
44. convince
45. persuade

Cooperation/Corporation

46. cooperation
47. corporation
48. cooperation
49. cooperation
50. corporations

Corespondent/Correspondence/
   Correspondents

51. corespondent
52. correspondence
53. correspondents
54. correspondence
55. correspondents

Corps/Corpse

56. corpse
57. corps
58. Corps
59. corpse
60. corps

Council/Counsel

61. council
62. counsel
63. council
64. council
65. counsels

Credible/Creditable

66. creditable
67. creditable
68. creditable
69. credible
70. credible

Deceased/Diseased

71. deceased
72. diseased
73. diseased
74. diseased
75. deceased

Decent/Descent/Dissent

76. descent
77. decent
78. Dissent
79. descent
80. dissent

Defer/Differ

81. defer
82. differ
83. defer
84. defer
85. differ

Deference/Difference

86. deference
87. difference
88. difference
89. difference
90. deference

Practice Exercises for Words From *Deprecate/Depreciate* Through *Executioner/Executor*

Practice Guide 6 (pages 191–196)

Deprecate/Depreciate

1. deprecate
2. depreciate
3. depreciates
4. deprecate
5. depreciate

Desert/Dessert

6. desert
7. desert
8. desserts
9. dessert
10. dessert

Device/Devise

11. devise
12. devise
13. device
14. devise
15. device

Dew/Do/Due

16. due
17. dew
18. do
19. due
20. due

Die/Dye

21. dye
22. die
23. die
24. dye
25. dye

Disapprove/Disprove

26. disapprove
27. disprove
28. disprove
29. disapproves
30. disapprove

Disburse/Disperse

31. disperse
02. disbursed
33. disburse
34. dispersed
35. disburse

Discreet/Discrete

36. discreet
37. discreet
38. discrete
39. discreet
40. discrete

Disinterested/Uninterested

41. disinterested
42. uninterested
43. uninterested
44. disinterested
45. uninterested

Done/Dun

46. dun
47. dun
48. done
49. dun
50. dun

E.g./I.e.

51. i.e.
52. e.g.
53. e.g.
54. e.g.
55. i.e.

Elicit/Illicit

56. elicit
57. elicit
58. illicit
59. elicit
60. illicit

Eligible/Illegible

61. eligible
62. eligible
63. illegible
64. illegible
65. eligible

Emigrate/Immigrate

66. emigrated
67. emigrated
68. immigrate
69. emigrated
70. immigrate

Eminent/Imminent

71. eminent
72. eminent
73. imminent
74. imminent
75. imminent

Envelop/Envelope

76. envelope
77. envelops
78. enveloped
79. envelop
80. envelopes

Every day/Everyday

81. Every day
82. Everyday
83. Every day
84. everyday
85. every day

Every one/Everyone

86. Everyone
87. Every one
88. everyone
89. everyone
90. every one

Example/Sample

91. sample
92. sample
93. sample
94. examples
95. example

Executioner/Executor

96. executor
97. executor
98. executioner
99. executioner
100. executor

Practice Exercises for Words From *Expand/Expend* Through *Formally/Formerly*

Practice Guide 7 (pages 199–204)

Expand/Expend

1. expend
2. expand
3. expand
4. expend
5. expand

Expansive/Expensive

6. Expansive
7. expensive
8. expensive
9. expensive
10. expansive

Explicit/Implicit

11. implicit
12. explicitly
13. Explicit
14. implicitly
15. explicit

Extant/Extent

16. extent
17. extant
18. extant
19. extent
20. extant

Facetious/Factious

21. facetious
22. facetious
23. factious
24. factious
25. facetious

Factitious/Fictitious

26. fictitious
27. factitious
28. factitious
29. fictitious
30. fictitious

Fair/Fare

31. fare
32. fair
33. fair
34. fair
35. fare

Farther/Further

36. further
37. farther
38. further
39. farther
40. farther

Feasible/Possible

41. feasible
42. possible
43. feasible
44. feasible
45. possible

Feat/Fete

46. fete
47. feat
48. feat
49. fete
50. feted

Fever/Temperature

51. temperature
52. fever
53. fever
54. fever
55. temperature

Fewer/Less

56. fewer
57. fewer
58. less
59. fewer
60. Fewer

Finally/Finely

61. finally
62. finely
63. finely
64. finally
65. finally

Fiscal/Physical

66. physical
67. physical
68. fiscal
69. fiscal
70. fiscal

Flagrant/Fragrant

71. flagrant
72. flagrant
73. fragrant
74. flagrant
75. fragrant

Flair/Flare

76. flair
77. flair
78. flare
79. flare
80. Flared

Flaunt/Flout

81. flaunt
82. flout
83. flouting
84. flout
85. flaunting

Flew/Flu/Flue

86. flue
87. flu
88. flue
89. flew
90. flu

Foreword/Forward

91. forward
92. forward
93. foreword
94. foreword
95. foreword

Formally/Formerly

96. formally
97. formerly
98. formerly
99. formally
100. formally

Practice Exercises for Words From *Former/Latter* Through *Ideal/Idle/Idol*

Practice Guide 8 (pages 207–212)

Former/Latter

1. former
2. former
3. latter
4. former
5. latter

Forth/Fourth

6. fourth
7. forth
8. fourth
9. fourth
10. forth

Fortunate/Fortuitous

11. fortuitous
12. fortunate
13. fortunate
14. fortuitously
15. fortunate

Good/Well

16. well
17. well
18. good
19. good
20. well

Grate/Great

21. great
22. grate
23. grate
24. grate
25. great

Guarantee/Guaranty

26. guaranty
27. guarantee
28. guarantee
29. guaranty
30. guarantee

Hail/Hale

31. hail
32. hail
33. hail
34. hale
35. hailed

He/Him/Himself

36. him
37. he
38. himself
39. he
40. him

Healthful/Healthy

41. healthful
42. healthy
43. healthful
44. healthy
45. healthy

Hear/Here

46. here
47. here
48. hear
49. hear
50. here

Her/Herself/She

51. herself
52. she
53. her
54. she
55. she

Hew/Hue

56. hewn
57. hues
58. hue
59. hew
60. hue

Hoard/Horde

61. Hordes
62. horde
63. hoard
64. hoard
65. horde

Hoarse/Horse

66. hoarse
67. hoarse
68. hoarse
69. horses
70. horses

Hole/Whole

71. hole
72. whole
73. whole
74. holes
75. whole

Holy/Wholly

76. wholly
77. holy
78. wholly
79. wholly
80. wholly

Human/Humane

81. human
82. human
83. Humane
84. human
85. humane

Hypercritical/Hypocritical

86. Hypercritical
87. hypercritical
88. hypocritical
89. hypercritical
90. hypocritical

I/Me/Myself

91. me
92. I
93. I
94. me
95. I

Ideal/Idle/Idol

96. idle
97. idol
98. ideal
99. idle
100. ideal

Practice Exercises for Words From *Imply/Infer* Through *Liable/Libel/Likely*

Practice Guide 9 (pages 215–220)

Imply/Infer

1. imply
2. imply
3. inferred
4. infer
5. Implied

In behalf of/On behalf of

6. in behalf of
7. in behalf of
8. on behalf of
0. in behalf of
10. on behalf of

Incidence/Incidents

11. incidents
12. incidence
13. incidence
14. incidents
15. incidences

Incite/Insight

16. incite
17. incited
18. insight
19. insight
20. incite

Indigenous/Indigent/Indignant

21. indigenous
22. indigent
23. Indigents
24. indignant
25. indigenous

Ingenious/Ingenuous

26. Ingenious
27. ingenious
28. ingenuous
29. ingenious
30. ingenuous

Interstate/Intrastate

31. intrastate
32. interstate
33. interstate
34. interstate
35. intrastate

Irregardless/Regardless

36. regardless
37. Regardless
38. regardless
39. regardless
40. regardless

Its/It's

41. it's
42. its
43. it's
44. its
45. its

Later/Latter

46. latter
47. later
48. later
49. latter
50. latter

Lay/Lie

51. lie
52. lain
53. lain
54. lying
55. lies

Lead/Led

56. lead
57. lead
58. led
59. led
60. led

Lean/Lien

61. lean
62. leans
63. liens
64. lean
65. lien

Leased/Least

66. least
67. least
68. leased
69. leased
70. leased

Lend/Loan

71. loan
72. lend
73. lend
74. loan
75. lend

Lessee/Lesser/Lessor

76. lessor
77. lessee
78. lessor
79. lesser
80. lesser

Lessen/Lesson

81. lessen
82. lessened
83. lesson
84. lessen
85. lesson

Levee/Levy

86. levees
87. levy
88. levy
89. levee
90. levies

Liable/Libel/Likely

91. liable
92. liable
93. libel
94. libelous
95. likely

Practice Exercises for Words From *Lightening/Lightning* Through *Overdo/Overdue*

Practice Guide 10 (pages 223–226)

Lightening/Lightning

1. lightening
2. lightening
3. lightning
4. lightening
5. lightning

Local/Locale

6. Local
7. locale
8. locale
9. local
10. local

Loose/Lose

11. lose
12. loose
13. lose
14. loose
15. lose

Magnate/Magnet

16. magnet
17. magnate
18. magnate
19. magnet
20. magnetic

Main/Mane

21. main
22. main
23. mane
24. main
25. mane

Manner/Manor

26. manner
27. manors
28. manor
29. manner
30. manner

Marital/Marshal/Martial

31. marital
32. marshal
33. martial
34. marshal
35. marital

May be/Maybe

36. may be
37. Maybe
38. maybe
39. may be
40. may be

Medal/Meddle

41. meddle
42. medal
43. medal
44. meddle
45. meddle

Miner/Minor

46. minor
47. minor
48. miner
49. minors
50. minor

Mode/Mood

51. mood
52. mode
53. mode
54. mode
55. mood

Moral/Morale

56. morale
57. morale
58. moral
59. moral
60. morale

Morning/Mourning

61. morning
62. morning
63. mourning
64. morning
65. mourning

Naval/Navel

66. naval
67. navel
68. navel
69. naval
70. naval

Ordinance/Ordnance

71. ordinance
72. ordinances
73. ordnance
74. ordnance
75. ordinances

Overdo/Overdue

76. overdue
77. overdo
78. overdo
79. overdue
80. overdue

Practice Exercises for Words From *Pair/Pare/Pear* Through *Practicable/Practical*

Practice Guide 11 (pages 229–233)

Pair/Pare/Pear

1. pare
2. pear
3. pairs
4. pare
5. pair

Partition/Petition

6. petition
7. partition
8. partitioned
9. partition
10. petition

Passed/Past

11. past
12. passed
13. past
14. passed
15. past

Patience/Patients

16. patients
17. patience
18. patients
19. patients
20. patience

Peace/Piece

21. peace
22. peace
23. piece
24. peace
25. pieces

Peak/Peek

26. peak
27. peak
28. peak
29. peek
30. peek

Peal/Peel

31. peal
32. peals
33. peel
34. pealed
35. peeling

Peer/Pier

36. peer
37. peers
38. pier
39. peer
40. pier

Persecute/Prosecute

41. persecute
42. persecuted
43. prosecute
44. persecute
45. prosecuted

Personal/Personnel

46. personnel
47. personnel
48. personal
49. personnel
50. personal

Perspective/Prospective

51. perspective
52. prospective
53. prospective
54. perspective
55. perspective

Peruse/Pursue

56. pursue
57. perused
58. peruse
59. pursued
60. pursued

Plaintiff/Plaintive

61. plaintiff
62. plaintiffs
63. plaintive
64. plaintiff
65. plaintive

Pole/Poll

66. pole
67. poll
68. poles
69. poll
70. polls

Populace/Populous

71. populace
72. populous
73. populous
74. populace
75. populace

Pore/Pour

76. pores
77. pore
78. pour
79. poured
80. poring

Practicable/Practical

81. practicable
82. practical
83. practical
84. practicable
85. practical

Practice Exercises for Words From *Pray/Prey* Through *Scene/Seen*

Practice Guide 12 (pages 237–241)

Pray/Prey

1. prey
2. pray
3. pray
4. prey
5. prey

Precede/Proceed

6. proceed
7. precede
8. precede
9. preceded
10. proceed

Precedence/Precedents

11. precedence
12. precedence
13. precedents
14. precedent
15. precedence

Presence/Presents

16. presents
17. presence
18. presence
19. presents
20. presence

Principal/Principle

21. principal
22. principal
23. principal
24. principle
25. principle

Propose/Purpose

26. propose
27. purpose
28. purpose
29. proposed
30. propose

Quiet/Quite

31. quiet
32. quite
33. quite
34. quiet
35. quite

Raise/Raze/Rise

36. rise
37. raze
38. raise
39. rose
40. razed

Real/Really

41. really
42. really
43. real
44. real
45. really

Reality/Realty

46. realty
47. reality
48. realty
49. reality
50. realty

Receipt/Recipe

51. receipt
52. recipe
53. recipes
54. receipt
55. receipt

Residence/Residents

56. Residents
57. residence
58. residence
59. residents
60. residents

Respectably/Respectfully/Respectively

61. respectfully
62. respectively
63. respectfully
64. respectably
65. respectively

Ring/Wring

66. wring
67. ring
68. rings
69. wring
70. wring

Role/Roll

71. Roll
72. role
73. roll
74. role
75. roll

Rote/Wrote

76. wrote
77. rote
78. wrote
79. rote
80. rote

Rout/Route

81. route
82. rout
83. route
84. routed
85. routes

Scene/Seen

86. seen
87. scene
88. scene
89. seen
90. seen

Practice Exercises for Words From *Set/Sit* Through *Sure/Surely*

Practice Guide 13 (pages 245–248)

Set/Sit

1. set
2. sit
3. sat
4. setting
5. sitting

Sew/So/Sow

6. sow
7. so
8. sown
9. sew
10. sewing

Shall/Will

11. will
12. will
13. will
14. will
15. will

Shear/Sheer

16. sheer
17. sheer
18. sheared
19. sheer
20. shear

Shone/Shown

21. shone
22. shown
23. shown
24. shone
25. shone

Should/Would

26. would
27. should
28. should
29. would
30. should

Soar/Sore

31. soar
32. sore
33. soared
34. soaring
35. sore

Sole/Soul

36. sole
37. sole
38. soul
39. soul
40. sole

Some/Somewhat

41. somewhat
42. some
43. some
44. somewhat
45. somewhat

Some time/Sometime/Sometimes

46. sometime
47. sometime
48. some time
49. Sometimes
50. some time

Staid/Stayed

51. stayed
52. staid
53. stayed
54. staid
55. stayed

Stationary/Stationery

56. stationery
57. stationery
58. stationary
59. stationery
60. stationary

Statue/Stature/Statute

61. stature
62. statue
63. Statutes
64. statue
65. stature

Straight/Strait

66. straight
67. strait
68. straight
69. Strait
70. straight

Suit/Suite	Sure/Surely
71. suite	76. surely
72. suit	77. sure
73. suite	78. surely
74. suite	79. surely
75. suit	80. sure

Practice Exercises for Words From *Tare/Tear/Tier* Through *Your/You're*

Practice Guide 14 (pages 251–255)

Tare/Tear/Tier

1. tare
2. tier
3. tear
4. tare
5. tier

Than/Then

6. than
7. than
8. then
9. then
10. than

That/Which

11. that
12. which
13. which
14. that
15. that

Their/There/They're

16. they're
17. there
18. they're
19. their
20. their

Theirs/There's

21. There's
22. there's
23. theirs
24. there's
25. theirs

Them/They

26. they
27. they
28. they
29. them
30. they

Threw/Through

31. threw
32. through
33. through
34. threw
35. through

To/Too/Two

36. too
37. too
38. too
39. to
40. Too

Tortuous/Torturous

41. torturous
42. tortuous
43. torturous
44. tortuous
45. torturous

Toward/Towards

46. toward
47. toward
48. toward
49. toward
50. toward

Us/We

51. us
52. we
53. we
54. us
55. we

Vain/Van/Vane/Vein

56. vain
57. vane
58. vans
59. vain
60. vein

Vary/Very

61. very
62. vary
63. vary
64. very
65. vary

Vice/Vise

66. vise
67. vices
68. vices
69. vised
70. vice

Waive/Wave

71. wave
72. waive
73. waving
74. waived
75. wave

Waiver/Waver

76. waiver
77. waver
78. wavered
79. waiver
80. wavered

Weather/Whether

81. weather
82. whether
83. whether
84. weather
85. weather

Who/Whom

86. who
87. whom
88. Whom
89. Who
90. whom

Who's/Whose

91. who's
92. whose
93. whose
94. who's
95. who's

You/You're

96. you're
97. your
98. your
99. you're
100. You're

Additional Practice Exercises for *Affect/Effect*

Practice Guide 15, Part A (pages 259–264)

1. effect
2. affect
3. affect
4. effecting
5. effect
6. affect
7. effect
8. effect
9. effect
10. effects
11. affect
12. affect
13. effect
14. effecting
15. effect

Cumulative Practice Guide 1

Part A (pages 263–264)

1. an
2. accept
3. adapt
4. advice
5. affect
6. already
7. altogether
8. elude
9. Almost
10. among
11. anyone
12. as
13. ensure
14. badly
15. biannually
16. capitol
17. site
18. complements
19. continual
20. council
21. dissent
22. deprecate
23. devise
24. due
25. disperse

Part B (pages 264–265)

1. elicit
2. emigrated
3. imminent
4. every day
5. everyone
6. further
7. fewer
8. formerly
9. well
10. hoard
11. me
12. imply
13. indigent
14. interstate
15. its
16. lie
17. liable
18. loose
19. martial
20. Maybe
21. morale
22. overdue
23. passed
24. patience
25. persecuting

Part C (pages 265–266)

1. personal
2. prospective
3. proceed
4. precedence
5. principle
6. quiet
7. rise
8. really
9. realty
10. receipt
11. respectfully
12. route
13. set
14. sow
15. sheer
16. sometime
17. stationary
18. stature
19. surely
20. than
21. their
22. too
23. waver
24. whether
25. You're

Section 8   Spelling, Proofreading, and Editing

Practice Guide 1 (pages 279–281)

1. We are in the process of planning fund raising activitie for the colleges proposed building program.

2. Since the exterminators must tent the building, all tenants will be required to vacate their offices from August 3 through August 6.

3. Perhaps we should engage a free lance photographer to obtain professional pictures for the sales brochure of our new Willowbrook Development.

4. During this 3-day Memorial day sale, you can save up to 50% on regular items that have been reduced temporarily for this sale.

5. In your job search, visit the web site of MedSearch America <http://www.medsearch.com>, this on line career center posts résumés and lists job opportunities in a wide range of health related occupations throughout the U.S.

6. New keys will be issued for the parking gates at entrances to all employees parking lots.

7. Before entering the premises, all visitors must stop at the kiosk to obtain a permit from the security guard.

8. Plan to register early for this conference; after November 2nd, registration fees ~~for this conference~~ will be $150.00.

9. You are among our preferred customers, and we are pleased to invite you to this special by-invitation-only sale.

10. We cannot accept any out-of-state or third-party checks; therefore, you will need to find another means for making this payment.

11. If you will fax me your E-Mail address, I will let you know the dates of the convention as soon as the executive board determines them.

12. Will you be able to attend the luncheon that ~~which~~ has been scheduled for Thursday, September 20th, at 12 noon?

13. Clini-Share has ~~have~~ been able to serve most of our patients' needs for medical equipment, medical supplies, and nursing care.

14. Ms. Deborah Martin has been appointed manager of the Accounting department; she will assume this position on July 1.

15. According to the sign posted, "Vehicles not displaying a valid parking permit will be towed away at owner's expense."

16. Stocks, corporate bonds, mutual funds, unit trusts, government bonds, tax-free municipal bonds, and precious metals, all of these investment opportunities are available through T. R. Noble.

17. For reservations for the nights of April 19 and 20 at the Park Regency hotel in Atlanta, your confirmation number is JRk1892.

18. Copies of the agenda, last year's minutes, a list of advisory committee members, a campus map, and a parking permit are ~~is~~ enclosed.

19. Do you foresee that these changes will affect our ability to market this high-end software to home computer users?

20. All of these grant proposals must be submitted to the appropriate office in Washington, D. C., by March 31, or they will not be ~~be~~ funded.

homework

workbook p. 151-53

proofreading p 3-14
              p 20-25

m w   f
    | K 2 80
  K118

Friday   p. 159- 163